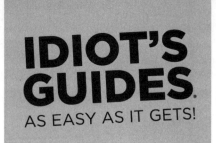

IDIOT'S GUIDES®

AS EASY AS IT GETS!

MAY 2014

Surviving Divorce

Fourth Edition

by Pamela Weintraub and Terry Hillman

ALPHA
A member of Penguin Group (USA) Inc.

ALPHA BOOKS

Published by Penguin Group (USA) Inc.

Penguin Group (USA) Inc., 375 Hudson Street, New York, New York 10014, USA • Penguin Group (Canada), 90 Eglinton Avenue East, Suite 700, Toronto, Ontario M4P 2Y3, Canada (a division of Pearson Penguin Canada Inc.) • Penguin Books Ltd., 80 Strand, London WC2R 0RL, England • Penguin Ireland, 25 St. Stephen's Green, Dublin 2, Ireland (a division of Penguin Books Ltd.) • Penguin Group (Australia), 250 Camberwell Road, Camberwell, Victoria 3124, Australia (a division of Pearson Australia Group Pty. Ltd.) • Penguin Books India Pvt. Ltd., 11 Community Centre, Panchsheel Park, New Delhi—110 017, India • Penguin Group (NZ), 67 Apollo Drive, Rosedale, North Shore, Auckland 1311, New Zealand (a division of Pearson New Zealand Ltd.) • Penguin Books (South Africa) (Pty.) Ltd., 24 Sturdee Avenue, Rosebank, Johannesburg 2196, South Africa • Penguin Books Ltd., Registered Offices: 80 Strand, London WC2R 0RL, England

IDIOT'S GUIDES and Design are trademarks of Penguin Group (USA) Inc.

International Standard Book Number: 978-1-61564-443-8

Library of Congress Catalog Card Number: 2013950651

17 16 15 14   8 7 6 5 4 3 2 1

Interpretation of the printing code: The rightmost number of the first series of numbers is the year of the book's printing; the rightmost number of the second series of numbers is the number of the book's printing. For example, a printing code of 14-1 shows that the first printing occurred in 2014.

Printed in the United States of America

Note: This publication contains the opinions and ideas of its author. It is intended to provide helpful and informative material on the subject matter covered. It is sold with the understanding that the author and publisher are not engaged in rendering professional services in the book. If the reader requires personal assistance or advice, a competent professional should be consulted. The author and publisher specifically disclaim any responsibility for any liability, loss, or risk, personal or otherwise, which is incurred as a consequence, directly or indirectly, of the use and application of any of the contents of this book.

Most Alpha books are available at special quantity discounts for bulk purchases for sales promotions, premiums, fund-raising, or educational use. Special books, or book excerpts, can also be created to fit specific needs. For details, write: Special Markets, Alpha Books, 375 Hudson Street, New York, NY 10014.

Publisher: *Mike Sanders*
Executive Managing Editor: *Billy Fields*
Senior Acquisitions Editor: *Tom Stevens*
Development Editor: *Ann Gilzow*
Senior Production Editor: *Janette Lynn*

Cover Designer: *Laura Merriman*
Book Designer: *William Thomas*
Indexer: *Heather McNeil*
Layout: *Ayanna Lacey, Brian Massey*
Proofreader: *Gene Redding*

Contents

Introduction

Idiot's Guide: Surviving Divorce, Fourth Edition, is a primer on the legal, financial, and emotional steps to ending your marriage and launching your life anew. Written for the person who may be too shell-shocked or upset to develop elaborate strategies himself, this *Idiot's Guide* presents a strategic plan of action for those in crisis. It also lays out useful solutions for the spectrum of day-to-day issues likely to emerge after your divorce has been decreed.

In an effort to cover the range of divorce issues, we have divided our volume into four distinct sections: deciding to divorce; legal concerns and the divorce process; financial issues; and co-parenting your children as you deal with matters from custody to the stepfamily to sharing time. Whatever your concerns, we have attempted to give you the basics. Because divorce is one of the most complex and emotionally loaded situations you will ever face, we have written this book as a bastion of simplicity. In the end, of course, you will make decisions with the help of your attorney—but you'll find this book a useful touchstone and the essential place to start.

In preparing the fourth edition, we took a look at some of the laws and practices of the divorce process around the globe. Our research revealed that governments and the courts worldwide have attempted to resolve the common legal, financial, and psychological situations families face when undergoing this difficult life change in similar ways. In all cases we examined, divorce laws have been fashioned with fairness in mind. When there are children involved, without exception, courts will rule in the best interests of the child. Legislators and courts continue to unify the laws and simplify the process to the degree their particular culture and system allows. We also discovered that divorce practice and laws have changed with the times, as new means of communication—such as texting—are now admissible as evidence during a divorce trial in countries from the United States to France.

Society's changing attitude towards traditional marriage and acceptance of same-sex love is an important milestone. This uneven legal development has added a new wrinkle and a bit of complexity to laws across jurisdictions worldwide for both marriage and divorce. We examine these laws and try to clarify a muddy terrain.

The internet has become the great facilitator for those contemplating or already involved in divorce, providing guidance and direct help. The various jurisdictions in almost every location have made access to their divorce laws—including child custody, division of property, spousal support, parenting plans, and child support guidelines—easy to find. In many cases, payment of child support can be made directly through a website. Government and court websites often provide child support calculators and links for accessing protection against domestic violence and enforcement of child support.

How This Book Is Organized

As you read this book, you will find that many issues affect divorcing people across the board: reestablishing self-esteem, making the best possible settlement, and managing your money. Other areas are more specialized. Not all divorced people, for instance, have children or wage custody wars; not all receive alimony; and not all must navigate the complexity of the step-family.

Part 1, Making the Decision, urges you to make sure ending your marriage is the right decision. After reading this section, you will be more certain of your choice. If your marriage cannot be saved, the rest of the book delivers a clear strategic plan for moving forward when you may still be too traumatized to chart the course yourself.

In **Part 2, Navigating the Law,** we cover everything you need to know about the legal journey you're about to make, including what to do and, perhaps most importantly what *not* to do, as you and your spouse begin to untie your marital bonds. All the options are spelled out, from mediating to settling your differences in a court of law. You will also learn how to find a good lawyer and how to make sure you're not paying too much for services.

Part 3, The Economics of Divorce, is all about managing your money: what you have, what you have to give up, what you might get, and what your kids will get. Finally, if you haven't been supporting yourself, we give you some tips to build a foundation for your financial future.

The last section, **Part 4, Focus on the Children,** is dedicated to your children, if you have them. Without doubt, making sure your children fare well during and after the divorce is what you care about most. We explain the concepts underlying custody of the children; provide a plan by age for sharing time with parents; and outline a plan for minimizing stress for children who must navigate new living arrangements, family members, and homes.

We've tried to give you food for thought and some comfort in knowing that this period in your life has a beginning and a middle, but also an end. It won't be an easy journey, but hopefully this guide will smooth out some of the bumps in the road.

Extras

Pay special attention to the sidebars scattered throughout. These provide real-life anecdotes, help you avoid common pitfalls of the divorce process, and familiarize you with the legal lingo. They will get you going in a positive direction and will give you some comfort when you need it the most. You'll come to recognize these icons as you read:

DEFINITION

Here you'll find definitions of commonly used terms in divorce.

RED ALERT

Know these pitfalls, and you will be ahead of the game.

SILVER LININGS

Every dark cloud has a silver lining. In these boxes you'll find some ways to look on the positive side.

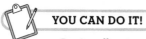

YOU CAN DO IT!

Don't wallow in your misery. Instead, take positive steps to regain control of your life and move on.

But Wait! There's More!

Have you logged on to idiotsguides.com lately? If you haven't, go there now! The worksheets and forms used in this book can be accessed online.

This icon 🖑 indicates material available to download. Just visit idiotsguides.com/divorce.

Acknowledgments

We want to thank Elayne Kesselman, Esq., who has provided the legal information for this book. As an experienced practicing attorney in New York City, Ms. Kesselman has shared the lessons from her many years as a skilled mediator and litigator. She has provided us with an inside look at what goes on in the mind of a judge and your spouse's lawyer, and what can make or break a settlement or trial. This information is invaluable.

We are also grateful to psychologist Mitchell A. Baris, PhD, a leading expert on the psychology of divorce, children of divorce, and parenting in the face of divorce, for sharing his observations and thoughts with us. We thank as well psychologist Carla Garrity, PhD who, along with Dr. Baris and other experts in this field, broke new ground by developing the concept of the *Parenting Coordinator*. Child psychologist Janet Johnston, PhD, generously spoke to us about her insights on children in high-conflict divorce.

Financial analyst Ted Beecher helped make our chapters on money management and settlement as detailed and timely as possible.

This is the first edition to be published since our beloved literary agent, Wendy Lipkind, passed away. You are in our thoughts.

Trademarks

All terms mentioned in this book that are known to be or are suspected of being trademarks or service marks have been appropriately capitalized. Alpha Books and Penguin Group (USA) Inc. cannot attest to the accuracy of this information. Use of a term in this book should not be regarded as affecting the validity of any trademark or service mark.

Making the Decision

For those of you who have picked up this book because you can't see your way out of a marriage gone stale, or because you've forgotten who you are, or perhaps because you've let yourself slip into a romantic relationship you were unable to resist, we urge you to take a step back and look again at what you now have. Perhaps you should be reading a guide to salvaging your marriage, not one on divorce.

The decision to divorce, or to stay together and work it out, is the most important you may ever make. In Part 1, we help you grapple with the decision to end or attempt to save your marriage, and we help you deal with the rejection if the decision to divorce has been thrust upon you by your spouse. Either way, we suggest some ways you can navigate your way to a new beginning.

Saving Your Marriage: When There's Hope

When you married a decade ago, you felt completely in sync. Both outdoor enthusiasts, you spent your weekends hiking and camping. Back in town during the week, your needs were simple—a night at home streaming the latest movie with a bowl of microwave popcorn or take-out Chinese food was all you needed to feel happy and at one with each other and the world. But somewhere along the line things changed. Your goals and values are no longer compatible, and you disagree about how to spend your time and money.

Your husband, always frugal, is happy with second-hand furniture and mismatched dishes, while you feel it's worth the expense to update your possessions as you become more successful in your careers. He's content to eat the same meals week in and week out, while you've developed a passion for cooking and love trying new restaurants. You still like each other, but you've grown apart. Your relationship is no longer fulfilling, and you long to be with someone who shares your interests and values.

In This Chapter

- When it's appropriate to try to save your marriage
- What therapy can do for you
- The pros and cons of divorce
- Telltale signs that your marriage should end

Or perhaps the following scenario more accurately describes your situation: At first you thought it was exciting, that fiery temper that flared up whenever she sensed a universal injustice or personal slight. You appreciated her strong opinions and her willingness to defend them. Yet now her discerning nature has begun to feel compulsive, and the passion has turned to venom—and it has turned on you. Whenever you leave your coat in the living room, whenever you disagree with her politics or her taste in film, her eyes widen in anger, and before you know it, a book or shoe has flown across the room. You'd like to work it out, but she wants a divorce. What, if anything, can you do?

Or does the following better describe your dilemma? You thought you would be faithful forever, but suddenly, at the cusp of middle age, you have fallen in love. You're excited by feelings you haven't experienced in years. It's thrilling to see his name pop up on your phone or email inbox. He makes you feel attractive, desirable, and interesting. As you and your spouse have yet another squabble about mundane household tasks, you find yourself daydreaming about a different life. It's wonderful to feel this way again, but could you really abandon your loving husband and the life you've built together?

A Difficult Decision

The decision to divorce is never easy, and as anyone who has been through it will tell you, this wrenching, painful experience can leave scars on adults as well as children for years. Before you and your spouse decide to call it quits, consider whether your marriage can be saved.

Colorado clinical psychologist and divorce expert Mitchell Baris, PhD, co-author of *Caught in the Middle: Protecting the Children of High-Conflict Divorce,* has some guidelines for those wrestling with this difficult decision. When is it possible, through diligent, hard work, perhaps in counseling, to save a marriage? And when is it generally impossible? When— despite the kids—are you doing the right thing by throwing in the towel?

There are, of course, many reasons for divorce, including sexual infidelity or abandonment, a lack of interest, a difference in values, continual emotional rejection and expressed desire for other partners, and certainly, physical abuse. When are the chasms just too wide to bridge? When can bridges be mended and relationships restored? "The decision to divorce is personal," states Dr. Baris. "But I think the point of no return comes with the loss of respect and trust. Those two feelings are particularly difficult to rekindle. Trust can be built back, but it takes years. Often, if trust and respect are gone, rebuilding the marriage is hopeless."

Dr. Baris also feels it might be difficult to rebuild a marriage when the animosity between two people builds to the breaking point. "I find couples are most likely to split when the intensity of negativity between them escalates." One couple, for instance, fought relentlessly about their son's bedtime, his eating habits, the duties of the cleaning service they had hired, and even the cable TV bill. For such couples, discussion on any topic—from the children to the brand of dog food they buy—might erupt into a negative and angry emotion. "These people will continually make destructive remarks about each other or just bring up the past," states Dr. Baris. "In therapy with them, you see this intense negativity and anger just pouring out."

What if children are involved? Dr. Baris explains that studies show that whether or not parents stay married is less important than whether they engage in fighting or conflict—and whether or not they drag the children into their disagreements. The degree of conflict in the environment is the critical factor that determines the ultimate psychological health of a child.

In other words, don't keep your marriage together for the children if that means exposing them to constant conflict and wrath. It's better for your children if you divorce amicably than if you stay together and continue at war.

SILVER LININGS

As painful as it may be to admit that your marriage is at an end, sometimes ending a painful or difficult marriage is the only way you can empower yourself to move forward toward emotional health and growth. We know that leaving a familiar relationship for the possible isolation and stress of single life (and perhaps single parenthood) is a rough road to travel. But after you have made the transition, you will find that you are open to new experiences and new relationships never before possible. If your marriage has been demeaning, painful, or even boring, take comfort in the knowledge that divorce might signify the beginning of something, not just the end.

Divorce often means relinquishing the comforts that defined your life in the past. Families who lived in the suburbs as a unit may now have to sell their house, leave the neighborhood, or move out to less expensive (and possibly less desirable) areas. Divorce means divesting the accoutrements of a shared life and starting out again—diminished in strength and often alone. The death of a marriage inspires, among other emotions, anger, grief, and fear.

Resolving Conflicts and Saving Your Marriage

Your marriage is at the brink of dissolution. You and your spouse have lost trust and faith in each other; your mutual anger is so palpable that you can no longer go out as a couple without breaking into a verbal sparring match or an out-and-out fight. Past hurts and wrongs haunt both of you, coloring your interpretation of the present; and perhaps most damaging, one or both of you have engaged in an extramarital affair.

Despite such problems, couples can and do put their marriages back together, although only through extremely hard work. But both members of the couple must do the work, or it will be doomed from the start. Generally, the best approach is finding a marriage counselor to help you.

There are many therapists out there, each with his or her own approach to counseling. What should you look for in a marriage counselor? What kind of therapist is right for you?

Some of the best advice we've heard comes again from Dr. Baris, who works with the divorced and the divorcing every day. Couples should look for someone who can help them restructure their communication and react to their partner in terms of the real situation, not ghosts of the past, Dr. Baris advises. "Some counselors look into the couple's deep past; they help them go over their own childhood experiences, their early family dynamic. Couples might explore the impact their past had on their marital choice and on the negative (and positive) patterns they carried into their marriage and up to the present."

Although different marriage counselors emphasize different strategies, we have seen the highest levels of success among those who focus on *conflict resolution*. When one spouse gets excited or angry, the ideal strategy for the other is to try to defuse the anger by soothing his or her partner. Going to war—or worse yet, dredging up the past—will only fuel the fires of conflict and weaken the relationship already on its last legs.

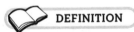 **DEFINITION**

> **Conflict resolution** is a peaceful and mutually satisfactory way to end or significantly—and hopefully permanently—de-escalate a conflict.

Couples in trouble might also benefit from lessons in fair fighting. In this technique, each partner listens to the other without being vicious or defensive—or striking back with hurtful insults or references to the past. One well-known doctor, who pioneered the technique of "restructuring" couples so that they can fight fairly, has an amusing approach. He keeps a piece of linoleum in his office and hands it to one person at a time. "Here, you hold the floor," he says to the person holding the linoleum. The other person cannot speak until the linoleum is handed over. The lesson for couples here: learn how to hear the other one through, and do *not* interrupt, especially to escalate the conflict.

How do you find the right therapist? The best way, our experts tell us, is to get referrals from satisfied friends. Make sure, of course, that you select someone who specializes in couples and relationships and that he or she is well regarded by other professionals. Make sure that whomever you choose feels "right." Is there a rapport among all three of you? Can you communicate easily with the therapist? Sometimes one spouse will come to feel the therapist has allied with the partner against them; if your spouse feels this way, perhaps it would be best to seek help from another counselor, one who can strike a better sense of neutrality as the sessions go on.

Once you find a therapist who meets these criteria, give therapy a fair chance. Be open to the possibility that your marriage can be saved—and be ready to do the work that it requires. Remember, therapy isn't always easy, especially if you're carrying painful emotional baggage from your childhood. But, if you and your partner truly love each other and are willing to alter some basic patterns, therapy can succeed.

Point of No Return

Sometimes, the best-laid plans are laid to waste. Despite all your hopes and dreams in the beginning, and all your good intentions now, it seems impossible to continue your marriage. For many of us, the notion of "till death do us part" has become an anachronism. When life becomes too painful, few of us question the notion, at least intellectually, of moving on.

Sometimes, Dr. Baris notes, so much hurt has been engendered over the years that it is simply impossible to get beyond it—at least in the context of your current relationship. When people harbor deep, abiding anger, and when, despite therapy, that anger cannot be resolved, it could be time to let go.

Even in the absence of anger, one or both partners might start to lose respect for the relationship and their spouse. That might signal the end as well. One couple we know divorced after the husband made some poor investments and lost his business and the family home. The woman, who insisted she bore no anger, said she could no longer remain married to someone for whom she had "no respect." In another instance, a man divorced his wife, whom he'd met in the fiction-writing workshop at the University of Iowa, after she gave up her literary career for a high-paying job at a public relations firm.

Sometimes, people divorce because they grow apart. One couple we know spent 20 years in a traditional marriage; he went off to work, and she stayed home in the role of homemaker. When the youngest child left for college and the couple had untold hours to spend together, focusing not on child or family issues but on each other, they found they had little in common. His involvement in business and marketing was simply boring to her, and he couldn't relate to her interests in gourmet cooking and international travel. Their taste in movies and even friends had become widely divergent. There were no affairs and no long-simmering anger or resentment issues. It's just that when both people reached this new crossroad, marked by the departure of their children, his arrow pointed east and hers west.

Younger people with relationships of much shorter duration often reach this juncture as well. When people get married too young, they might find they have gone through enormous changes during the relationship and have grown apart. They've simply gone through more personal development; they have a stronger sense of identity, and in light of that, they would not make the same marriage choice today. Frequently, in such cases, the decision to divorce is mutual. Often, these people can walk away from marriage without feeling particularly angry, especially if they don't have any children.

When Is It Over?

How do you know when you've finally reached the point of no return, when putting your relationship together again is simply too much of a stretch? In the end, the answer is personal. But if your answers to the following questions are irrefutably "yes," it might be time to let go:

- Does every situation, no matter how seemingly trivial, evolve into a fight?

- Do you or your spouse continually refer to hurtful events in the past?

- Is all the respect gone from your relationship? Do you feel it is impossible to bring that respect back?

- Have your goals and directions changed whereas your partner's have stayed the same? (Or vice versa.)

- Is your partner no longer fostering your individual growth?

- Have you and your partner both changed so much that you no longer share moral, ethical, or lifestyle values?

- Have you and your spouse lost the art of compromise? When you disagree, are you unable to forge a path together that is acceptable to both?

- Do you and your spouse have a basic sexual incompatibility? Have you stopped making love?

- Does your partner continually push your "pain" buttons by keeping you emotionally insecure and off-balance?

Be Absolutely Certain

The decision to divorce should never be made in the aftermath of a fight. Divorce is final and should be considered carefully, not just for its impact on you, but also for its impact on your children. When you divorce, what ramifications will reverberate through your life and the life of your family? Will you have enough money to sustain your lifestyle—including important small details such as trips to the movies, piano lessons, or your weekly dinner out? Are you ready to leave the family house for a tiny apartment? Are you ready to divide the valued possessions you've collected together over the years?

The answers, for many, might be straightforward: the emotional relationship with their spouse is largely negative, for one or more of the reasons listed previously. Why else would divorce be in the air?

Nonetheless, sometimes couples in conflict can overlook the benefits of being in a relationship. For instance, if you have a child, have you considered how difficult it might be to either take on total responsibility or to have restricted visitation? Will you miss your in-laws, friends who might have to choose your spouse over you, or neighbors you might have to leave? Have you considered the stress of the dating scene? Perhaps most important, will you be relieved or paralyzed by the solitude you might be subject to, day in and day out, once you and your partner split?

Should you decide that divorce is your best option, we suggest that you proceed with caution and be aware of what you could lose. If you move forward heedlessly, you might lose more than you need to, or more than you can bear.

 **RED ALERT**

If you're considering ending your marriage, especially if you have children, understand and weigh what you now have with what you stand to gain or lose. Will you miss the adult companionship if repairing your relationship is still a possibility? Finding another partner—if that is what you want—may take longer than you think. If you have children, expect an earthquake in their lives and yours. They will be travelling between two homes while their familiar world shatters around them. You will only see them during fixed time slots, and you may miss important occasions, from birthdays to holidays. Think carefully before you finalize your decision.

The dangers of moving too quickly to divorce can be illustrated by Melanie's experience. When Melanie met Brad, she thought she had found a good partner to balance her impulsive, outgoing nature. Stable and sober, Brad seemed to have a plan for everything, from buying a house to having kids.

Before long, it became clear that Brad had an agenda for Melanie, too. In almost every situation, he had an opinion about what she should say, think, and feel. It was Brad who insisted she work outside of the house, spending less time with the kids, since it was so easy for him to conduct his business from home.

Melanie began to feel repressed and confused. She suffered from depression and self-doubt, all the while living the so-called dream. Despite her love for her children, she felt strangely disenfranchised. No longer comfortable with her instinct and spontaneity, she felt like a stranger to herself.

It's no wonder she responded strongly when Rick, an old flame from high school, contacted her after his own divorce. Rick seemed to approve of everything she said and did. With a new love in her life, her motivation to divorce Brad quickly and move on was high. Yet the price she paid to be rid of Brad was high, too. As the work-at-home parent (who had a higher income), he maintained physical custody of the children. Instead of seeing her children each night, Melanie now saw them every other weekend and one evening during the week. Meanwhile, Brad encouraged their animosity toward their mother. And he managed to secure a significant portion of Melanie's salary for child support.

According to Melanie's interpretation of her situation, she needed out of this marriage. But her haste caused her to suffer irretrievable losses, most notably the inability to be a daily part of her children's lives.

Before making such a drastic decision, Melanie could have communicated her feelings to Brad. With the help of a marriage counselor, she might have helped him see how lonely and disempowered she felt. The counselor might have helped Brad communicate how overwhelmed or overworked he felt, as well. In short, therapy might have helped Brad and Melanie rebalance their relationship. Brad might have become aware of his controlling behavior and tried to change. Melanie might have realized that she could put the brakes on her new romance, avoiding the losses she ultimately sustained.

Married people often develop routine patterns and an interpersonal chemistry that becomes entrenched without realizing the affect they have on each other. Even the suffering partner may not be conscious of why unease sets in. Melanie's urge to escape the marriage could have been understood as a warning sign rather than a cause for action—unless the action was to tell Brad how she felt.

Of course, working it out may have been impossible. If so, Melanie might have acted far more strategically before requesting a divorce. Depending on her job, she might have requested a flexible work schedule, for instance, so that when the court decided custodial care of the children, the balance would have been equal and the time shared.

In the end, Melanie's romance with Rick came to a crashing halt, anyway. It simply could not survive the loss of her children in daily life and the pain that caused.

Had Melanie been less impulsive and more thoughtful, had she been able to see the future more clearly, her life might have taken an entirely different turn.

There's a lesson in this for most of us. When it comes to divorce, there is always a cost. You must calculate the cost/benefit ratio before you move forward with your divorce. If the price is too high, you may decide to hold off—or at least wait until you've positioned yourself in such a way as to rebalance the equation and come out ahead.

Take some time to consider your losses—and there are sure to be some—before your decision to divorce is set in stone.

When Divorce Is Urgent

We end this chapter with one final caveat. Occasionally, the decision to divorce is mandatory. In instances of spousal or child abuse (mental or physical)—in fact, whenever your safety is in jeopardy—you don't have the luxury of merely thinking about a separation. If your life, limb, or sanity is threatened, it's important to make a quick and abrupt break. If you or your child are in danger, do not wait to organize your finances, collect your valuables, or even see a lawyer. Just get out.

 RED ALERT

Sometimes, people in destructive relationships have trouble removing the shackles and setting themselves free, and for good reason. Studies reveal that the most dangerous time for a domestic violence victim exists when he or she first tries to leave—or does leave—the abusive relationship. If you're in this situation, call law enforcement officials or your local domestic violence hotline for your protection and safety.

One woman we know had been abused for years when, in the aftermath of one final, brutal-izing battle, she phoned her oldest friend and one-time college roommate. The friend came over with her husband and a couple of shopping bags and gathered what she could: some clothes, a toothbrush, and spare cash. Then, the friend and her husband escorted the badly beaten woman out the door. The woman never went back; however, to this day, she states that if she had not been ushered out by her friend, she might still be in that abusive relationship.

When it comes to domestic violence, women are most often victimized. Yet almost 5 percent of battering victims are men, and the trauma can be similar regardless of the victim's gender. At the center of abusive relationships are issues of power, with the batterer using violence to maintain control over the relationship and his partner. Victims are often in denial about their situation, but it is hard to deny some typical battering tactics:

Isolating the victim from family and friends. This keeps the victim locked in the relation-ship because she is cut off from her support system.

Intimidation. The abuser intimidates the victim through looks, actions, and gestures. For example, perhaps the couple is at a party and the wife is talking to a man across the room. The batterer looks across the room and clenches his fist. She sees this gesture and knows the subtext: she will be assaulted when they get home. He might also intimidate her by destroy-ing her personal property or displaying weapons around the house.

Name calling. This is a prime feature of emotional abuse, wielded by men and women alike.

Threats. Batterers might threaten their partners as a means of coercion. Threats might be directed at the victim, at the victim's family and friends, or even at the batterer himself. Threatening to commit suicide if the victim leaves is not uncommon.

Economic abuse. Batterers often control family finances and might keep the victim on a weekly allowance to take care of the household. Victims of abuse might not have access to family bank accounts or might be prevented from taking or keeping a job.

Minimizing the violence. Almost universally, batterers minimize violence they perpetrate by saying such things as, "What's the big deal? I didn't really hit you; I just slapped you." They will often deny the violence outright and tell their victims that it was all imagined.

Blaming the victim. Batterers will blame their partners for the violence, saying they were provoked.

Using the children. Batterers may use the children to relay intimidating messages or harass the victim during child visitation.

What can family and friends do if they think someone's in an abusive relationship? First, provide unconditional support. And second, provide a safe haven so the victim has somewhere to go.

YOU CAN DO IT!

If you are the victim of verbal abuse from your spouse or ex, you should move to de-escalate the situation immediately. As soon as you notice the first sign of verbal abuse, put up your hand and say "Stop." If the verbal abuse continues, you should deal with your spouse or ex only through a third party. Be aware that "verbal abuse," depending on the circumstances, can be considered "harassing" or "threatening" criminal conduct, and as such, could support the issuance of a protective order.

What can you do if you are being abused? The first step is recognizing the telltale signs, and the second is seeking help and removing yourself from the situation as quickly as you can.

The Least You Need to Know

- Think long and hard before you move forward with your decision to divorce, as it might be impossible to reverse.
- If you want to save your marriage, therapy based on conflict resolution might help.
- If your marriage is rife with conflict, don't stay together for the children. Exposure to conflict is worse for them than a divorce.
- If your physical or mental safety is threatened, separation from your spouse is mandatory.

Planning for Divorce

There comes a time when you have to bite the bullet and admit that your marriage is at an end. You've tried living together and sorting things out; you've tried couples therapy; and you've tried living apart. The truth is, unless you sever ties and go your separate ways, you'll never have a shot at the happiness you both deserve.

Divorce is a major step for you and your family. You will be making life-changing decisions under extreme emotional conditions. At times, your head and mind will be pulled in opposing directions. In order to craft the best outcome, you need a clear mind and a strategic path forward.

This chapter covers critical information to consider before you move ahead with divorce proceedings.

In This Chapter

- Ways to strengthen your position before asking for a divorce
- Securing your legal position when you learn divorce is in the cards
- Protecting your money and reducing your liability before the legal proceedings begin
- Strengthening your right to custody and visitation

Think Before You Act

Before you move forward with divorce, the savviest attorneys would advise you to make some preparations. It might seem heartless, but if you plan to ask your spouse for a divorce, or if you think your spouse might want one from you, there are some matters you should take care of first. Attend to these issues before you or your partner decides to call it quits, and you'll be ahead of the game during legal negotiations.

We know that the notion of a pending divorce—even one not yet discussed with your spouse—can send you into a tailspin. The mere thought of divorce might evoke a range of emotions, including relief, fear, disappointment, excitement, and dread. After years of frustration, you're finally ready to divest yourself of some old and uncomfortable life choices for a world of new possibilities and, you hope, lower levels of conflict and pain. But no matter what you feel, you must push these emotions aside and take some practical and highly strategic steps before anyone gets the ball rolling.

Consider Your Legal Options

Until you have embarked upon the journey of divorce yourself, you might have some unrealistic notions about what is involved. Ideas about the painful process derive not just from family and friends, but also from Hollywood movies and websites that focus on extraordinary circumstances or the extraordinarily rich and famous. When you read about divorce on the internet, the principals are celebrities like Ashton Kutcher and Demi Moore—not Mary and Tom from down the street. Contested divorce for the wealthy has always been a high stakes game involving costly attorneys, each negotiating (and sometimes litigating) for a client's part of the marriage "pie."

For the rich, much about divorce is likely to remain this way. However, divorce proceedings can be different for those of more modest means. Most middle-class divorces today are conducted through a variety of venues. Many middle-income people hire attorneys for just part of the process and increasingly handle paperwork and logistics themselves. Others opt for low-conflict resolutions. This includes not just mediation, in which a neutral third party—the mediator—helps the parties reach a compromise, but also the newer method of "collaborative divorce." In collaborative divorce, each party has an attorney, but the adversarial milieu is replaced by a philosophy of harmony and the goal of getting along. In collaborative divorce, the two attorneys work together as a team, with the goal of problem-solving, not duking it out.

From the do-it-yourself divorce (referred to as *pro se* or *pro per*) to the mediated divorce to all the variations in between, divorce has become a consumer's marketplace. If you have limited funds, you no longer have to spend them all on your attorney just to sever your marriage.

On the other hand, extra choice means extra risk and responsibility. Should you find a brick-and-mortar or online store and offer your credit card for a $99 divorce, leaving the details to an attorney (or more likely, a paralegal)? Even if you do, one thing is for sure: you must educate yourself so you can be fully protected. As you begin to investigate divorce logistics, stay alert and remain skeptical. The choices you make now could impact your financial and familial situation for years or even decades, so make sure you are doing things right.

Consult and Hire an Attorney

As soon as you think you will be seeking a divorce, you must speak with an attorney. This is the first step in your journey, and an essential one. Even if you have been married for only a short time, even if you have no property or children, and even if you plan to mediate your divorce or handle it all yourself, you still need to take this step. An initial consultation with a divorce lawyer can be free, but even if it costs you a few hundred dollars, it's a worthwhile investment.

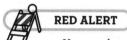 **RED ALERT**

You may have friends or family members who have gone through a divorce. Listen to their experiences, but don't rely on their advice in lieu of meeting with a divorce lawyer. Every case is different, and a qualified attorney is the only person who can accurately assess your individual situation.

You may think your situation is so simple, or your assets so negligible, that you have nothing to worry about and nothing to lose except for the attorney fee. But you could be wrong. From lingering debt to funds in a pension or retirement plan, there are many assets and liabilities even the most modest couple is sure to have. You may make fatal errors before you have a chance to tell your spouse what's on your mind. Should you move to another apartment now? Might you lose your chance at custody of the children? Can you date? Should you take money out of your bank account? In short, are you at risk in any way?

A qualified divorce attorney will help you avoid traps you could never know about on your own. During the meeting, the lawyer will ask you questions that will allow him or her to evaluate your case. Building on this knowledge and knowing the law and the court system, the lawyer will be able to answer your questions and offer appropriate strategies. Whether you end up hiring this lawyer or not, you will gain a better strategic sense of what's ahead.

Although the wealthiest individuals often pay their full service attorneys' hefty retainers to start work, those of more modest means may now purchase legal services à la carte through a new style of practice called "unbundled" law. In this method, an attorney will look over your shoulder if you can't afford "full service," and no retainer may be necessary. He or she can help you strategize, write a legal letter, or review a mediated settlement agreement.

Should you decide to handle many of the details and do the bulk of the work yourself, it is nevertheless in your best interest to have an attorney on call who is familiar with your case. Even if you and your spouse have "worked everything out" or have chosen a mediator, your own lawyer will advise you about rights you probably don't know you have.

You don't need a prominent divorce lawyer, but you should find someone who has handled divorces before, someone you can afford, and someone with whom you feel comfortable. You are going to have to live with your divorce settlement for the rest of your life. Make sure you don't sell yourself short.

How do you find an attorney? Word of mouth is usually a good way to begin, but don't go by recommendations alone. Other resources are your local Bar Association, or if you are really strapped for cash, you can try legal aid. Don't settle for the first attorney you meet. You must find someone you like, and that individual must practice the kind of law that meets your needs. If you want someone to offer services by menu, then a full-service powerhouse may not be for you.

Meet with a few lawyers before making up your mind. Even if you have to pay for these consultations, you'll learn a little about the differences in legal style and home in on the qualities you prefer.

Know Your Spouse's Annual Income

One of the first issues you'll be settling in your divorce agreement or in court relates to money. Whether for spousal support or child support, you will have to know your spouse's earnings and assets to calculate a reasonable figure. If it doesn't make sense to ask your spouse, you might have to do some digging before that information becomes unavailable.

If your spouse has a salaried position or is paid by the hour, the information should be on a recent pay stub. Alternatively, look at last year's tax return. If your spouse is self-employed, a tax return might not tell you the full story. Do a little detective work. Be creative, but be careful not to break government privacy rules.

Ultimately, you might have to rely on your spouse to furnish this information, but it's prudent to know as much financial information as possible before taking it up with him or her. One wife we know happened to be enrolled in a course on money management when she decided to move ahead with her divorce. Before she informed her husband, she asked him to help her fill out an income-disclosure form—ostensibly her "homework." When she began divorce proceedings, she had the information she needed—in her husband's handwriting, no less.

Even if you're not enrolled in a class, requesting such information should be fairly straightforward. Why do you want the details? In this day and age, our financial status is something we must all be on top of. Just tell your partner you feel foolish without a handle on the economic underpinnings of your life.

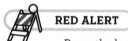 **RED ALERT**

Be on the lookout for financial information that is distorted or intentionally incomplete. If you suspect any shenanigans on the part of your spouse, consult a forensic accountant. When fishing for information about your spouse, do not explain, explicitly, why you need this information. Whoever you're asking might well figure out your motivation. Therefore, you must make it understood that discretion is essential. But do so subtly; the less said, the better. Remember, even a friend can be forced to testify against you under oath.

Assess What You Can Earn

Even if you are not used to earning money for yourself, you could well have to go to work after the divorce. Have you been out of the job market for a while? Perhaps you need some time to get your skills up to speed before taking the plunge. Or, better yet, get a plan to make yourself more marketable and ask your spouse to support you while you go to school or get that extra training. Has business been off lately? Keep a record of that now so no one later accuses you of deliberately reducing your income to negotiate a more favorable settlement.

Understand Your Family's Financial Holdings

Remember, as you wind your way through the divorce maze, you will only be able to share in assets you know about, so you must find out exactly what the two of you have. For most, that's probably easy. There may be a house (with a mortgage), a car (perhaps leased or encumbered by a loan), a pension or retirement plan (not yet vested), and a little bit of savings.

But for some, property ownership is more complicated. For instance, businesses created during the marriage are assets to be valued, and a judge can distribute their value upon divorce. The same may go for an academic degree or even part of the value of a summer house—one you inherited during the marriage—depending upon the facts of your case.

Assess Your Family's Debt

Often, the allocation of debt is harder to prove or negotiate than the division of assets. What debts do you have? Credit card, personal loans, bank loans, car loans? How much does it cost to pay these debts each month?

As for tabulation of assets, a good source for this information is your family's tax return. Most tax returns will have the name of your bank(s) and the account numbers. If you don't have the tax return and are afraid of raising suspicions by asking for it, write the Internal Revenue Service or other appropriate taxation agency for a copy (provided it was a joint return), but it could take several weeks to receive it. If you have a family accountant, you can also ask him or her to send you copies of statements and returns.

Make Photocopies of All Family Financial Records

Canceled checks, bank statements, tax returns, life insurance policies—if it's there, copy it. You might never need this information, but if you do, it's good to have it. If it's in electronic form, save it on an external hard drive as well.

Take Stock of Your Family's Valuables

Organize and make a list of all your individual and joint financial assets, and get the documentation in order: your brokerage accounts, checking accounts, savings accounts or IRAs, life, car, and health insurance policies, deeds to your properties, and so on. Get the name and phone number of your financial advisor and insurance broker if you don't already have it.

Inventory your safety deposit box or family safe, and take photographs of the contents. Do the same with jewelry or any furniture, paintings, or other items of value. You needn't list every worn-out piece of furniture, but anything with a value of more than $300 should be included. Property insurance policies can be helpful here because many companies ask you to list the valuables you want insured. Some people keep a list of belongings in a safe, also for insurance purposes. If you've done that, start with that list. There's no need to reinvent the wheel.

Understand Your Household Costs

Whether you plan to stay in the house or leave, you won't know how much money you need unless you know the monthly costs of running your household. If you pay the monthly bills, your job is easy. If you don't, look through the online accounts or the checkbook—see how much you pay in monthly rent or on your mortgage; check utilities, including electricity, heat, cable, and phone; and look at sundry costs from snow plowing in winter to lawn care and gardening in spring.

One woman we know, a well-educated social worker with a full-time career, didn't know the first thing about the family's monthly expenses because her husband's assistant made out the checks and paid the bills from the office. She was embarrassed to confess her "ignorance," but she is hardly alone. Use the worksheet for calculating expenses at the end of this chapter to help you understand your finances.

 **SILVER LININGS**

Although your reasons for seeking out financial information may be painful, you will greatly benefit from knowing where money comes from and how it is spent. You'll soon learn how to manage your money, which is empowering, both now and after your divorce.

Determine Where You Will Live After Separation

If you're the spouse who plans to move out, decide where you're going to live, and figure out how much it will cost, month-by-month, beforehand. Maybe you plan to move in with your romantic interest. Although that might be tempting—it might be the reason you want to divorce—it might also be a case of going from the frying pan into the fire. How is your spouse going to react when you want to bring the children there? Will this make your case a thousand times more difficult to settle? Will your spouse have an adultery claim that can hurt you later? If you answered any of these questions with a "yes" or an "I don't know," move somewhere else.

Look through the real estate advertisements to learn about rents. Consider what it will cost to move, and calculate start-up expenses, including telephone installation and turning on electricity, internet, and cable.

Start Saving Money

One unemployed wife of an electrician wanted a divorce immediately. Her friend, a paralegal who worked in a law firm specializing in divorce, convinced her to hold off for a while. Instead, the friend advised her, it would be best to wait a solid year before starting the divorce action. During that time, she was instructed to save money—enough, hopefully, to be able to pay the rent for a place of her own after she asked for a divorce.

It wasn't easy, but the wife saved enough to move out and pay rent for a year. As it turned out, the judge ordered the husband to pay her monthly rent until the divorce was final; but without the initial savings, she wouldn't have been able to move out in the first place.

Build Up Your Own Credit

If you don't have credit cards in your own name, apply for them now. You might be able to get them based on your spouse's income, and you will probably need credit later. Use the cards instead of cash and pay the entire balance by the due date every month. Don't charge more than you can pay; you'll be creating even more problems for yourself!

Stay Involved with Your Children

First of all, this is important for your children—especially because they will need all the support and reassurance they can get during the turbulent times ahead. In addition, because courts consider the depth and quality of your relationship when making custody and parenting time decisions, such involvement now could translate to more time with your children and the likelihood of shared custody after the divorce.

Do a self-check: have you been so busy earning a living that you've let your spouse bear the brunt of child rearing? If so, now is the time to reallocate your priorities. If you have school-age children, help get them off to school in the morning, help them with homework at night, and help get them to bed. Learn who their teachers are, who their pediatrician is, who their friends are. If your children are not yet in school, spend as much time with them as you can before and after work. Be an involved parent—for now and for your future together.

YOU CAN DO IT!

With a major disruption imminent, your kids will need the reassurance of your extra attention. Fear of abandonment by one or both parents is the number-one reaction of children faced with divorcing parents. On the legal front, the more involved you are with your kids now, the more chance you will have to stay involved—by court order, if necessary.

Withdraw Your Money

If you fear your request for divorce will send your spouse straight to the bank or brokerage accounts, withdraw half of the money in all your savings accounts first. (If you have an IRA, consult your accountant about how to approach this.) Place the money in a new account, and keep it there until you and your spouse can work out the distribution of property. Do not spend the money if at all possible.

If the money is in a checking account and you know the account is nearly emptied every month to pay bills, do not withdraw any of that money; you'll create financial havoc if checks bounce.

Consider Canceling Charge Cards

If you pay the credit card bills, consider canceling your accounts—or at least reducing the spending limit. In one case, the wife's announcement that she wanted a divorce sent the husband on a $50,000 shopping spree—and she became liable for the home theater and the hot tub (installed, incidentally, in a house she stood to lose). If you cancel or reduce lines of credit, of course, you must inform your spouse to save embarrassment and, later, anger. You can say the family needs to cut back, which is probably going to be true.

Decide How to Tell Your Spouse

Here, you might need professional advice or advice from a battle-worn friend. Would your partner accept the news more easily in a public place, such as a restaurant, or in the privacy of your home?

One husband we know delayed telling his wife he wanted a divorce because she threatened suicide each time he mentioned separating. The wife was an unsuccessful actress with a flair for the dramatic who dropped her suicide threats once the husband agreed she could take over their apartment. Still, some threats must be dealt with seriously.

If you're afraid your announcement will send your spouse off the deep end, be sure that you have consulted a professional counselor beforehand. Although there is often no way to lessen the hurt and rejection, a professional therapist might be able to supply you with strategies for leaving your spouse with as much of his or her self-esteem intact as possible.

Decide How to Tell the Children

You might want to consult with a professional about this. Would the news be best coming from the two of you together or from one of you alone?

One husband we know planned to tell the children that he was moving out on Christmas. He thought that would be a good time because the whole family would be together. His lawyer tactfully suggested he choose a different day.

Safeguard Your Property

High school yearbooks, jewelry, computer flash drives, your grandmother's family heirlooms, whatever—if it indisputably belongs to you and you fear your spouse might take it for spite or leverage, move it out of the house. If you have several such items, move them out slowly, over time, before you announce your plans. Depending on the size of the objects, you might store them in a safe-deposit box, a storage facility, or the home of a trusted friend.

 YOU CAN DO IT!

Before you start divorce proceedings, you might want to consider the legal difference between divorce and separation (see Chapter 4). If you want finality in your marital status, it is certainly preferable to be divorced. Alternatively, if you are not ready to be divorced, a judgment of separation is preferable. We suggest that, to the extent possible, you investigate these alternatives in advance.

Avoid Unnecessary Major Purchases

When there are suddenly two households to maintain, you might find your financial freedom drastically curtailed. The number of people who buy brand new cars while they're starting divorce proceedings is staggering. The payments could financially devastate you, and your spouse can use the existence of your new car as proof of your ability to pay for all sorts of other expenses. Sorry, guys and gals: resist.

Tell Your Spouse First

Although you might consult with friends before you take the plunge, be sure that they know if word gets around before you have told your spouse you want a divorce, it could spell trouble for you down the road.

Stay in the Marital Residence If Possible

Depending on your circumstances and the laws of your jurisdiction or country, you could weaken your position on custody and possibly your personal or *marital property* if you move out. You should discuss any plans to move from the marital residence with your lawyer before making a decision. As always, take immediate action if abuse is at issue.

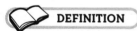

DEFINITION

Marital property, also called *joint property,* is generally what a husband and wife acquire during the marriage. In some jurisdictions, inheritances, disability awards, and gifts received from a third party—that is, not the spouse—are not considered marital or joint property, even if a spouse received them during the marriage. Other exceptions may exist as well.

When It Comes as a Surprise

You may be shocked to learn that your partner wants a divorce. Barbara thought she and her husband were, for the most part, getting along well, with only some small disagreements. They had a beautiful one-year-old son whom they both adored. One night, her husband announced he wanted a divorce. At the same time, he refused to move out of the house for another year because he wanted to bond with his son. Barbara had no recourse. She lived under those strained circumstances until they worked out a settlement. Only then did he move out.

No matter what your circumstances, if your spouse's desire for divorce takes you by surprise, you will probably feel as if the bottom has dropped out from under you. You're likely to need months to lick your emotional wounds, restore your self-esteem, and start to heal. Nonetheless, as raw and beaten as you might feel, you will need to follow a plan of action if you want to protect your legal rights, financial assets, and access to your children. We know you'll have plenty of time to think the details through, but for now, when the pain is so enormous you can hardly think at all, these actions will shore up your strategic position for later.

The second you're told you will be involved in divorce, hire a lawyer. Be sure to tell your lawyer about any problems that might require relief from the court: the need for money for yourself or your children; the need to decide, at least on a temporary basis, where the children will live and what the visitation arrangements will be; and in some cases, the need for protection from the other spouse.

If you are a parent, the most important thing to do is to consult your lawyer to make sure that you are doing everything possible to protect your rights with regard to your children.

You must also avoid trampling on the rights of your spouse, no matter how you feel about him or her. You may be furious, but don't make the fatal mistake of locking your spouse out of the house or abandoning your marital residence with or without the children. If you do so, you stand to damage your position with regard to custody and assets. If you leave, the judge could order that your spouse remain in the residence—with the kids—until things are settled. If you lock your spouse out, the judge could order you to let him or her back in. With emotions at peak levels, this situation would be uncomfortable at best.

Never act out of revenge. Do not put the children in a loyalty bind. Resist any urge to do "revenge spending." It might be used against you later if your case goes to court.

 **RED ALERT**

Alberto was so furious at Sarah for divorcing him, and then suing for 90 percent of the estate, that he sent her a cockroach in the mail. Aware of her fear of insects, he chuckled to think of her reaction upon opening the clever "gift." But at trial, the so-called antic served merely to enrage the judge. He found the "trick" so reprehensible and Alberto's character and sense of justice so skewed that all discretionary decisions were made in favor of Sarah. Please keep your anger in check. Angry or aggressive acts can be used against you once the legal system is involved.

It goes without saying, of course, that if your spouse has asked for a divorce, you will also need to follow the strategic tips provided at the beginning of this chapter. First, protect your financial position by learning all you can about your family's finances. Be sure to photocopy all relevant documents and photograph your valuables, including those in the safe deposit box.

You must protect yourself against any preemptive moves your spouse may have taken without your knowledge. Directly ask your spouse for any papers that are suddenly missing. Make sure that the safe deposit box or family safe has not been raided. With your lawyer's help, you can get restraining orders against the use of specific bank accounts.

Now is the time for some financial strikes of your own. If it's not too late, collect any diaries, calendars, or other items and remove them from the house. If your spouse hasn't yet raided the bank accounts, withdraw half of the savings accounts and open a new account. Do not spend that money if at all possible. If the credit cards are in your name, or if you pay the credit card bills, cancel them. Tell your spouse you've cancelled the cards. Since he or she has announced plans to divorce, this should not come as a surprise.

On the other hand, if you have not yet established credit in your own name, now is the time to do so; use your spouse's credit lines to build some credit of your own. Obtain and complete applications immediately.

If the two of you are going to live together until the divorce is final, decide where you'll sleep. Note that because your spouse told you that he or she wants the divorce, you have the upper hand and can probably successfully demand use of the bedroom. If you and your spouse can still have a civil conversation, decide how and what the two of you will tell the children.

Finally, consider therapy if you feel it might help. There are going to be many stresses in the future, emotional as well as financial, and the better you can cope with them, the smoother the divorce process will go for you.

Use the following worksheet when assessing your expenses. You'll need this information later, no matter which side of the divorce proceedings you find yourself on.

Worksheet for Calculating Expenses

Item	Amount
Housing Expenses	
Rent	_____
Mortgage	_____
Property taxes	_____
Condominium charges	_____
Cooperative maintenance charges	_____
Outstanding loan payments	_____
Gardening	_____
Cleaning person	_____
Household repairs	_____
Painting	_____
Furniture, linens	_____
Cleaning supplies	_____
Utilities	_____
Water charges	_____
Electricity and gas	_____
Landline	_____
Mobile phone	_____
Cable and internet	_____
Appliances and upkeep	_____
Transportation Expenses	
Car payments	_____
Car insurance	_____
Car repairs	_____
Fuel	_____
Public transportation	_____

Children

Children's tuition   _____

Summer camp   _____

Babysitter/childcare   _____

Allowance   _____

School transportation   _____

Child support (from previous relationships)   _____

Lessons (music, dance, etc.)   _____

Sporting goods   _____

Personal Expenses

Food   _____

Clothing   _____

Laundry   _____

Dry cleaning   _____

Books   _____

Magazines   _____

Newspapers   _____

Cigarettes   _____

Gifts   _____

Beauty/salon   _____

Lunches at work   _____

Courses   _____

Hobbies   _____

Insurance

Life insurance   _____

Personal property insurance   _____

Fire, theft, liability insurance   _____

Medical Expenses

Medical insurance _____

Medical _____

Dental _____

Optical _____

Pharmaceutical _____

Entertainment

Vacation _____

Movies _____

Video rentals/downloads _____

Theater _____

Dining out _____

Parties/entertaining _____

Miscellaneous Debts and Expenses

Credit card debt _____

Alimony (from previous relationships) _____

Church or temple dues _____

Charitable contributions _____

Income taxes _____

Other (Have we missed something essential to your life? You fill in the blanks.)

_____   _____

_____   _____

_____   _____

TOTAL: _____

A quick glance at this chapter might turn your stomach in knots. The advice may seem aggressive and sometimes even adversarial, but you must protect yourself. Getting divorced is one of the great stressors in life, but you can get through this. Trust us. It may seem impossible right now, but time will heal this wound.

The Least You Need to Know

- As soon as you know you will be involved in a divorce, consult an attorney.
- Find out your family's income and assets.
- Find out your family's expenses and estimate your future expenses.
- Photocopy all business records.
- Get any incriminating information—particularly personal diaries—out of the house, but be prepared to produce this material during the discovery process.
- Care for your children. Their road will not be easy.

Love in Ruins

One of our friends was devastated when, during her last year of medical residency, her husband, a wealthy surgeon, left her for someone else without explaining, even briefly, what went wrong. The couple became involved in a protracted court battle regarding finances and issues of child custody. As trial date after trial date was postponed, issues of spousal maintenance and child support, division of property, and a permanent custody decision were put on hold.

In all that time, the ex-husband—by now living with his new partner—refused to tell his former wife why he'd left her, for fear it would weaken his case. But here's the thing: this woman would have traded untold thousands of dollars for a simple explanation. "I'll tell you after the case is closed," her former spouse often promised during their infrequent moments of civility. If only that moment had arrived.

In This Chapter

- Understanding the emotional journey to divorce for the "dumper" and the "dumpee"
- How to tell your partner it's over and the importance of honesty
- How to work through the pain and get on with your life
- Protecting your custodial, property, and financial rights in the aftermath of separation

In truth, it's impossible for you to shield your partner from pain if you are rejecting him or her. It's going to hurt—especially if you are forthright and direct in your communication. And yet, as you and your partner face this final stage of your relationship, the most important gift you can give is honesty.

Breaking the News

The inevitability of divorce is often experienced quite differently by the person who has done the rejecting (the *dumper* in divorce lingo) and the rejected individual (the *dumpee*). If you are the partner initiating the divorce, the emotional journey from your marriage toward a new life began long ago. However, your spouse, although sensing difficulties, might not realize how far you have traveled from the nucleus of your relationship. Your spouse might not feel just hurt and angry, but also shocked, when you announce the news.

You owe an honest explanation to the person you have married about why you want to leave. Again and again, divorce psychologists report that the complaint they hear most is, "I want one adequate explanation. I never knew what went wrong."

After you have provided your spouse with an explanation of what went wrong, expect powerful emotions ranging from sadness to anger to fear. Remember, the divorce might sadden you, too, but you have had time to get used to the idea. Your partner has not. You will have to give some time and some leeway for your spouse to catch up.

Receiving the News

If your spouse has asked you for a divorce, you might find yourself reeling with disbelief, pain, and, after the shock wears off, anger. You must remember that these feelings are entirely normal. Indeed, the grief one feels at divorce is in some ways comparable to the grief experienced when a loved one dies. According to psychologist Mitchell Baris, PhD, the grief is experienced in phases.

"Initially," he explains, "You go through a phase of sadness, anger, and heightened feelings of rejection. There may be very different rates of acceptance for one partner than for another," Baris states. Eventually, even the rejected individual will come to see separation and divorce in a more positive light. The divorce decision, although initiated by one person, becomes mutual.

It only makes sense that the person who initiated the decision comes to accept the reality of divorce sooner. "That individual is a little bit more advanced; they have been working through their initial feelings of acceptance, of realization that the relationship is over," says Dr. Baris. "The sadness, the sense of failure, has begun to fade, and he or she has already begun to envision the single life—whether as a single parent or as a single individual. By the time that person has announced a desire to divorce to a spouse, the idea of separation has already been worked through. The rejected individual, on the other hand, is typically several months behind in terms of working through the grief."

Famed death researcher Elisabeth Kübler-Ross defined the stages in the grieving process over the death of a loved one. Those facing divorce, say psychologists, can expect a similar, though perhaps not identical, process. Psychologist Mitchell Baris has altered the well-known Kübler-Ross list slightly in its application to divorce:

Denial. This is your basic state of shock. You cannot believe it's true.

Anger. The rejected individual, "the dumpee," will direct anger at the rejecting spouse and the world. Get it out. It's okay.

Guilt and depression. Feelings of guilt are inevitable, more often in the one initiating the divorce, but in the recipient as well. Depression is a common emotion, even in those who badly want to divorce and move on. After all, it is still the end of something you once hoped would endure. It's important to turn guilt and depression into something constructive: an examination of the role you played in the breakup of your marriage. Life is about growth, after all, and if you can't see yourself clearly, you won't be able to move on.

Acceptance. Reality has sunk in. It's not one of those bad dreams from which you will awaken; it's real. You accept this as your reality and move on—however awkwardly, however tentatively—with your life.

 **RED ALERT**

Those who remain stuck in a morass of anger, self-pity, and self-imposed isolation might be helped by psychotherapy. The right counselor can do wonders for someone who needs to change his or her view of the world, embrace creativity in life, and, most importantly, start feeling good!

Envisioning the Future

If you have children, and often even if you don't, your relationship with your soon-to-be former spouse will change. As you both move on in your lives, the intense hurt and anger you are now experiencing will lessen. It is easy for us to say, "we've seen it before," but trust us, we have.

Your feelings will change over time. You will meet new people and become involved in new interests or jobs. Other, unrelated issues will take center stage in your mind. Your children's activities will continue to engage you. Just watching them grow and change will give you immense pleasure as you rebalance your emotional life.

 YOU CAN DO IT!

You will be involved with your former spouse regularly if you have children. For the children's sake, as well as your own sanity, civility is all-important during the breakup period of your marriage. Fostering bitterness will only root you in your current upset and pain. Instead, as you go through the beginning of the end, you must refocus your thoughts on your new life. This will hasten your healing, empowering you to move on.

At some point in the years to come, you'll be surprised to find that watching your son's baseball game with your ex-spouse just a few rows back or even on the same bench is not as painful as it had been. You might even be able to chit-chat about the kids. Who would've guessed!

Emotions Can Have Legal Implications

Even before the shock, disbelief, and confused feelings have abated, you are faced with a legal situation: what happens now for the two of you? Both of you will have to consider the legal implications of your behavior from now on.

It's not fair, you say? Sorry, but the truth is, many states courts are set up so that the circumstances leading one person to leave another have no bearing on the division of marital assets, child support, or parental time sharing.

That's right: if your spouse has left you for another love, in most cases, it will have no impact on the division of the worldly goods you have built up during your time together or on other issues in your separation and divorce. In a pure no-fault state, the dumper and the dumpee are on equal footing in the eyes of the law. Check the laws in your jurisdiction and country.

Despite common "no-fault" divorce laws, the emotional turmoil of impending divorce often causes one partner to concede his fair share of the marriage spoils in a negotiated settlement. As you plan your separation and, ultimately, divide your marital assets and other arrangements, be aware that the emotional tenor created as your marriage crumbles and then dies can influence a divorce settlement in unforeseen and irrevocable ways.

Our friend Tonina provides the perfect cautionary tale. A reserved individual who always wanted space and "more time for me," Tonina often felt overwhelmed by her outgoing, gregarious, and attention-seeking spouse, Leo. She'd been ambivalent about their marriage for years, spending much of her free time selling her homemade jewelry at craft shows, often far from home.

Over time, the discontented Tonina found companionship in a recently divorced fellow craftsman, a gentle bead-maker who also made the rounds of craft shows. With so many hours together, their booths side by side, the friendship between Tonina and the sensitive bead-maker eventually blossomed into more. Finally, Tonina realized she'd found the soul mate she had always needed. Although Leo had been good to her and truly loved her, and although he would be devastated, she knew she had to tell him she had reached a fork in the road, and she could no longer travel his way.

In the days following "the announcement," Tonina moved into a spare room in the home of a female friend and participated in counseling with Leo. Leo had pressed for the sessions; his fervent hope was to use the counseling to convince Tonina to recommit to him. Tonina, on the other hand, hoped the therapist could convince Leo to let go. Eventually, that is just what occurred.

Six months after her announcement, Tonina had moved into her own apartment, a bastion of the space and solitude she had so long craved, but also a haven for nurturing her new romance. Leo, on the other hand, continued to live in the couple's home, where he often found the loneliness crushing. He signed up for several online dating services and went out several times a week, but he found it hard to shake his fear that Tonina could never be replaced.

It was a full year after Tonina moved out that the divorce was finalized—a year of new awakenings for Tonina and agony for Leo. There was only one benefit to the underdog position that Leo could discern: despite their 20 years of marriage, Tonina had demanded far less than her fair share of the marital estate than she was legally entitled to. Pressured by Leo at the outset not to obtain private counsel, but to work with a mediator of his choosing, Tonina agreed as part of her "penance."

In her desire to sever ties as quickly and cleanly as possible, she agreed to the stern terms Leo put forth in the mediation sessions each week. She literally (and knowingly) allowed Leo to shortchange her in settlement by waiving her rights to marital property belonging to them both. Not only did she agree to give Leo the house and the car free and clear, she also requested none of his 401(k), to which she was entitled.

If Tonina had been less wracked by guilt and Leo had been less hurt during those months of separation, the division would have been more equitable. But with Tonina feeling too guilty to hire a lawyer to negotiate on her behalf and with Leo too upset to abide by the standard of fairness he usually embraced, Tonina was left without a dime.

Our advice to those about to end a marriage is to be aware of how the emotional underpinnings of your initial breakup can affect the financial and legal terms of your final settlement. If you are the leaver, we beseech you to be emotionally kind to your soon-to-be ex when you break the news. The angrier your spouse becomes during this delicate time, the more unyielding he or she will be in reaching a reasonable settlement.

This is not only the empathetic path, but also the strategic one. If you feel too much guilt, or if you are the object of too much anger, you may find yourself accepting unfair terms.

Even as you remain kind, you must also stay steadfast in your demand for what is your legal due. You are breaking up your marriage for a reason, after all. In the end, it takes two to ruin a marriage; if the law, generally, does not distinguish between dumper and dumpee, neither should you.

If you are the one who's been left, on the other hand, this may be your best chance to strike the most favorable deal possible. Like Leo, you might be able to obtain greater concessions from your spouse in the early days of the announcement, when the hurt is still raw and the guilt most pronounced. This is all provided you keep your anger—but not your sense of disappointment and betrayal—to yourself.

 RED ALERT

Be aware of your emotions as you begin divorce proceedings. It is tempting, in the interest of peace and economy, to go with a mediator. But if you feel so guilty you might cave during negotiations—if you have any doubt about your ability to demand economic fairness because you feel you inflicted emotional pain on your spouse by leaving—you would do well to hire someone to negotiate on your behalf.

Remember that your spouse may be most likely to leave with less when you seem bereft and alone. Even if your partner has left for another love, he or she will be less likely to make concessions in settlement if you seem happily ensconced with a new love, too. This is just human nature. You have already been rejected; a better divorce settlement is hardly compensation, but you should still opt for whatever advantage you can.

The Least You Need to Know

- Be honest with your spouse about your reasons for moving on.
- Realize that although you are now in emotional turmoil, time will assuage your shock or your guilt.
- In most cases, the law does not distinguish between *dumper* and *dumpee* in terms of custody or distribution of wealth.
- Protect your financial and property interests through any legal means available to you, even if you feel guilty, as soon as it is clear that divorce is inevitable.

Separation

Couples considering divorce often achieve a new balance during a period of separation, which can be one of the first emotional and legal steps down the road to divorce.

Separation (be it legal or physical) generally commences on the day a couple begins to live in separate residences with the intention of continuing to live apart. As you consider separation, familiarize yourself with the local law on living outside the family home. Laws on separation vary by jurisdiction, and they can affect the legal status of your marriage as well as the eventual division of property, should there be a divorce. In some places, separation for a prescribed period of time is grounds for divorce. If you've decided to live separately just to try it out, find out first if you fall into this category. On the other hand, in New York State, the law requires that the parties live separate and apart for one year after the execution of a written separation agreement.

In This Chapter

- How physically separating can help you understand what you really want
- Using the period of separation to come into your own
- Whether to leave home or stay until the divorce is final
- Understanding the law on separation in your jurisdiction

If you do not reside in a place where separate residences will have an impact on you legally, you have the luxury of time away from your family situation to contemplate your life choices.

Beginning of the End, or a New Beginning?

In most jurisdictions, separation, whether physical or legal, does not have to end in divorce. Sometimes separation can be a time of forgiveness and renewed commitment. Many times, couples will separate in hopes of saving a marriage. Sometimes, this can work. After all, just getting distance from a painful, antagonistic situation can provide you with enough perspective to come back together weeks or months later and sort things out.

One couple we know did just that. The man, a newspaper reporter, left his wife in Boston and went on assignment in Iraq for a year. Their marriage had been on the rocks, but during the year apart, the two developed an email correspondence that brought them new intimacy and understanding. When they came back together after 12 months apart, they were ready to really commit to the relationship and even decided to start a family.

In other marriages, separation—as opposed to divorce—becomes a permanent way of life. We know of a couple who has been legally separate but married for over 25 years. The woman, happily living in a townhouse in Miami, plays tennis during the day and spends evenings with her lover, another woman. The man, who enjoys the city life in a Manhattan penthouse, runs a successful business and has pursued a series of monogamous relationships that fell apart, one by one, when he refused to commit to marriage. He had the perfect excuse. He was not yet divorced from his estranged wife. For this couple, divorce holds nothing positive. It would erode their joint fortune and diminish the money available to their two children. In the man's case, getting a divorce would only make him available for remarriage, an idea he hardly relishes.

This estranged couple had their relationship formalized in a legal agreement drafted by their attorneys. For them, it was the best route to new and separate lives.

 **RED ALERT**

While some couples are able to sort things out during time apart from their spouses, it's not always the case. The flip side is that some couples who separate just to "get a little distance" find they like the distance just fine.

Preamble to Divorce

As the name implies, separation can be the first step along the journey to separate lives. Not quite permanent or irrevocable, separation enables the two individuals to get a taste of what it would be like to exist apart—to manage separate households, separate finances, and separate selves.

Most of the time, separation is a preamble to divorce—even if that was not the original intent. A Dallas couple we know opted for a long-distance relationship as a means of gaining perspective. The decision to separate was facilitated when the woman was offered a job in Des Moines. Unfortunately, her husband began feeling so resentful when she really left that, ultimately, he could not accept her back into his life. He felt this way despite the fact that he was the one who had encouraged her to leave in the first place.

Another example involves a woman who married the first boyfriend she ever had right after college. As the marriage went on, he became increasingly critical, commenting on everything from her friends to her weight to her work habits to her clothes. Yet because she'd never really been alone, she could not imagine life without him. Finally, through therapy, she was able to take what she thought would be a short hiatus from the marriage. She never imagined that during this break she would experience a return of self-esteem, enthusiasm, and even joy. This separation was just what she needed to realize she could go it alone over the long haul.

As a step before divorce, physical separation has emotional and legal implications that you need to understand. Decisions made during separation often become carved in stone, and anyone separating without the appropriate strategizing and protections can suffer unpleasant repercussions for years. Indeed, the legal arrangements made for separation often cannot be renegotiated for the divorce; those who decide to let things go, thinking they will have another chance at a fairer deal later, are sorely disappointed most of the time.

Remember what we said in Chapter 3: the emotional tenor of your break-up and, by extension, your separation can impact the legal outcome of your divorce. Separation is such a naturally turbulent and overwhelming period that it lends itself to rash decisions driven by emotions like guilt and anger. In a cooler moment, you may have made a more strategic deal, but you will not generally have the luxury of negotiating twice. If you are separating, you should attend to the fine print of your future life now.

There are couples who treat separation casually and live apart without any formal legal agreement. If you and your spouse are quite certain that your separation is temporary, and that you will be using the time to reconcile, a casual attitude may work well. You can date your spouse—even have sex with your spouse—because as far as you are concerned, divorce is not in the cards.

However, please be careful. If you have filed for a fault divorce (covered in Chapter 6), you may lose grounds for divorce in your jurisdiction if you date or have sexual relations with your spouse during a period of separation. If separation is likely to be the first step in your journey to single status, we suggest you enter it seriously and formally—with a signed agreement and full awareness of the potential errors, many of them impossible to reverse later on.

Separating Peacefully

As with the decision to divorce, the party who initiates the separation experiences it differently from the spouse who is caught unaware. Whether you are the dumper or the one dumped, your future will be impacted by your decisions during this critical time.

It makes sense that the person who initiated the divorce may come to embrace the single life of separation sooner; that individual has been living with the decision for quite a while. Given this fact, the individual who has initiated the divorce should see the separation as a means of providing his or her partner with time. Even though you might be saying, "Okay, we're going to end the relationship. Let's get working on the terms of the separation. Let's see if we can mediate this," your partner is still reeling from the pain. At first, he or she will not be nearly as ready to negotiate the terms of the agreement—certainly not in any sense that could be favorable to you.

If you have been rejected by your spouse, on the other hand, use the separation period to help yourself heal. As you go through the stages of grief we covered in Chapter 3, you will come to see yourself as a solo act. You might need to utilize this time to brush up on job skills, gain self-confidence, or simply come to know yourself as an individual who stands alone. You'll know you have arrived when you too can say, "Okay, I can see our incompatibility. This needs to end. At this point, I would also choose to end this relationship and go on in a new direction."

Remember, the process is painful. If you're like most people, you won't pass quickly through the emotional gauntlet of separation. Typically, psychologists say, the first year following initial separation is most difficult. During this period, you're most likely to experience mood swings, sadness, feelings of loss, and anger. If you remain on this emotional roller coaster for more than a year, however, you are not progressing fast enough. It is time to seek counseling or some other form of psychological help.

Published research bears this timetable out. According to a study from California clinical psychologist and marital transition expert Joan Kelly, Ph.D., couples report that conflict drastically declines after 12 months. Other research indicates that conflict and anger tend to diffuse after a period of separation, and if couples have not continued to interact, at the end of two years, most of the conflict will be gone.

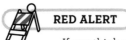 **RED ALERT**

If you think you are going to divorce and you might want custody of your children, some judges might hold your move from your children's house against you. Be careful. Don't let a short-term goal interfere with what you really want.

Surviving Forced Togetherness

Sometimes, despite the positive impact of physical separation, couples stay together in the same physical space for legal and financial reasons until the day of the divorce decree. There are a number of reasons why this is often legally advisable. If you seek full or joint custody of the children—or if you just want a generous visitation schedule—staying in the house will help your cause. Leaving, in fact, often puts you at a tremendous disadvantage in any legal proceeding. Although the opinions expressed here, as in the rest of the book, do not constitute legal advice, the decision to stay or leave is so important that we strongly advise you to consult your attorney before you do anything.

Your leaving might make it easier for your spouse to delay the signing of divorce papers, putting you at a strategic disadvantage. Indeed, many times, a spouse will just want you out of the house but will be reluctant to move forward with divorce because of economic circumstances. Once you leave, your spouse will have little incentive to move quickly. The longer your spouse delays the divorce, the more frustrated you will become, and the more likely you will be to sign an agreement less favorable to you. On the other hand, if you stay in the home, your spouse will be the frustrated one; you will have the upper hand during negotiations.

Finally, consider the financial implications. The longer you and your spouse share the same home, the more money you will save.

If you've decided to stay in the house until the divorce is over, turn one section into your "camp." If you move out of the bedroom, do not—we repeat, do not—leave your clothes, jewelry, and other possessions in the dresser, especially if you plan to use them on a daily or weekly basis. Instead, choose a spot—the den, the guest room, or even the basement—and move all your clothes and possessions there so that you and your spouse have as little negative interaction as possible. (Workday mornings can be pretty negative even in the happiest marriages!)

If you have been advised by your attorney to stay in the house, try to do so as amicably as humanly possible. Of course it will be difficult, but adding any more hatred or animosity to the marital pot is toxic.

 **SILVER LININGS**

> During your first year of separation, you might find comfort and camaraderie in one of the myriad support groups for the divorced. As you go about choosing a group, however, do be cautious. Some divorce groups are wonderfully supportive and nurture healing. Others foster conflict and fan the flames of anger. It will not help you to associate with a group that feeds the anger. Find a support team that facilitates positive, constructive solutions for your life so you can get beyond your relationship and divorce and move on.

Making Your Move

If life in the house is intolerable and you know custody is not in the cards for you, a move might be wise. It could take one to three years for your divorce to be final, and neither you nor your spouse could cope with one to three more years of tension. More important, it's not good for the children. Again, check with a lawyer before making a decision.

Before you move, discuss the division of personal property with your spouse. You might not be able to take anything with you yet (one woman we know stayed with 10 friends during the 12 weeks it took her to locate an affordable apartment), but at least you'll both understand that by moving out, you're not giving up your rights to property. Your lawyer might want this in writing. If you don't have a lawyer, write down that you are not giving up any rights by moving out and ask your spouse to sign what you've written.

If life in the house is intolerable and you want custody of the children, talk to your lawyer about moving out with the children. Your lawyer might want to first obtain an order from a judge, giving you temporary custody of the children, thereby giving you the right to take the kids with you when you leave.

Reading the Fine Print

It's important to understand the legal implications of separation, including the difference between an informal break and a legally binding agreement. Remember that separation laws vary by jurisdiction and country. In some jurisdictions, for instance, all assets and debts acquired after the date of the agreement are excluded from consideration as marital property. Without a legal agreement, you are considered married in every sense of the word—and held liable for every cent your partner spends.

For this reason, a formal separation agreement can go a long way toward protecting your financial assets, your custodial privileges, and your personal rights. After all, the separation agreement covers essentially the same ground as a divorce agreement: division of assets and debt, child support and custody, visitation, and spousal support. A separation agreement can be the blueprint for the divorce settlement, and is not easy to change after it has been set forth in a fairly drafted agreement. (Of course, terms of support and custody or visitation are subject to change upon proof of change in material circumstances.)

 YOU CAN DO IT!

More and more couples are choosing to handle their divorces without attorneys, that is, *pro se* or *pro per*. Even if this is your plan, we urge you to consult attorneys at the outset and to put your separation agreement in their hands. In fact, we suggest that if you spend money anywhere it is up front, in drafting a separation agreement. A carefully constructed separation agreement may be the best investment you make; but if you aren't careful, a separation agreement can be your ruination as well. We urge you to do whatever you can to make sure your separation agreement protects your assets, your income, your children, and your rights.

Remember, a separation agreement is a binding contract—one that is put in writing, signed by both parties, and typically notarized. Each separation agreement is different, based not only on the laws in your area, but also the circumstances of the couple involved.

As you and your lawyer render this document, you will establish the ground rules: who stays in the marital home and who leaves; who pays support and to whom; who has custody of the children and how each of you will contribute to their support and care; and not least, how you will divide your marital assets and debts. These issues and a few others, including how you deal with income and debt accrued during separation, will be part of the boilerplate in any separation agreement.

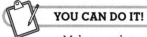

YOU CAN DO IT!

Make sure that even though you are moving out, your spouse understands you are not giving up the right to property. Some spouses, out of guilt, may give the other so much money that they have to move into a single room where they cannot bring the children to visit. Don't become one of them. Ask your attorney to protect you as vigorously as possible through a legally binding separation agreement.

Here are a few other points you may want to attend to:

- Continuation or cessation of certain benefits, ranging from medical and dental insurance to sharing a credit rating.

- The issue of who may deduct alimony payments on the tax return.

- Who pays for college expenses. Unless this is spelled out, the noncustodial parent may not be required to contribute.

- Rights to a pension benefit.

- Access to liquid assets like cash, bonds, and credit cards.

- Ground rules for dealing with credit cards owned jointly.

The Family Plan

For couples with children—who must interact with each other to co-parent, even in the face of divorce—a separation with a parenting plan goes a long way toward easing conflict. In some places it's required. If you're in this situation, you're stuck with your soon-to-be ex-spouse for better or worse. You've got to figure out some way to manage the conflict and get over it so you can see your ex from time to time and reestablish a businesslike relationship that works.

Psychologists advise these parents to create every opportunity for complete separation so that full emotional disengagement can take place. After a period of time—generally about a year—they can relax the separation. Without the hiatus, say psychologists like Baris, some parents may find it more difficult to end the conflict.

In light of all the work you and your spouse will need to do during your physical separation, this is a poor time to invest in a new relationship. You must give yourself the time and space to find some new personal definition and direction. A time of separation is a perfect time to look inward, asking yourself how you contributed to the relationship's end. Some people have difficulty assuming responsibility for creating negative situations for themselves and so look to blame anybody or anything else. You must let go of this "victim" mentality if you want to avoid making the same mistakes again.

The Least You Need to Know

- Physical separation allows a time to assess your feelings about remaining married.
- While many couples see the value in remaining married, others find they are happier living on their own and begin the divorce process.
- If you will live apart for some time, a formal separation agreement negotiated with attorneys will protect you.
- If you remain in the home for legal reasons, but that situation becomes intolerable, ask your lawyer what you should do. Do not just leave; you might compromise your legal standing.

When There's No Turning Back

After the decision to separate and divorce is made, you must—each of you, alone—take some practical steps to protect your interests. As unfortunate and as heartless as it sounds, you have moved on to another stage. You have stopped trying to patch things up in the realm of the heart and have begun instead to negotiate the real world of lawyers and courts, bank accounts and mortgage payments, and, most critically, the custody of your children.

Where to Begin the End

If you and your spouse still get along and you are both fully aware of the family's financial situation, you can sit down and work out an allocation of assets and liabilities. You might also be able to agree on custody and visitation. The two of you together could conceivably decide who takes the children when and for how long; how to structure visitation; how to arrange for childcare; and how to cooperate so that you are there to back up each other in the parental role, although you no longer function as husband

In This Chapter

- Documenting your complete financial history
- How to practice discretion if you decide to date
- When to hire a private investigator
- How to review your prenuptial agreement
- How to craft your own settlement agreement

and wife. Each of you can then find a mediator or lawyer. One attorney will draw up documents, and the other will review them.

The problem is, things don't always go this smoothly. Even the best-intentioned couples find themselves arguing over anything from the custody of the family dog to who gets the football season tickets. If you're like most people, sitting down over a cup of coffee and dividing up the hard-earned fruits of your marriage is just not going to happen.

What then? Follow the scouting motto: be prepared. In Chapter 6, we provide some additional tips to help you lay the groundwork for this preparation. We'll assume, of course, that you've already followed the steps recommended in Chapters 2 and 3. By now, you have consulted a lawyer and have taken stock of your family's financial situation, including any income, property, or outstanding debt. But as the dust begins to clear, as reality sets in, you will be dealing with the details—the accumulations, the detritus, the remains of your relationship, and the vestiges of your shared life. As you set out to settle the score—divest some baggage, work through pain, or simply clear the field—you'll need to attend to the special issues discussed in this chapter.

Gathering Your Financial Documents

You've already collected financial statements readily available around the house. It's important to have copies of tax returns, bank statements, insurance policies, and loan applications going back as far as possible. If you or your spouse has destroyed documents after a decade, as some people do, it could work against you. Such documentation might be especially critical if there's a gap between your reported income and your standard of living.

The Bright family, for instance, reported income of $50,000, but the two children attend private school ($20,000 per year total); the Brights take two very nice vacations a year ($5,000 total); the monthly mortgage on their house is $2,000 ($24,000 total); the monthly mortgage on their summer house is $500 ($6,000 total); and each party drives a leased car at a combined cost of $500 a month ($6,000 total). Grand total: $61,000. That's $11,000 more than their reported income, without even taking into account taxes, food, utilities, clothing, pet supplies, and so on. Clearly, there's more income than has been reported. Bank statements, credit card receipts, canceled checks, and the like all help prove real, as opposed to reported, income. You might also need tax returns simply to prove how much income you or your spouse earns, even if you work for someone else.

If you can't find any of these documents (or you never saved them), you can write the Internal Revenue Service for copies of joint returns, or you can ask your accountant for copies. The bank might keep copies of loan applications and might be willing to release a copy of your application to you. For a fee, although it tends to get expensive, you can obtain copies of canceled checks and your bank statements. (Before incurring that expense, check with your attorney. He or she might be able to get the same information directly from your spouse's attorney. In most instances, the divorce law of your jurisdiction entitles you to this information if your spouse has it or has access to it.)

As you document your deep financial history, make sure that you include these assets:

CASH AND VALUABLES

Savings accounts

Checking accounts

CD accounts

Options to buy stocks

403 accounts

401(k) accounts

Individual retirement accounts

Cash value of life insurance

Businesses

Loans to others

Educational degrees

Security deposits

Bonds

Notes

Stocks

Real property

Jewelry

Antiques

Artwork

Vehicles

Business assets, including accounts receivable, work in process, inventory, hard assets, computer equipment, and software programs

The point is, once the dust has cleared and you can focus, you might need to do a little digging in preparation for the legal proceedings to come. A divorce trial can sometimes be like a war, and you want to go to battle fully armed. Who wouldn't?

The Price of Dating Before Divorce

As you continue to plan strategically for your divorce in these early stages, you need to consider the impact dating will have during your day in court. You do not have to be a hermit just because you are divorcing, unless your attorney tells you otherwise. Usually, discretion is the key. For example, if your divorce is not yet final, never have a friend of the opposite sex sleep at your home or spend time alone with you in your bedroom while the children are home. Similarly, if you are claiming that your spouse was unfaithful, and it is important to your case that you have been faithful, do not become involved with anyone until the divorce is final.

Even if your lawyer tells you it's okay to date, avoid going places where you might run into your spouse. In one case, a husband took his new girlfriend to his wife's favorite restaurant. (She found out when the credit card charges came through.) She was furious and refused to cooperate in settling the case.

Don't bring the children along on a date and don't introduce your friend to them. Unless your case is over or it has been dragging on for many years, it's too soon for the children, and it will only hurt and anger your spouse.

Hiring a Private Investigator

Depending on your circumstances, you may feel compelled to do some investigative digging. Perhaps you suspect that your spouse is having an affair, and you want the goods on him or her. Should you hire a private eye?

The days when you needed compromising pictures of your spouse in the arms of another are long gone. In all states, you can get a divorce on grounds other than adultery. Still, there are people who firmly believe that if you could catch your spouse "in the act," he or she will "cave in" and give you an enormous settlement rather than risk disclosure of the infidelity.

In our opinion, this works on television and in the movies, but not in real life. Sometimes, the two-timing spouse is relieved to have his or her relationship out in the open; other times, he or she just doesn't care. Paying a private eye, at a hefty hourly rate, usually is not worth it.

There is one exception. If custody is going to be an issue in your case, the work of a private investigator might pay off. If you suspect that your spouse ignores the children or relegates their care to someone else (ranging from grandparents to babysitters), or if there is an unknown person living with your spouse and your young children, you might consider calling a private investigator. Evidence for any of these scenarios could be vitally important in a custody case, particularly if you and your spouse are otherwise equally capable parents.

Finally, here's a word to the wise: never conduct surveillance yourself. Secret recordings of your spouse might prove harmful. In one difficult case, the husband, who sought custody of his two young sons, provoked his wife into an argument while the children were in the same room. Secretly, he recorded 10 minutes of his wife yelling and the children crying and played the recording in court. The husband lost custody. The wife testified that the husband had started the argument. What kind of father, her lawyer argued, would deliberately subject his children to an argument between their parents to create evidence for court?

Generally, it's against the law to tap a phone line, so don't do it unless you have permission from a court. Furthermore, there is not much to be gained from a phone tap. A recorded phone conversation probably won't do you much good and could result in your prosecution, unless it somehow directly bears on the issue of custody.

One woman we know lost custody of her son because, following a benign voicemail message to her ex, she accidentally failed to turn her cell phone off. With her ex's answering machine still running, she said terrible things about him to her little boy. The recording was later produced in court—and provided the judge with all the evidence he needed to remove the child from his mother. As the "alienating parent," she was permitted to see the boy for just an hour a week, in therapy.

Reviewing Your Prenuptial Agreement

If you and your spouse signed a *prenuptial agreement,* this is the time to pull it out. You might be surprised to read what the two of you signed in the throes of new love.

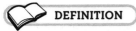 **DEFINITION**

A **prenuptial agreement** is a written contract entered into by a couple before marriage to establish their rights in the event of a death or divorce. The validity of such agreements depends on state law. Have your own attorney review the document.

Prenups, as lawyers call them, used to be popular mostly with older people who were marrying for the second time and wanted to protect the inheritance rights of their children in the event they died. However, now, young people marrying for the first time often inquire about having a prenup. Some stand to inherit money from parents, and the parents want the prenup. Others are wealthy in their own right and have heard so many divorce horror stories that they want to protect their assets.

If you signed a properly executed prenuptial or postnuptial agreement (an agreement entered into after your marriage), there is little to discuss if the marriage fails. Judges will generally uphold the terms of the prenup with a couple of exceptions. In general, judges will not uphold provisions in a prenuptial agreement stating who is to have custody of children and how much child support is to be paid. The care and support of children is usually subject to court review. In addition, judges will not support your agreement if you can prove it was the product of fraud, coercion, distress, or some other unfairness the laws of your state allow you to assert.

What, exactly, will a judge consider unfair? Did you each have your own attorney when you signed the agreement? Did you each reveal how much money, assets, and debts you had before you signed the agreement? How close to your wedding date was the agreement signed? (Signing it on the day before might be construed as undue pressure.) Did you understand the agreement? Is it so unfair to one party that a court won't enforce it? Were you tricked into signing it? If you can prove any of these unfavorable conditions existed, a judge might invalidate the prenuptial agreement.

Starting the Divorce Action

To get the divorce process rolling, someone will need to file. The spouse who starts the legal proceedings is called the plaintiff or petitioner, and the one who responds is called the defendant, or respondent.

If you have hired a full service attorney, he or she will decide when to start legal divorce proceedings, usually based on a number of different factors. Maybe you need some kind of immediate relief, such as support, and your spouse has refused to provide it. If you are fully represented, your lawyer must go to court and ask a judge to order your spouse to pay. The only way the lawyer can go to court is to first start a divorce action, and therefore you would be the plaintiff, or petitioner. If you are handling your case pro se, or if you have hired a lawyer to advise but not represent you, you will initiate the action yourself.

Perhaps you've decided to start your divorce action a few months before you get that bonus, thus excluding the money from marital property. Depending on the laws of your jurisdiction, such strategy may or may not be completely effective. Even if a bonus is paid after the date of separation, it might be deemed joint property because it was earned during the marriage. If you have hired a full-service attorney, he will know just what you should do. If you are filing on your own, this is one of those areas where legal advice should be sought.

Whatever the details, if you and your spouse have worked out a mutually agreeable deal, when it's time to file, the lawyer (or individual) who has been doing the paperwork simply files. Either spouse can file first.

In short, who becomes plaintiff and who becomes defendant depends on a number of factors. Although it might not sit right with you to be the defendant or respondent, gone are the days when such labels matter much.

 YOU CAN DO IT!

You might convince a judge to throw out a prenup if you didn't have an attorney, you were unaware of your spouse's assets or liabilities, you did not understand the agreement, you were tricked into signing it, or you signed it very close to your wedding day.

Working Out a Settlement Agreement

Whether you call it a Separation Agreement or Divorce Settlement, in the best of all possible worlds, you and your spouse would sit down like two civilized adults and pound out a fair deal between yourselves.

In one difficult case, a 60-year-old man was divorcing his second wife. (His first wife died after 30 years of marriage.) Discussions between the lawyers went nowhere, and the parties' grown children from their first marriages weren't helping with their endless "suggestions." Finally, the husband met his wife for breakfast at a diner one Sunday morning. Monday, he came to see his lawyer with the details of a settlement scribbled on a napkin. The lawyers got busy writing up the settlement agreement.

The moral of the story? You and your spouse should do whatever you can to settle the case. You'll save legal fees and headaches. There is only one caveat. Do not sign anything until you speak to a lawyer.

Indeed, we conclude this chapter by stating the obvious. Always check with an attorney before signing any agreement or taking any major steps such as moving out, withdrawing money from joint accounts, stopping credit cards, hiring a private investigator, or trying to tape conversations.

The Least You Need to Know

- Photocopy all the financial documents you can find.
- Be discreet if you date.
- Only consider hiring a private investigator when appropriate in issues concerning child custody.
- Make sure to review your prenuptial agreement as early in the game as possible.
- Confer with a divorce attorney before taking signing documents or taking any major steps.

Navigating the Law

After you digest the fact that your marriage is really ending, you must negotiate its conclusion as gracefully, efficiently, and inexpensively as you can—in a way that's advantageous to you. This simply won't be possible unless you learn all you can about matrimonial law. Only through such knowledge will you be able to protect your rights and your self-esteem.

Consider Part 2 your gentle introduction to divorce law. In the next several chapters, we help you take stock: should you attempt to settle your case out of court, on your own, or with the help of an attorney? Should your legal counsel deliver services à la carte or in full? Should you seek a peaceable settlement through mediation or proceed to the battleground of a trial, armed with attorney, financial documents, and more stamina than you have ever needed before?

Part 2 also examines the legal challenges in marriage and divorce for same-sex couples as well as the divorce laws and processes in Europe.

The Art of the Deal

After months or even years of negotiating, most spouses reach divorce agreements without anyone ever setting foot in a courthouse. This chapter tries to help you reach this goal quickly, saving tens of thousands of dollars and untold years.

"No-Fault" Divorce

In many jurisdictions, provided you've resided in the same state or territory for a minimum amount of time, you do not have to prove *grounds* to get divorced. In such jurisdictions, all you have to plead is incompatibility or irreconcilable differences leading to the irremediable breakdown of the marriage, and a judge will grant you a divorce.

In This Chapter

- The "no-fault" divorce
- When to pursue a quick divorce and when to avoid it
- Constructive approaches to bargaining and compromise
- The cost of a quick divorce
- Your lawyer's role in a quick divorce

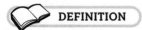

DEFINITION

Grounds are the legally sufficient reasons required for divorce. Although many jurisdictions are "no-fault," where no grounds need be asserted other than incompatibility or irreconcilable differences, others require the plaintiff to prove grounds, including adultery, abandonment, or mental cruelty.

This is quite a change from the days when private detectives hid in hotel room closets with cameras to prove adultery. Some jurisdictions, however, still maintain a "fault" system. You have to prove one of several grounds to get divorced. Grounds usually include mental cruelty, abandonment, adultery, or imprisonment. When people living in "fault" jurisdictions cannot prove grounds, they sometimes move to no-fault jurisdictions to get their divorce.

You might qualify for a no-fault divorce, but that doesn't mean the real issues—custody, support, visitation—are going to be easily resolved. If any of those areas presents a problem, you might still need a judge, even though the divorce itself is a given. Types of fault, meanwhile, depend on the location. With the specifics of each jurisdiction so variable and so subject to change, we hesitate to list every last detail here. Information is readily available on the internet if you search for grounds for divorce and add your jurisdiction and country.

Quick and Easy

Regardless of the requirements for divorce in your area, the real measure of how quickly you'll get your divorce through the courts is how quickly you and your spouse agree on the issues that exist between you. If you have no assets or debt, if you have no children, and if you've only been married a short time, your divorce should be relatively quick and easy. We know several couples who lived together peacefully for years, got married, and were divorced two or three years later. Maybe it was being married, or maybe the relationship had run its course. Whatever the reason, the divorce was merely a matter of filling out the right papers and submitting them to the court. As long as you and your spouse agree that your marriage is over, you both know what assets and debt you have, and you agree on how you'll divide them, a quick divorce could work for you.

Not So Quick and Easy

A woman who had been married to a wealthy businessman for 12 years left him for her son's ninth-grade history teacher. She insisted that all she wanted was the dinnerware they had bought during a trip to Paris. Her lawyer begged her to demand a fairer deal, wrote her letters stating she was making a mistake, and even threatened to stop working as her attorney if she took the deal. But she ran off with her new love and the Limoges. Four months later, when her relationship with the teacher ended, she wanted to reopen her case—but it was four months too late. She got a quick divorce, but hardly a fair one.

What's the moral of the story? A quick divorce works fine if it's fair, but not when it occurs because one side feels guilty or pressured. Remember, never sign papers dividing assets or debt without first consulting an attorney. Never sign papers while you are in an overly emotional state. You can feel sad or even depressed about the breakup, but if you're in a major depression, or you're enraged, spiteful, or blinded by love, wait until your emotions settle down before you commit yourself to a deal you might regret later.

 SILVER LININGS

If you haven't received what you want in the divorce decision in terms of custody or property, you will usually have the right to appeal. If you have been treated unfairly by the judge, the situation might be rectified. However, depending on how backlogged the appellate court is, it could take months or years to get back in front of a judge. Worse, appellate judges often defer to the trial judge, especially in custody cases where the trial judge had the opportunity to view not only the evidence but also the parents' behavior in court. The appellate judges had no such opportunity.

Working Through the Issues

What if you and your spouse just can't agree? What if there are issues that promise to complicate the situation for years to come? Can you get a quick divorce anyway? Sometimes you can, with the help of a judge, but it depends on where you live.

In major metropolitan areas, where the court dockets are crowded, it could be months, even as long as a year, before your case can be tried. In smaller communities, it is possible you can get your day in court much sooner.

Bargaining and Compromise

It's difficult to negotiate for yourself, particularly when emotions are involved. For many couples, trying to negotiate is like reliving the worst moments of the marriage. After all, if the two of you got along well enough to work out a divorce, you might not be divorcing in the first place. Does this mean you have to abandon all hope and leave everything to the attorneys? Not necessarily. Here are some tips that might help you reach a settlement without going to court:

Never present your bottom line early in the negotiations. It might sound childish, but it happens to be true. When negotiating, don't present your bottom line first; that could end up being the high figure, and it can drop from there.

Argue issues, not positions. It might sound obvious, but it isn't always. For example, you and your spouse are discussing who will pay for your children's college education. Your spouse says the two girls will go to state schools. You say they'll go to the best school they get into. The two of you are arguing positions, not issues. The issue is the cost of college and how you'll finance it.

YOU CAN DO IT!

Focus on the problem, not on your feelings. Say you want to live in the family home until your youngest child graduates from high school, but your husband wants to sell the house now. The issue is whether you can afford the house and whether your spouse needs the sale proceeds. However, your husband's real concern might be that you'll remarry and have someone else move into "his" house. If that issue surfaces, it can be addressed by agreeing that if you remarry, the house would then be sold.

Make rules for your discussion. If you and your spouse are meeting alone, write out a schedule of topics to be covered and stick to it. Agree that neither of you will interrupt the other. If you're meeting with your spouse and with the lawyers (commonly called a four-way meeting), you and your attorney should plan the meeting. You should have an agenda, preferably in writing, and you should know when to talk and when not to talk.

Before one four-way meeting, one husband's lawyer asked him not to talk to his wife. After just three minutes, the husband was shouting at his wife, and she was yelling right back. The husband's lawyer was doodling, and the wife's lawyer was trying to calm her client. Considering that the combined hourly billing rate of the two lawyers probably exceeded $1,000 an hour, the husband (and wife, for that matter) was spending their money at a rapid rate.

Be flexible. That doesn't mean cave in. It means be ready to compromise. Remember the example about the two girls and what college they'd attend? Suppose you don't want to pay anything for college, and your spouse wants you to pay half. What about paying one third? What about paying half only if your income is at a certain level by the time the girls go to college? What about agreeing to pay half but also stipulating that any loans or scholarships the girls receive offset your half?

Be open to ideas. As long as you stay locked into one position, it will be hard to settle your case. You might have to get some advice from your attorney, from your accountant, or from friends who have been divorced.

Be ready to trade. Say that you really want the gold necklace your husband bought you on your third wedding anniversary, and he really wants the cookware. You want the cookware, too. Decide which one you want most, and, if the values are about equal, make the trade. It sounds obvious, but when emotions are running high, it might not be.

Leave heated issues for last. This is a lawyer's trick. Resolve everything you can and save the heavy issues for last. Maybe you both want custody of your child. If you start off discussing that sore point, you'll get nowhere with any other issues. If you first sort out the house, the car, and the debts, you might make better progress on the last, toughest issue.

Have a judge or neutral third party, like a mediator, help resolve the issues you can't resolve. Maybe you and your spouse have worked out everything except custody. A custody trial will still be cheaper than a trial on all the other issues, too. Don't throw in the towel on your settlement agreement just because you can't resolve everything.

If things get too emotional, step back. Maybe you and your spouse have met with the best intentions, but before you know it, you're back to the old routine that never got you anywhere in your marriage. Break for a few minutes or a few days before trying to hammer out an agreement again.

Don't expect improved behavior from your spouse. Behaviors are not likely to change during or after divorce. If your spouse was irresponsible with money during your marriage, don't be shocked when he or she is late with the support check or if your joint savings have mysteriously been depleted.

Remember, getting divorced does not turn a frog into a prince. If you negotiate in good faith but lose track of who you are dealing with on the other side of the table, you could be in for disappointment.

Give up if you're getting nowhere. Maybe you've met alone, maybe with lawyers, maybe with a priest or an accountant, and you've agreed on nothing. It might be time to move on to the next step, which could be a trial in front of a judge. Some spouses need to be told by a judge the way it's going to be.

In one case, the father would not voluntarily relinquish custody of the children (teenagers who wanted to live with their mother), no matter what. If a judge had told him he had to let them go, however, he would have complied.

As it turned out, the case did not go to the court. The lawyers finally worked out an agreement without using the word "custody." The children stayed with their mother during the week and with their father most weekends. The father could live with this arrangement because technically both parties still had custody.

Impediments to Settlement

Once you both feel you know what is and is not in the marital pot, the biggest impediment to settlement is usually emotion.

Maybe you're not ready to let go, so just when it seems like you're about to make a deal, you find a problem with the agreement. If the real problem is that you do not want the marriage to end (whether it's because you still want to be married or you don't want to give her the satisfaction of being divorced), then you should tell your lawyer to stop negotiating for a while. You need time to think things through, and there is no sense incurring legal fees by having lawyers draft and redraft the agreement when you know you're never going to sign it.

Maybe you're ready to be divorced—maybe it was your idea—but you're convinced your spouse would not agree to a deal unless he was hiding something. Despite all the financial disclosure, you're just not sure that you really know what assets your spouse has.

If this is the problem, tell your lawyer you want a representation in the agreement that your spouse has fully disclosed assets and debt, and if it later turns out your spouse lied, you have the right to reopen the deal.

 SILVER LININGS

If your spouse isn't getting back to you about the agreement, saying he's too busy right now to look at it, maybe he is. One couple was on the verge of settling their case when tax season began. The husband was an accountant who relied heavily on returns for his income. He said he was just too busy to review the agreement; his wife was sure he was delaying. The truth was that the husband was too busy working to focus on the agreement, and negotiations had to wait until early May.

Some people reject settlements because they don't understand the law, and they think they'll do better in court. For many people living in jurisdictions where no-fault divorce is available, it is difficult to understand how a spouse can just walk out of the marriage without paying some kind of penalty. The "penalty" sought is usually an extra share of the marital assets. The law might provide, however, that no matter the reason for the divorce, assets are to be divided on a nearly 50/50 basis. An individual who refuses to accept this will never be able to settle on a 50/50 basis and might have to go through the expense of a trial just to hear a judge say the exact same thing.

Some people reject settlements because they feel the deal has been "shoved down their throats." Perhaps a lawyer was too pushy, and although the client didn't complain during the negotiations, she balks when it comes time to sign. Whatever the problem, discuss it with your lawyer. If yours is a case that needs to be decided by a judge because you just can't work out or sign a settlement agreement, stop the settlement process now before any more money is spent.

When to Reject an Agreement

At what point is it worth throwing in the towel during settlement negotiations? Here are some criteria to consider:

You think your spouse is hiding assets. You can have an expert locate them and testify to their existence in court. Remember, if you're sure that he's hiding assets but you can't prove it, a judge probably is not going to accept your position. Always consult with an attorney.

The deal is too vague. For example, the proposal is that "visitation will be agreed upon later" or that "bank accounts will be divided according to the parties' wishes." Any proposal that's merely an agreement to agree is just putting off conflict, not resolving it. Reject it in favor of a specific proposal.

The deal is unfair. Although that might seem obvious, it's not always easy to know when a deal is unfair. Here are some examples:

- You and your spouse ran up the credit card bills together, buying things for the family, but only one of you is going to be responsible for all the debt.

- You filed "aggressive" joint tax returns, but now only one of you is expected to pay the debt.

- You own two apartments, and your spouse wants both of them.

- The test lawyers use for fairness is the law and the case law. You can use the "objective test": if you were not involved in this case, would you think the proposal was fair?

Accepting the Package and Moving On

If the problem holding up the deal is the feeling that your spouse is hiding assets, but you can't prove it, you probably should take the deal.

If you're running out of money to pay a lawyer, and the deal is reasonably fair, you probably should take it.

If neither one of you is completely happy—in fact, you're a little unhappy with the deal—you should probably take it. It's been said many times that the best deal is the one where both sides leave the table a little dissatisfied.

When the Settlement Is Reached

When everyone agrees on the settlement, an attorney hired by one partner usually writes it up in a document called the settlement agreement or stipulation of settlement. Most of the agreement will have boilerplate language—language lawyers use all the time in agreements. For example, there's usually a provision that neither side will bother the other or that each side is responsible for his or her debts. The heart of the agreement—custody, visitation, child support, or property distribution—can take a lawyer longer to draft. The agreement will be binding, just as though a judge had arrived at the decision after trial. The lawyers must make sure that there are no mistakes.

If your lawyer is the one who has drafted the agreement, he will review it with you and then send it to the other lawyer, who reviews it with your spouse. Finally, when the terms and language of the agreement are acceptable to everyone, you both sign on the dotted line. Usually, you need to sign five copies—one for the court, one for each lawyer, one for you, and one for your spouse. Some lawyers like clients to initial every page in addition to signing the agreement. That way, no one can later claim they didn't know what was written.

 YOU CAN DO IT!

Sometimes, when a divorce settlement is ready for signature, one or both parties will look for excuses not to sign. This represents a sudden, deep realization that the marriage has truly ended. It is a bittersweet moment—bitter because of the anger and hurt you've experienced, but sweet because a great weight is about to lift from your shoulders. You may still feel resentments or regrets, but over time, those will fade into a daily routine that includes new projects and people. So pick up the pen, and sign the agreement. It's okay to cry (or have a drink!). If you truly feel the divorce is in your best interests, sign the document and move on.

The Cost of a Quick Divorce

Many couples we know have gotten their divorce for the cost of the court filing fees (usually under $1,000) and some photocopies. Others still needed a lawyer to work out the language of an agreement setting out their rights and responsibilities, tallying up costs of some $5,000 between the two of them.

In general, the less work the lawyers have to do, the cheaper your divorce will be.

Your Lawyer's Role

Even without a trial, if you have important issues to resolve, it's best to have a written agreement that you and your spouse can sign. The lawyer will draft that agreement, go over it with you, and send it to your spouse's lawyer, who will review it and then go over it with your spouse. After the document is agreeable to everyone, one of the lawyers will probably also have to draft papers that can be submitted to a judge, who will sign them and grant the divorce.

In some jurisdictions, even when everything is in agreement, one of you might still have to go to court to testify. Your lawyer would conduct your examination, asking you legally required questions about the breakdown of your marriage, while you sit witness in front of a judge.

Do you need a lawyer if you and your spouse have agreed on everything? In that instance, is there anything for an attorney to do? Of course, you can get a quick divorce without a lawyer. However, if there's a chance you and your spouse will have outstanding issues, you're better off having legal counsel from the start.

The Default Divorce

Some spouses never answer the divorce papers they receive. They just don't care, or they figure they'll let you do all the work to get the divorce. Do you have to wait until your spouse responds before you can move ahead?

The answer is usually no. If you can prove that your spouse personally received the papers the law requires you to have served, you may be able to get a divorce on default—your spouse's failure to respond. Although, by law, your spouse might have had 20 or 30 days to respond to the divorce papers before you are entitled to a default judgment, your judge might want you to wait three months before actually submitting the rest of the papers you need to be granted a divorce, just in case your spouse decides to respond after all. Check the laws in your jurisdiction, as default divorce may not apply everywhere.

There are some downsides to a default divorce:

Your spouse may be able to open the default after it is granted. In some jurisdictions, if your spouse is able to show "good cause" within one year of the divorce, he or she can have the default opened. That means your spouse can march into court and claim she never got the papers, or was sick at the time, or didn't understand them, and she wants a second chance. If the judge agrees that there is a reason to open the default, he will, and your divorce will in effect have to start all over again.

People tend to follow agreements more than they follow orders. If you and your spouse negotiated an agreement, the chances are better that your spouse will abide by it than if a judge set down in an order what your spouse has to pay because he didn't come to court.

You might actually do better if your spouse shows up in court. Maybe you can't prove how much money she earns, but if she were there, your lawyer could cross-examine her in such a way as to let the judge know that the tax return does not reflect all her income.

The judge might refer certain issues to another judge, such as a special referee or master. This can prolong the amount of time it will take to complete the case. Maybe the judge wants to give your spouse another chance to show up, so he refers the support hearing to another judge and tells you to notify your spouse about the new date. It's not fair, but courts tend to try to ensure that everyone has his day in court, even when the person who's getting the second chance is the defaulting party.

The scenarios described in this chapter provide some insight into what it takes to make a settlement happen. If you think you can settle and avoid litigation, it is in your best interest to make that settlement happen. Remember, the only winners in a protracted litigation are the lawyers! Judges in a trial will often try to give something to each party in the divorce, thereby imposing a form of settlement. Why not work out the issues yourselves? You and your spouse know better than anyone what's most important to each of you. If your marriage is at an end, orchestrate its conclusion in the least expensive, most expeditious way possible. Compromise where you're comfortable, and weigh the cost of waging an all-out war. Push your pride and hard stance aside, but don't give up what's most important to you.

The Least You Need to Know

- Even if you qualify for a no-fault divorce, you might still need to resolve other issues, such as custody, visitation, and support.
- Never sign important papers without first consulting an attorney.
- In negotiations, be flexible; come up with new ideas. Argue issues rather than positions.
- Even with a quick divorce, you might still need a lawyer to draft documents.
- If you want to reject a deal, make sure the basis for the rejection is rational, not purely emotional.

How to Find and Retain an Attorney

If you had a sizable wedding, you probably followed these traditions: you listened to various bands before choosing the music; you tasted food from different caterers before hiring a chef; and you studied portfolios before selecting a photographer. In this respect, at least, getting divorced is easier than getting married. You probably only need to find one person: a competent lawyer you like, trust, and can afford. And your spouse doesn't have to agree!

Do You Need a Lawyer?

If you've been married a relatively short time and you don't have kids, if you don't have many assets or much debt, or if you and your spouse have worked everything out, you might be able to proceed without a lawyer. Court clerks are usually not allowed to give legal advice, but that doesn't mean they can't tell you where to file certain papers. And these days, with the new trend toward *pro se* divorce, legal forms are available for the taking on many government websites. If all else fails, legal form publishers sell "divorce kits" that you can use to do all the paperwork yourself.

In This Chapter

- Choosing the right lawyer for you
- What to expect from your lawyer
- An introduction to fees
- Evaluating references
- How to interview a prospective lawyer

On the other hand, if you have children, if you have acquired assets (even if it's just a house and a pension or retirement plan), or if you and your spouse cannot agree on anything, you would be well-advised to seek legal counsel. Even if you agree on everything, getting a consultation is still money well spent. It's perfectly acceptable to present a lawyer with the agreement you and your spouse have drafted and ask for comments. Many law offices offer "unbundled" and à la carte legal services, so you may not need to break the bank to get all the protection you need.

One young father assumed that if his wife had custody of their young son, she would be free to move anywhere in the country. He was surprised, and relieved, to learn from his attorney that he could include a stipulation in his agreement that his wife not move more than 75 miles from her present location—provided he had not already moved himself. That was a provision he wanted, and got, in the agreement. For him, the money spent on attorney's fees was well worth it.

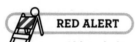 **RED ALERT**

Although divorce forms are now ubiquitous on the internet, not all of them meet court standards. The court clerk in your county will be able to help you determine what forms you need, and perhaps even provide them and help you fill them out.

How to Choose the Best Lawyer for You

Even if your case seems pretty straightforward, go to someone who has handled matrimonial cases before. You don't need an attorney who works solely in that area, whose fees might be very high. But you do want someone who knows which papers have to be filed in which courthouse and who can take your case to trial if need be. Now is not the time to do your third cousin a favor by hiring her son, who was recently admitted to the bar.

Some very competent matrimonial lawyers will tell you from the outset that they do not go to court. They might be very good negotiators, but if your case doesn't settle, they will recommend another attorney, either in their firm or at another, to take over the case. For some people, that's fine. Others prefer to have an attorney who will go the distance. Be sure to ask.

YOU CAN DO IT!

If you live in the United States, The American Academy of Matrimonial Lawyers in Chicago is a good source for names of qualified attorneys in your area. This organization sets high standards for membership. If you have allocated a sizable budget for your divorce case, this is the best place to start, although by all means not the only source for those of more modest means. You may reach them by phone at 312-263-6477 or via their website at www.aaml.org.

When you call the lawyer, ask whether there is a fee for the initial consultation. Don't be shy. Some lawyers will see you for free; others will charge their usual hourly rate, which might be as much as $700 an hour in major metropolitan areas. Others only bill you if they take your case. Still others bill by the task: so much for a finished separation agreement, so much for help in writing a motion, and so on.

As you go about choosing an attorney, you might want to work other factors into the equation as well. How does the office look? You don't need skyline views, but if the office is dirty, or the magazines are months old, be wary. Will your legal papers be cared for the same way? On the other hand, some attorneys do share space with others, and upkeep of the office is not within their control.

Be sensitive, as well, to the amount of time you're kept in the waiting room. Your attorney's office shouldn't be Grand Central Station, after all. A small wait isn't always a bad sign, but if you are kept waiting more than 15 minutes, you might want to think twice about using that attorney. He or she should want to impress you most before you sign on. If you have to wait a long time before the initial consultation, what will it be like after you're a client?

Once you begin your meeting inside the lawyer's private office, are you constantly interrupted as the attorney takes calls? An emergency call is one thing, but a constant stream of interruptions is another sign that this lawyer might just be too busy—or too disinterested in your case.

RED ALERT

Make sure you choose an attorney you can afford. Some lawyers want a large retainer, but their hourly rate is relatively low, or they have a junior attorney who can do some of the work at a lower hourly rate. If you want to hire a lawyer for only certain aspects of your divorce, you might prefer someone who specializes in unbundled services. If you have millions of dollars at stake, a legal powerhouse could be best for you.

Your First Meeting

When you're with an attorney for the first time, he or she will ask you for some background information about your situation. You should be told, briefly, how the laws work in your state and what that will mean for your case. The lawyer can also tell you which court will handle your case. Is the court in your jurisdiction backlogged? Knowing this could determine your strategy in resolving your case—is it helpful to drag out the divorce or to end it quickly?

A lawyer who knows the judges and their individual biases and personalities will be ahead of the game. Unfortunately, a carefully weighted decision by a judge is not a guarantee. Some, for instance, may see all mothers as overprotective or all fathers as bill payers. Sometimes a decision can be made simply on the basis of whether the judge had a fight with his or her own spouse that day! A savvy, experienced attorney will be able to maneuver around a judge's personality or bias with more agility than someone who is new to the field or to the area.

Fees and Billing

During the first consultation, the lawyer should also explain his or her fees. Does she take a retainer—a lump-sum payment—up front? That practice is common. As the lawyer works on your case, she subtracts an amount equal to her hourly rate from the sum you have pre-paid. For example, if you paid Attorney Greenfield $5,000 and her hourly rate is $500, you would have bought 10 hours of work in advance. Most will quote a flat rate for the retainer.

Other lawyers do not take a retainer and simply bill you every month as the case moves along. Some lawyers require that a cushion remain in the retainer until the case is concluded—for example, a few thousand dollars to cover the closing of a matter or to refund to you at the conclusion of the case. Whatever the arrangement, determine the details now. Remember, never sign on with a lawyer unless you have these financial details in writing. Be sure to read the fine print in your retainer agreement. More about fees in Chapter 14.

Consider the Opposing Counsel

If your spouse has already hired an attorney, find out whether that individual has had any dealings with the lawyer you hope to hire. Remember, lawyers develop enemies and make friends. A lawyer will rarely come right out and say he hates your spouse's attorney and can't even call him or her, let alone negotiate, so you need to be crafty. Watch the attorney's reaction when you mention the lawyer's name. Ask whether they've had any cases against one another. Ask about the other lawyer's reputation.

SILVER LININGS

You and your spouse are in a better position to resolve your case amicably and efficiently if your lawyers know each other and get along.

You might even tell a white lie; say that you've heard the other attorney is impossible and ask whether there's any truth to it. A lawyer might be more willing to agree with an assessment that he or she thinks someone else has made.

Good Referral Sources

The internet has many sources of matrimonial attorneys in your area. Most bar associations have websites and list the members of their family law sections. There are also websites that specialize in divorce, such as divorcesource.com and divorcemagazine.com, and of course you can simply Google "divorce lawyers" plus your location. It goes without saying that you should do your due diligence for all lawyers found on the internet.

Our preference is to consult with and possibly hire a divorce lawyer through the recommendation of a professional. This is a safer alternative to randomly selecting an unknown entity from company ads on the internet. Clergy, therapists, and marriage counselors might all be able to suggest divorce attorneys. Probably the most common way to get the name of a matrimonial attorney is through another attorney. You might already have a business lawyer, or maybe the lawyer who drew up your will is a friend and can recommend someone. Suppose you've gone to see one matrimonial lawyer, and you want the names of a few others. He or she will not be reluctant to give you some, especially if you explain that you can't afford the quoted fees.

Another source of referrals is friends who have been divorced. Sometimes they will recommend their ex-spouse's lawyer over their own, particularly if they thought they got the short end of the stick in the settlement. This, too, is a good way to get started.

Your local bar association is an important source for family law attorneys as well. If you can afford it, a certified family law or matrimonial specialist is preferable, if your jurisdiction has such a certification. If you are on a tight budget, try to find a lawyer recommended by people you trust. Although a lawyer can be listed as a member of the bar association simply by joining and without indicating any particular level of expertise, some may provide a consultation at a low fee or for free. You might find a suitable attorney by going through the list and checking their websites, if they have one.

What Legal Style Is Right for You?

There are as many different legal styles as there are attorneys. Some attorneys are tough and aggressive and give you an immediate feeling of confidence or dislike, depending on your perspective. Others seem too nice or too soft-spoken, and you can't imagine them standing up to your spouse, let alone a judge.

Your attorney's legal style has to make you feel confident and comfortable. Of course, you want someone who will deftly help you negotiate and win power points in court. By the same token, if your lawyer is so aggressive you're afraid to speak up and voice your concerns, all that aggression won't do you much good. In the end, it's a huge plus if you simply like your lawyer. Are you compatible? Can you be straightforward without feeling he or she is judgmental or condescending? Is your attorney genuinely concerned about you and the outcome of your case?

Some lawyers act one way when they are with clients, another when they're in front of a judge, and still another when they're with opposing counsel. That's not always inconsistency; sometimes, it's just smarts. The best thing you can do is to watch prospective attorneys perform in court; this is difficult, of course, because legal schedules change at the drop of a hat.

Some lawyers are skilled negotiators, and others ace litigators. Some will take a case only if they are hired to handle everything. Others earn a living by selling a menu of services—one motion, settlement agreement, and counseling session at a time.

 **RED ALERT**

> Resist the temptation to hire a lawyer based on your notion of how that lawyer might relate to your spouse. You might think it's important for the lawyer to be able to stand up to your spouse. The truth is, the lawyer usually won't even speak to your spouse, only to his or her lawyer. Thus, the way your lawyer gets along with your spouse's lawyer is the issue. Don't worry about your spouse's opinion of your lawyer.

At the opposite end of the spectrum from tough, aggressive attorneys are the lawyers we refer to as "peacemakers." Specialists in collaborative law, these attorneys work together to provide clients with a structured, nonadversarial alternative to the contentious system of dispute resolution. The collaborative movement in divorce law grew out of the realization that "some litigation, like nuclear war, is unwinnable," according to the Collaborative Law Center, based in Cincinnati.

If you require that counsel attend to your rights with more vigilance than could ever happen in mediation, but at the same time you want to avoid conflict, a collaborative attorney could be for you. Of course, a collaborative attorney can only sign on if your spouse hires a collaborative attorney. For a peacemaker to step in, you will both need to be on the same page this one last time.

No matter what kind of lawyer you hire, you should request a client reference. Some attorneys might feel uncomfortable with the request because of confidentiality issues, but others might have clients who would be willing to talk.

How to Interview a Lawyer

What exactly do you need to know before you hire a lawyer? Here are some questions to ask before you write a retainer check or sign on the dotted line.

Concerning general experience, ask these questions:

- How many matrimonial cases have you handled?

- How many of those cases went to trial? (An attorney who has done a lot of trials might not be a good negotiator. Keep that in mind, especially when the lawyer hasn't been in practice very long.)

- How many of these cases involved custody, support, business valuations, large financial settlements, or other issues pertinent to your situation?

- Where did you go to law school? (Don't ask if the diploma is staring you in the face.)

- Are you experienced in unbundled divorce (or collaborative divorce, or whatever style of divorce you hope to enter)?

- Do you have the time to take on a new case now?

- Do you know my husband (or wife)?

- Do you know his or her attorney?

Ask about day-to-day operations:

- Will anyone (usually an associate) be assisting you on my case?

- What is his or her experience?

- Can I meet the associate now?

- What work would the associate do and what work would you do?

- Which one of you will negotiate the case? If you want to be sure that the lawyer you are seeing is the negotiator rather than a potentially inexperienced associate, say so.

- Who will try my case?

- Are you available to take phone calls?

- Is the associate available to take calls?

- What hours are you usually in the office?

- Do you have any time-consuming trials coming up?

- Will I get copies of all papers (letters, faxes, legal papers) in my case? (Be sure the answer is "yes.")

Make sure the fees are clear:

- What is your hourly billing rate?

- What is the associate's billing rate?

- If both you and the associate are working on my case at the same time, am I billed at your combined rates? (Some firms do that only if two attorneys are needed, such as at trial. Others do it routinely, and others only bill you at the higher attorney's rate.)

- Is your fee for trial different from your hourly rate? (Some attorneys charge a set fee for every day they are in court.)

- Do you charge a retainer, and how much is it?

- Will the billing arrangements be set out in writing? (Insist that they be.)

- What happens when the retainer is used up?

- Will you keep me informed each month as to how much of the retainer has been depleted?

- What happens if I get behind on the bills?

- Can you collect your fees from my spouse?

- How much am I billed for copies of all relevant documents? (If the fee is too high, you might want to make copies on your own.)

- What extra fees should I expect? (Your retainer will spell out your responsibility for "fees"—what the lawyer charges for his or her time–versus "costs"—things like court filing fees, process server fees, excessive postage, messengers, stenographers, or similar out-of-pocket expenses.)

- Are those fees due in advance, and will I know in advance what they are?

- Am I billed for telephone calls?

- Do you have a minimum unit of time you bill me for? (Some lawyers will bill you for 5 or even 15 minutes when a call takes only 4 minutes.)

Ask these questions about handling the case:

- Will I have input in decisions concerning strategy in my case?

- Will I be kept informed of all developments?

- What problems do you foresee arising in my case?

- What are your personal feelings about joint custody versus sole custody? (Sometimes a lawyer has strong convictions one way or the other that could potentially affect the outcome of your case.)

- Based on your experience, how much do you think my case will cost?

Before you make the final decision to sign on with a lawyer, be sure to fill out the following attorney information sheet. It will guide you in your decision—and serve as a reminder about your agreement in the months to come.

ATTORNEY INFORMATION

Name of attorney _____

Address _____

Size of firm _____

Style of law practiced (e.g., traditional, unbundled, collaborative) _____

Recommended by _____

Date seen _____

Consultation fee   _____

Office   _____

    *Is it an easy location for me to
get to?*   _____

    Was it relatively neat and clean?   _____

Attorney's Education   _____

                                             _____

Experience   _____

    Was I kept waiting?   _____

    Were we interrupted?   _____

    Did I feel comfortable?   _____

    Did the attorney listen to me?   _____

Fees   _____

    What is the hourly billing rate?   _____

    *What are the rates of others
who might work on the case?*   _____

Retainer fee   _____

    *What happens when retainer is
used up?*   _____

    How often am I billed?   _____

    What happens if I can't pay?   _____

    *Will attorney agree to collect from
my spouse?*   _____

    *Who pays for disbursements and
extra services?*   _____

Handling the case   _____

    *How long does the attorney think it
will take to complete the case?*   _____

    *Has the attorney handled cases
like this before?*   _____

You're Hired!

After you have decided whom you want to represent you, a reputable lawyer will send you his or her written agreement concerning fees and will give you time to ask questions about the agreement before you sign it. If a lawyer asks you to sign an agreement in his or her office without giving you the chance to think it over, look for another lawyer. Sometimes it's worth showing the agreement to your business or personal lawyer, whom you trust. If and when you do return the written agreement, you usually have to include the retainer check required as your initial payment.

The Least You Need to Know

- Hire a competent attorney who makes you feel at ease, whom you like, and whom your best instincts say you can trust.
- Hire an attorney with experience in the kind of representation you seek, whether it is unbundled services or collaborative law.
- Make sure you can afford the attorney's fees or are able to work out an arrangement for payment.
- Never pay a retainer fee without a guarantee that the unused portioned will be returned.
- Know whether an associate will be working on your case and determine the associate's billing rate. Find out whether you'll be billed for both the associate's time and the primary attorney's time when both are working on the case.

The Full-Service Attorney

Divorce settlements can be negotiated with the help of a mediator, or even by you and your spouse, if the case is simple (no kids, no substantial assets, usually of short-term duration). If, on the other hand, your marriage is more complicated or there is conflict, you will need legal assistance. In many areas of the country you can decide how much legal help to buy, depending on your budget and your needs. But if you have a difficult case, you might need a full-service attorney.

Is Full-Service Representation Right for You?

As you go about investigating your options and interviewing attorneys, the first thing you will need to decide is whether the traditional, full-service attorney is for you. It's important to state up front: you're likely to have a better outcome with a full-service attorney, provided you're able to pay the bill.

In This Chapter

- How to decide whether you need full representation
- What to expect from your lawyer
- How and when to call your lawyer
- The client-attorney relationship

Since so many people need legal services but aren't able to pay the hefty price, the legal profession has adopted a new business model: limited scope legal assistance, also known as unbundled legal services. This legal option, although by definition limited, can end up being far more comprehensive in the long run for those on a budget than filling out forms from a website or even handling the divorce entirely *pro se*. Many middle-class couples seeking a divorce run into trouble when they pay a hefty retainer to a full-service attorney. If the retainer runs out before the work is completed—a common scenario—the client will have to pay more for additional services. If the client has run out of funds, he will be forced to handle the rest of his divorce without any legal input at all. On the other hand, if the client purchases legal services only for the most complex tasks, he winds up with more comprehensive legal representation for the duration of his divorce.

So while full representation is certainly in your best interest, this is only true if you can afford it. If you lack the tens of thousands of dollars required for such an investment, signing on with a full-service lawyer is risky, indeed.

If you have substantial property at stake, or if you are facing a custody war, it may be worth your while to go into debt to finance full-service legal representation for your divorce. If you are well-to-do, you should, by all means, sign on with a full-service lawyer or firm as your best means of protection.

However, if you are a person of modest means with no extraordinary issues at stake, you might do well to embrace the adage, "less is more."

What to Expect

You have reviewed your personal circumstances and, after much soul searching, have decided that a full-service attorney is right for you. You have interviewed a number of attorneys, considered personal references, and finally, put down a hefty sum to retain the legal representation of your choice.

What should you expect? After you hire your matrimonial attorney, get ready to have a long, intense relationship with the person who will be your closest ally in the days to come. You will be putting all your trust and faith in this person, and he or she will be your most effective support during the separation and divorce process.

Your relationship with your matrimonial attorney can be smooth or rocky, close or business-like. You might come to think of your attorney as your confessor, therapist, knight in shining armor, but if you're going to make it through the divorce, you must banish these notions.

Instead, it is to your advantage to learn (quickly) how to utilize your attorney in the most effective, cost-efficient way possible.

 **RED ALERT**

Don't confuse your lawyer with your therapist and waste your precious dollars using your attorney to vent your anger, assuage your guilt, or comfort your feelings of loss. Seek the help of a qualified counselor if you need it, and let your lawyer focus on the legal issues.

What Your Lawyer Should and Should Not Do

The practice of law is not a science, but it's not exactly an art either. There are certain things your attorney can and should be doing. On the other hand, watch for red flags if you believe your lawyer is behaving inappropriately.

Your Lawyer's "To Do" List

Plan ahead. Your lawyer should have an overall plan for your case. This might simply mean that she plans to meet with your spouse's lawyer within the next month and settle the case, have documents drawn up within two weeks after that meeting, have them signed within two weeks after that, and then submit them to court.

Maybe it means she's going to make an immediate request for support on your behalf and start demanding financial documents, with the goal of having your case ready for trial within six months.

Maybe your lawyer can't say when things will happen because too much depends on what the other side wants; still, she should have a general idea of how the case will proceed from your side given any number of scenarios.

Request financial documents. Early in your case, your lawyer should demand any and all financial documents in your spouse's possession so that you can learn what there is between you to divide up.

Find out about employee benefits. If you or your spouse has a pension or any kind of employee benefit, your lawyer should get a copy of the appropriate plan documents and account statements for the past few years. We know of more than one case where the lawyers agreed a pension would be divided up, only to discover that, under certain circumstances, the company had no obligation to pay the pension at all.

Arrange for expert testimony. Your lawyer should assess whether any experts will be needed in your case. If your wife has a hat-making business she established during the marriage, you might need a business appraiser to estimate the value of that business. Your lawyer should locate a well-respected forensic accountant or business appraiser now for possible later use.

Maybe custody will be an issue, and you'll need an expert to testify on your behalf.

In some jurisdictions, the judge will appoint an expert to report to the court, but you still might need someone to support your case. Your lawyer should start getting you the names of qualified people.

Negotiate. Your lawyer should, under almost all circumstances, tell your spouse's lawyer that you are willing to listen to any reasonable settlement proposal and to negotiate. Cases have been settled on the steps of the courthouse on the day of trial, so it's a good idea to leave the door open at all times.

Communicate. Your lawyer should promptly respond to letters and phone calls and keep you informed of all such communication. Copies of letters should be sent to you within 24 hours of the lawyer's receipt. He or she should notify you about important phone calls—those concerning settlement proposals, for instance—as soon as possible. If the court hands down any decisions regarding your case, your lawyer should notify you at once.

Your attorney should return your calls within 24 hours unless there's some reason why that's impossible—for instance, if she's in court or in the middle of a trial. On the other hand, you should only call when you have something to ask or something important to say. It's a good idea to write down questions and save them for a few days (unless they are urgent) so you can ask several at once. Some lawyers bill you a minimum of 15 minutes per call, so you might as well take up the time you'll be billed anyway.

Prepare witnesses. If your case is heading to trial, your attorney, with your input, should begin to interview and line up witnesses as needed. She should be sure to give your witnesses ample advance notice of the trial date.

Prepare you for trial. If your case actually goes to trial, your lawyer should fully prepare you. If possible, you should visit the courthouse and even the courtroom in advance. Your lawyer should review the questions he himself plans to ask and alert you about what to expect during cross-examination.

One attorney we know even tells her clients how to dress on the day they will be in court. "Go for the schoolteacher look," she likes to say, "and leave the jewelry and fur at home."

Anticipate the outcome. Throughout your case, your attorney should give you some sense of whether the law supports your position. No attorney worth her weight will guarantee you a victory, but a knowledgeable lawyer should be able to tell you whether there is a basis for your position and what is likely to happen if the case is tried.

Provide advice. If your case ends with a defeat at trial, or if there are any defeats along the way (say you lose a motion when the judge denies your request for something), your lawyer should be able to provide you with sound advice about whether to appeal or seek reconsideration at the trial level.

 YOU CAN DO IT!

If this is your first time hiring an attorney, keep in mind that he or she is working on your behalf and at your expense. Don't be intimidated as you pass through the glass doors into a beautifully furnished office with mahogany desks. Your goal is to get the help you need to resolve your divorce in your favor in the least amount of time and at the lowest cost. Be prepared to present your position and have a list of questions for the attorney at every meeting.

Red Flags

Your lawyer should be your advocate and defender, and he or she should always act with professionalism and integrity. Keep you eye out for these red flags. If you feel your lawyer is behaving inappropriately, say something.

Don't get too close. Although your lawyer might know more about you than your accountant, your therapist, or even your spouse, it's probably not a good idea to become drinking buddies. You want your lawyer to make objective decisions, not to cater to your demands because you've become best friends.

Keep family separate. In general, it's probably not a good idea for your lawyer to meet your kids. If the children are teenagers, and their testimony is essential, then of course your attorney must meet them. But in other instances, they'll feel as though they're being made to take sides. Your attorney also runs the risk of being called as a witness in the case by virtue of his or her contact with the kids. (If your lawyer does become a witness, he or she will no longer be able to represent you.)

Observe proper procedure with your spouse. Your attorney should not be in contact with your spouse if he or she has an attorney, unless his or her attorney has agreed to such contact.

Maintain professionalism. Your attorney should not "come on" to you in any way whatsoever, nor should you treat him or her as a romantic prospect. (Agreeing to discuss your case on a Friday night at a fancy restaurant is not a good idea.) It doesn't matter if the attraction is mutual. If it's real, it can wait until your case is over. If your attorney does cross this line with you, report him or her to your state bar's ethics committee.

Avoid conflicts of interest. Your attorney should not have a business relationship of any kind with your spouse or his or her family. For example, if the attorney you want to use drew your will and your spouse's will, he or she should probably not be representing you in the divorce. (If your spouse consents, it might be okay, but the wiser course would be to find someone else.)

Similarly, if the attorney had a prior business relationship as counsel for your jointly owned business, the attorney might be disqualified from representing either you or your spouse. It is better to stipulate that a lawyer who has been representing you both in business activities should not act as a lawyer for one of you in a divorce.

The Client-Attorney Relationship

You expect your lawyer to act professionally, and you must act professionally, too. To maintain a good working relationship, keep in mind that communication is paramount and avoid common client behaviors that can jeopardize your case.

How and When to Call Your Lawyer

Many clients aren't sure when they should contact their attorney about a potential problem—something that might be important to the case.

For instance, say your husband consistently brings the kids back a half hour late. Should you tell your lawyer? It depends. If your attorney is hard at work on a motion about visitation, it's important that she know about the problem right away. If a conference between the lawyers is not going to take place for another two weeks, it's probably better to save the call for later, when you have more questions to add.

The bottom line is this: if you're not sure whether something merits a call, call your attorney. When you're through speaking about the problem, ask whether you should call about this sort of issue in the future. Maybe your lawyer will simply ask you to keep a diary, which you can hand over for later use in your case. Maybe he'll want to be kept informed immediately by phone.

With luck, you have hired a lawyer with whom you feel comfortable, and you can talk to him or her as you would a friend. Nevertheless, it's important to maintain the boundaries that should exist between any professional and client. Keep your conversation focused on the reason for the call, and avoid raising issues your lawyer has already addressed. If your lawyer starts saying such things as "We're going in circles," or "I think we've covered that," it's a gentle hint to move on to the next topic or say goodbye.

When on the phone with your lawyer, avoid the tendency to speculate. No single activity wastes more of your legal fee dollars than speculating on why your spouse has done something, what he or she might do, what a judge might do, or what the other lawyer might do. The list is endless. Discussing the merits of your position is one thing; trying to figure out why something was done or what someone else will do is usually a waste of time.

If too much time has elapsed since you and your lawyer agreed on a plan of action (your lawyer was supposed to call your husband's lawyer last week and hasn't done it yet), then make the call. The squeaky wheel gets oiled, but be reasonable. If your lawyer said he or she would call you as soon as there is a decision in your case, don't call every day to check whether the decision has come.

Check Your Behavior

Many attorneys will never let you know when they are annoyed with you. After all, they get paid to listen to you, and the more they listen, the more money they'll make. Indeed, for some, if you complain endlessly about your ex, you might unwittingly be filling his or her otherwise empty time sheet. But let's assume you hear testiness in your lawyer's voice, or you think he or she is tired of your case. What do you do?

The best thing to do is to raise your concern. "You sound upset. Does it have to do with my case?" is one good opener. "Have I done something to annoy you?" is another. If you have, your attorney will appreciate the opportunity to let you know. Maybe your payment check bounced; perhaps you've been yelling at the secretary or keeping the attorney on the phone too long. Perhaps you told your spouse something your lawyer said to keep under wraps.

Apologize and make sure that the problem has not become so big that your lawyer feels she can no longer enthusiastically represent your case.

RED ALERT

The most common reason lawyers seek to terminate clients is their failure to pay bills. Even if you've spent tens of thousands of dollars with a lawyer, if you are unable to meet a payment schedule, most lawyers will not want to continue representing you.

When to Fire Your Lawyer

One woman we know is in the fourth year of her divorce case—and on her third lawyer. Is she an exception? Not necessarily. Firing a lawyer is more common than you might think. Why does this happen? When is it warranted? And how do you pull it off?

Sometimes, lawyers are let go due to a straightforward personality clash. Characteristics you were willing to overlook when you hired your lawyer (a brash, aggressive personality or perhaps a cloying patronage) now bother you so much that you can't talk to him or her anymore. Maybe you feel that your lawyer has mishandled your case. You've gotten a second opinion and learned about strategies that could have saved you time and money. When you ask your lawyer about them, she just shrugs. Sometimes, it's just a feeling that your case needs fresh ideas. Your attorney seems tired of the whole thing and no longer has the enthusiasm she had when you first hired her. You might also feel that your lawyer is giving in too easily to the other side or that trust has been breached. You tell your lawyer something you do not want repeated to your spouse's lawyer, and your attorney goes right ahead and does just that.

How do you fire your lawyer? The easiest way is to hire the replacement lawyer before you tell your present lawyer that you're making a change. Then, your new lawyer makes the call to your current lawyer and arranges to get your file, and you don't have to worry about the awkward moment of telling your lawyer it's over.

If you feel some personal statement of closure is in order, of course, you can send your attorney a short note. Depending on why you're "breaking up," you can simply send a thank-you for past services or write a brief statement stating your beef. As with any close relationship, your lawyer might already be suspicious that you are unhappy with him or her, so your note might not be a total surprise.

Remember, most lawyers will expect to be paid in full before they release your file. Depending on where you live, your lawyer might be required to release your file even if you have yet to pay for all services—but the bill won't go away. If you have a problem paying the bill or a disagreement over the bill, discuss this with your present lawyer and work out an agreement. Or if agreement isn't possible, check if there is another source for arbitration to resolve fee disputes between attorneys and clients. (Many jurisdictions even offer free arbitration for this purpose.) Otherwise, have your new lawyer work things out for you.

The Least You Need to Know

- Before you hire a full-service attorney, make sure you can afford it.
- Your lawyer should have a game plan, be on top of your case, and keep you informed of all developments.
- Write out questions and call your lawyer with several at once, if possible. When in doubt about whether to let your lawyer know something has happened, call.
- Don't stick with your attorney if lines of communication have broken down.
- Find a new attorney before you fire your old one.

Handling Your Case *Pro Se*

If methods of divorce are viewed along a spectrum, at one extreme are those employing full-service attorneys, and at the other are those using no attorney at all. Despite the old adage that only a fool has himself for a client, an increasing number of people are forgoing the expense of a lawyer and going *pro se,* Latin for "on one's own behalf." A person who divorces *pro se* acts as his or her own attorney.

This chapter will help you decide whether you're prepared to represent yourself, and provide guidance if you choose the *pro se* route.

Why Go *Pro Se?*

Sometimes people go *pro se* because they believe their divorce is intrinsically simple—perhaps they have been married for just a short time, or they have no assets or debts and no children, and they want to cleanly sever ties. Other times, people divorce *pro se* without that having been the original intent, often because the money has run out mid-way through the divorce process. Without the ability to pay an attorney, these people are on their own.

Then there are those who never had the money for a lawyer in the first place. Instead of seeking legal solutions, they accept informal—and thus, unenforceable—agreements for things like child support and distribution of assets and debts. When these unbinding solutions fall apart, the couple joins the great tide of people seeking divorce remedies *pro se.*

Is *Pro Se* Divorce for You?

If you have been married just a short time, or if both you and your spouse have few or no assets and no children, *pro se* divorce could be your ticket. But those who go down this path, while potentially saving money, place themselves at risk.

"Self-representation is a heavy burden for persons exercising this right," says Barrie Althoff, an attorney in Washington State. "It is a right that most unrepresented persons would gladly give up if they could afford to retain legal counsel."

Indeed, the sheer legal logistics of the divorce effort can be tedious and enormously time-consuming, involving many individual steps and requiring meticulous attention to detail. Some of the tasks you must attend to include drafting pleadings, including all accompanying forms and affidavits; filing the pleadings with the court; paying the court fees or applying for a waiver for indigent litigants; and fulfilling and documenting any mandatory requirements, such as attending a parenting class.

Are you attentive to detail, comfortable with paperwork, persistent, and able to meet deadlines? Are you comfortable using a legal library (you may need a subscription to online legal source www.lexis.com for in-depth research), super organized, and able to read others' reactions and modify your actions? If not, despite your best intentions—and unless you have no other choice—*pro se* divorce may not be for you. You may want to talk to a lawyer about your case before deciding to represent yourself.

The Impact on the Court System

The glut of *pro se* divorce has brought chaos to family courts in jurisdictions around the world. *Pro se* litigants are often confused about which forms to sign. When they submit the right form, they may fill it out incorrectly. Some exploit the system in ways that attorneys would not, prolonging an action just to punish a spouse. The do-it-yourself approach to divorce has cut costs for many, but it also clogs a system never meant to serve amateurs.

When a *pro se* case goes wrong, husband and wife—neither represented by counsel—might end up before a judge and start fighting. Often the divorcing spouses become aggressive and contentious, not just to each other, but to the judge, and they have little understanding of the law or their rights under it. Clueless about courtroom basics, including procedure, rules of evidence, legal reasoning, and even appropriate behavior and dress, these unprepared *pro se* couples blunder through, introducing uncensored emotion and angst into a situation meant to be orderly and controlled. Their lack of knowledge leads to unreasonable expectations and impossible demands, all requiring a response from the judge.

Do Your Homework

When the court is inconvenienced, those causing the inconvenience may suffer when decisions are taken out of their hands. Inexperienced litigants who argue over their possessions in front of a judge may be forced to sell them without getting the chance to negotiate for what they truly want most. Those who make unreasonable demands for custody or visitation—lacking the lawyer's knowledge of permissible limits and norms—may receive less time or access than those who go in knowing the protocols and the expectations of the court. Therefore, *pro se* divorce participants must be more educated, more attentive, and far more on top of details than those with representation to get the outcomes they want.

 YOU CAN DO IT!

Familiarize yourself with your jurisdiction's divorce statutes. You should be able to find a copy of the statutes at your local courthouse or library or online. Remember, not only are you bound by these statutes—the judge is, too. Make sure that you study the types of proceedings and hearings that govern divorce in your jurisdiction and the order in which they take place. If you are your own representative, you cannot afford to miss a beat.

Legal Information vs. Legal Advice

With the *pro se* movement taking off over the last decade, help has become easier to access than ever before. But that doesn't mean that *pro se* couples can relax. Even with more help available, many still get tripped up over the distinction between legal information and legal advice.

Part of the confusion for such couples stems from a judicial code of ethics in the United States and elsewhere that specifically prohibits judges from dispensing advice or doing anything that would undermine their basic fairness and impartiality. Given these constraints, judges and other employees of the court may dispense information, but decline to provide anything that might smack of advice. If a *pro se* litigant does not understand the difference between information and advice, he or she might make an unfavorable deal or even a grievous mistake.

Remember, even though the court clerk and judge are there to help you, there are limits. The line between legal information and legal advice still may not be crossed. Richard Zora, author of *The Self-Help Friendly Court: Designed from the Ground Up to Work for People without Lawyers*, provides a clear example so that lay people may understand the difference between the two. "If you ask a question of two lawyers, and get two different answers, and neither lawyer is committing malpractice, that is legal advice," he explains. "But if there is only one right answer, that is legal information." It is your right to obtain legal information from the court. Neither the judge nor the clerk may provide you with legal advice.

 **RED ALERT**

Judges and clerks afraid to appear partial may sometimes opt for passivity instead. In an effort to meet the letter of that law, some courts and judges may feel compelled to withhold not just advice, but also important information, sitting by as *pro se* litigants blunder through.

Getting the Help You Need

More and more, courts and judges have realized that withholding help is not a workable plan. So over the last few years, many jurisdictions have stepped up to the plate. They've decided that, at the very least, court staff should be able to explain the processes and procedures to *pro se* litigants and tell them how to bring their problems before the court. The newest consensus: *pro se* litigants deserve to know the rules of the game—not only because it is their right, but also because their confusion can clog the courts. Toward that end, many jurisdictions have established outreach efforts to help the do-it-yourselfers going through *pro se* divorce.

In Ventura County, California, for instance, the Family Law Self-Help Centers offer walk-in assistance four full days a week to help residents fill out forms and understand the basics of the law. For those who need help after business hours, there are online video workshops on divorce, separation, child custody, and child support. The specific forms required for divorce in the jurisdiction are online as well. Many court systems across the country offer similar services.

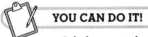 **YOU CAN DO IT!**

Ask the court clerk for permission to look in the court computer, write down the case numbers of five divorce cases that are at least one year old and have the clerk tell you where to find them. Take the time to study them, with an eye to finding one similar to your own. If the first five cases don't resemble your situation, ask to see more. Studying these documents will be a guide as to how forms are filled out in your jurisdiction. The experience of your fellow litigants should be an education, as well. Photocopy documents if you can.

Tips for Do-It-Yourselfers

There are a number of things you can do to make your do-it-yourself divorce a little easier. Ask the court clerk how or where to find documents approved by the court, either in a store or online. These documents are often called divorce kits, and are available in many jurisdictions around the world.

You can also ask the clerk to refer you to your jurisdiction's free walk-in center—or alternatively, to recommend a few paralegals—to help you fill out these documents and forms correctly. Make sure the clerk provides you with a list of local rules and filing fees. Get a list of the proceedings and the order in which they are handled by your jurisdiction.

Whenever you send anything to the court, remember to send a copy to your spouse or the other parent, if it is a parentage case. If the other party has a lawyer, you must send the copy to the lawyer. Be sure to use your case's docket number on anything you send to the court.

You must provide complete financial information when you are asked. If you try to hide income or property, the court will not trust you, and you could be prosecuted for a crime.

Remember, the only time you may talk to the judge or magistrate is in a court hearing. The judge or magistrate is neutral and may not talk to parties about their case except in court. You may not try to talk to the judge or magistrate when the other party is not present.

You must know the facts of your case and be able to present them to the judge or magistrate. The judge or magistrate will know little or nothing about you, your spouse, your children, or your concerns when the case begins. You need to know what is important to you and what information you want the judge to know. Do not waste your court time on matters that do not help the judge or magistrate to decide your case. Listen carefully to what is said. Make sure your presentation is relevant and to the point.

In most jurisdictions, you must file an appearance form—or something comparable—with the court clerk's office. It includes your name, address, telephone number, and signature. It tells the court that you are representing yourself. Filing it allows the court to contact you about all court events in your case.

Court clerks can give you information only. They cannot give you legal advice, such as telling you what you should do or what option makes the most sense in your particular case. However, courthouse law librarians can show you how to research a legal question or issue or where to find a particular case or court form.

Finally, keep in mind that you must follow the same court rules as lawyers or solicitors. Just because you're doing it yourself doesn't make you exempt from proper procedure.

 **RED ALERT**

A *pro se* divorce is not free. Expect to spend money on forms, copy costs, filing fees, court fees, certification fees, notary fees, and service of process fees. Other costs might include medical expenses for things like paternity tests, expert witnesses, and consultation and paralegal fees, among others. You may even need to pay to park your car when you go to court. It all adds up.

These are simple tips and guidelines, but it is amazing how many *pro se* individuals are completely unaware of them.

Another thing many *pro se* litigants involved in divorce fail to realize is that most divorce cases are resolved through settlement, not trial. Having come to court, they may rely on the judge to impose an external decision. Just because the couple has decided to divorce *pro se,* and no attorneys are involved, there is no reason for them to stop negotiating. It is often through negotiation that you arrive at a deal best for both of you. Do not let the excitement or immersion of representing yourself in court blind you to the possibility that you can walk away before trial and sign a deal of your own, if you so wish. If your budget permits, have the document reviewed by an attorney for your protection.

It is not our goal, in this chapter, to provide a manual for *pro se* divorce. Indeed, the instructions vary by jurisdiction from city to city and nation to nation around the world. Personal situations vary to such a degree that everyone needs a manual of his or her own. Your best bet, if you are considering *pro se* divorce, is to get feedback of the most local variety possible. Contact your local family court to see what kind of help is available for free.

The Least You Need to Know

- *Pro se* is becoming a more popular divorce option, and jurisdictions around the world have established outreach efforts to help those going through *pro se* divorce.

- A *pro se* divorce may be less expensive than hiring a lawyer, but it is not free or easy. The sheer legal logistics of the divorce effort can be tedious and enormously time-consuming.

- The procedures for *pro se* divorce vary by jurisdiction. Contact your local family court and educate yourself on the process in your area.

- It's in your best interest to consult a lawyer before deciding to represent yourself.

Hiring a Lawyer for Specific Tasks

If you have been married for more than a few years, if you have children, if you have received an inheritance, if you own a home or a business, or if you have a pension plan or other retirement assets, then your divorce is going to involve some complexities. Under these circumstances, and many others, specialized legal knowledge could benefit you enormously. In fact, hiring an attorney to handle your case is probably required to make sure your rights are protected.

But what if you simply don't have the money to pay a full-service attorney's hefty retainer fee? Should you risk representing yourself as many now do? In the past, with most attorneys worried about the liability of handling cases piecemeal, hiring an attorney to represent you might have been your only option. Fortunately, things have changed.

In This Chapter

- What to do if you can't afford a full-service attorney
- Hiring a lawyer to handle only what you can't do yourself
- Finding an à la carte attorney
- Understanding the role of the limited scope attorney

The Unbundled Divorce

People of modest means are increasingly hiring limited scope attorneys as consultants and "piece-workers," paying for services that are especially complex and demanding of true expertise, but handling the rest themselves. This style of divorce is called *unbundled divorce,* meaning that legal services are dispensed individually—one motion, agreement, or issue at a time.

The limited scope attorney will unbundle the full spectrum of services traditionally sold as a package and sell one service or task at a time. The client and lawyer together can decide upon the service needed most, thus conferring some protection at a fraction of the cost.

This option has become so popular that the American Bar Association has developed new professional standards to ensure that individuals who use lawyers for a part of their legal service are adequately protected. For the latest American Bar Association standards, visit their website, www.americanbar.org.

Many legal ethicists have signed on as well, agreeing that, for divorcing couples who cannot afford full legal representation, the middle path—limited scope representation that confers attorney-client privilege—is the most viable choice and far more protective of their rights than going *pro se.* Even if you can't afford a full-service lawyer, you can improve your chance of success if you obtain some legal help instead of going it totally alone.

 **RED ALERT**

Some pundits have suggested that a little legal service can be more harmful than none at all. But in the vast majority of cases, the more legal help you have, the better.

Obtaining Limited Scope Legal Assistance

If you are seeking true, unbundled legal representation for your divorce, your best bet may not be the storefront or online legal service that promises to take you through the process for anywhere from $99 to $399. Unless you're in a very simple family situation with few assets and no children, you'll need some professional legal advice.

Although such options can yield appropriate legal feedback, we suggest you start your search for limited scope legal representation offline, in the same place you would go for guidance as a litigant—the *pro se* assistance programs now available in many jurisdictions, often state-sponsored and associated with the courts. They can provide forms, videos, brochures, and general legal information, but you'll sometimes find attorneys working there and willing to provide advice. If the assistance program can't help you, they frequently can refer you to attorneys willing to help, one issue at a time.

 RED ALERT

Buyer beware! Many websites that dispense legal services may provide initial legal advice on the cheap, but only as a loss leader for additional costly services. Many, ultimately, charge substantial fees.

If you aren't satisfied or if these attorneys charge too much, contact your local Bar Association to see if you can tap what is often known as the "reduced fee panel," whose members charge for legal services based on income. Some won't handle divorce cases, but many do.

As you search for a limited scope divorce attorney, remember that this is a specialty, just like any other area of law. Sure, you could go to the highest-powered divorce firm in your city and request services à la carte, but that is unlikely to do you much good. Full-service divorce attorneys won't be seduced by the few thousand dollars you can part with to manage your marital woes. Even if they made an exception for you, they wouldn't be accustomed to delivering what you need.

Likewise, storefront legal offices that function as "paralegal paper mills" are likely to consider your request to focus on an outside-the-box or individual issue a disruption to the workflow. Instead, seek out an attorney who specializes in unbundled divorce—the kind of lawyer who handles family law as a solo practitioner or as part of a small firm, who has recently decided to join the growing contingent of attorneys selling divorce services à la carte.

 YOU CAN DO IT!

If you are beginning the divorce process and haven't had legal input, a single session of legal advice can prove invaluable. Be sure to bring a checklist of any items or issues you'd like to cover to make sure no concern is overlooked.

The Limited Scope Consult

Popular perception has it that an initial consultation with a divorce attorney is merely an opportunity to learn about fees and services, but Debbie Weecks, a limited scope attorney from Sun City, Arizona, says there's no reason why the initial consultation can't "be several hours long with an express understanding that the attorney's role is limited to offering advice both procedurally and substantively based upon the information the client is able to provide."

 **RED ALERT**

Courts have held that lawyers who handle cases this way are not responsible to the client for malpractice in the same way they would be if they were handling the entire case. You get what you pay for: limited service, limited duty to the client.

The initial divorce consultation might be all you need to get through the rest of the divorce procedure on your own. "Interview and advice services may be the only ones a limited service lawyer provides to a client," according to the American Bar Association. "The attorney-client relationship begins at the start of the interview and ends when it is over." In other words, the interview and advice (as opposed to mere information) comprise a discrete unit of legal work. While full-service attorneys often provide the initial consultation for free, as just the beginning of a long relationship, limited scope lawyers virtually always charge at this point—it is often the first and last time the client will walk through the door.

The limited service lawyer could, for instance, give you preventive advice. Let's say you anticipate a custody battle and fear your spouse might run off with your child; in a single session with a knowledgeable attorney, you might learn how to file a motion requesting an emergency custody order and a requirement for your spouse to turn over his or her passport. Even if you have no money, you might be surprised how much emotional and financial risk you face when your marriage ends. A limited scope attorney will keep you informed: do you know how to protect your credit rating, not to mention your level of future debt, from a spouse on a spending spree? Are you aware that if you use your newly inherited money— no matter how small the amount—to pay household bills or if you combine it with marital monies in any way, it might become community property in some jurisdictions?

Perhaps you are furious because your spouse is preventing you from seeing your daughter or son. A common assumption is that visitation is somehow tied to child support payments—no kid on Sunday, no money for your soon-to-be ex on Monday, regardless of what the judge ordered. The limited scope attorney will quickly set you straight, letting you know in no uncertain terms that those issues are generally unrelated under the law, but by withholding payment, you risk not just child-support arrearages but criminal charges as well. On the other hand, if you continue to make the payments, you can correct the visitation situation *pro se*—with the attorney's behind-the-scenes advice.

In fact, if your rights are being violated in any way, the limited service lawyer can tell you how to select and complete a simplified complaint form, request an order of default or evidentiary hearing, prepare and present the required testimony, and obtain a final order and judgment. Believe it or not, if your issues aren't outrageously tangled and messy, all of this can be accomplished in a single session, in the course of an afternoon. Depending on your city, you might be asked to pay the limited scope attorney up to $500 an hour for his legal advice. This may sound like a lot, but the savings—not just in money but also heartache—could be immense.

 **SILVER LININGS**

Limited scope legal assistance carries with it attorney-client privilege, but also limited attorney liability.

Coaching, Ghostwriting, and Other Assistance

If your divorce is complex, you will benefit from additional meetings with your limited scope attorney who can help you as a consultant, ghostwriter, and coach without ever talking to your spouse's attorney or spending a day in court.

Limited service lawyers frequently prepare, or help clients to prepare, pleadings in divorce, child custody, child support, guardianship, and other domestic relations cases. "In many of these cases, filing the complaint triggers a default process—in effect, it tips the first domino in a row of legal dominos," the American Bar Association says. "When the last domino falls, the default judgment is entered, and the case is over."

Limited Scope Assistance for Simple Cases

In one common "domino" process, a husband and wife may have no substantial property—not even stock options or pension plans—and no children. If they want to sever ties amicably and inexpensively, one of them can be designated the initiating party, the so-called plaintiff or petitioner. The plaintiff will consult a limited scope attorney, who may start by advising him on grounds for divorce. The most typical might be a no-fault petition based on irreconcilable differences or a mutual separation without co-habitation for a fixed period of time, depending on your local law and the facts of your matter.

Then, at the appropriate juncture, the limited scope attorney will help the plaintiff draft a complaint or petition requesting relief, in other words, a divorce or dissolution of marriage, depending on the language your jurisdiction employs. The plaintiff will file the complaint, and his spouse, by prior mutual agreement, simply will not respond. The plaintiff—with an attorney as a behind-the-scenes ghostwriter and coach—then files a motion for default judgment (a final judicial decision against a party who fails to file a required pleading or make an appearance in court). Again, the spouse does not contest.

Finally, the limited scope attorney advises his client to produce a witness who can appear at a default judgment hearing to substantiate that the divorce grounds are real. By prior arrangement, the opposing spouse, the "defendant" or "respondent," will not appear. After all the dominos have tumbled here, the judge enters a judgment of divorce, and a divorce decree is issued.

The whole process has been swift and equitable—and for this particular couple, orders of magnitude less costly than full-service representation or even mediation. Alternatively, attempting this without a legal professional by going *pro se* might have required months of false starts and might even have failed.

Limited Scope Assistance for More Complex Cases

Couples engaged in serious litigation involving custody disputes, child support, or abuse, on the other hand, would be best served by full representation; but even in these contentious situations, traditional legal help may simply be financially out of reach. In such instances, limited scope attorneys can guide the way.

It might work like this: a victim of domestic violence, operating on instructions from her limited scope lawyer, files a petition alleging abuse. After an *ex parte* hearing, in which she is representing herself, a judge may grant her an emergency protective order.

So what exactly has the limited service lawyer done? He or she has helped the client fill out the petition, prepare supporting documents (*affidavits*, in legal speak), and prepare for the hearing.

 **DEFINITION**

The Latin phrase **ex parte** literally means "by, from, or for one party." So, an ex parte hearing is a proceeding brought by one person in the absence of another. An **affidavit** is a statement of facts, which is sworn to (or affirmed) before an officer who has authority to administer an oath (for example, a notary public).

If the facts are in dispute, the attorney's role will be more pronounced. For one thing, the lawyer may accompany the client to an initial hearing, during which the other spouse may object. The result may be a second, adversarial hearing where both parties present evidence—and the limited service attorney will want to appear there as well. In the aftermath of the hearing, the judge will often grant a longer-term protective order, frequently effective for six months or more. The order typically may enjoin the abuser from contact with the abused, ordering him to leave the family home. Temporary custody of children is then typically awarded to the abused, with a temporary visitation schedule for the noncustodial parent. Emergency family maintenance and attorney fees might also be awarded to the petitioner.

So what does all this have to do with divorce? For a small sum of money to purchase limited legal representation, the abused party in the aforementioned scenario has set a powerful legal precedent likely to carry over when she files for divorce. "The protective order can establish presumptions about how the similar divorce issues should be resolved," the American Bar Association says. "These 'benchmarks' can substantially help the *pro se* party in the later divorce case."

In short, this is the domino theory of divorce at work, again.

How to Benefit from Unbundled Divorce

You will be most successful using unbundled services if you pick an attorney who specializes in the unbundled approach. According to Forrest Mosten, a pioneer in the unbundled movement, the most suitable lawyers want to "spend more time in direct contact with clients" and are "flexible with changing roles." Attorneys providing limited representation prefer "to teach clients skills and concepts" that will better their client's chances of winning—and maybe even improving their lives. If you want your divorce settled expeditiously, moreover, you should seek someone who appears at once proactive and nonadversarial. If the attorney can help you "prevent problems from ever ripening into conflict," Mosten explains, he or she is well-suited to the task.

Who is best suited for an unbundled divorce? Of course, the major qualification is financial: If you lack the money to pay for full-service representation, you may have no choice. Still, California attorney M. Sue Talia has some guidelines and tips.

If you choose limited representation, she says, you "must be prepared to live with the consequences of [your] decisions, even if they turn out differently than you hoped or expected." Talia says that the best candidates for this kind of legal help are able to emotionally detach from their situation. As with the most competent *pro se* litigants, they must be able to handle legal paperwork and juggle details, including financial details, in an organized and thorough way.

"In many situations, people who are less than ideal have no choice other than to accept limited representation and, therefore, to partially represent themselves," the American Bar Association says. In such instances, the litigants should try to assume only the simplest of the tasks and might seek further assistance from the self-help *pro se* programs in their jurisdiction.

The Least You Need to Know

- Many couples choose to divorce *pro se*, but by doing so, they place themselves at risk. Most would come out ahead by hiring an attorney for the complex parts of their case.
- Look for unbundled divorce services through the same centers that dispense legal information to individuals divorcing *pro se*.
- If you cannot afford a full-service attorney and your legal funds are extremely limited, the best money you ever spend may be for a consultation with a limited scope attorney.
- Even if you are a *pro se* litigant, your limited scope divorce attorney can help you draft documents and prepare your case every step of the way.

Mediation, Arbitration, and Collaboration

In the best of all possible worlds, couples facing divorce would work out agreements between themselves. That's often difficult, of course, because it's the very tendency to argue and diverge that leads to divorce in the first place. The most common solution is hiring attorneys—adversaries—who help the couple duke it out privately or in court. But for those who cherish the notion of an amicable parting, mediation is a popular and relatively inexpensive alternative.

Gentle Tactics

In *mediation*, you and your spouse settle the issues of your divorce with the help of a mediator, who could be a social worker or an attorney. This person has multiple tasks, including the following:

- Hearing the issues

- Understanding the personalities

- Explaining the divorce laws that form the necessary background to the mediation sessions

In This Chapter

- The advantages of mediation

- How to choose a mediator

- The mediation process from beginning to end

- When to go into arbitration

- Why collaboration might be right for you

- Facilitating discussions
- Suggesting solutions to disputed issues
- Bringing the parties to a settlement agreement

A deft mediator will be able to handle two individuals who have been a couple, sleuth out the dynamics of their marital relationship, and bring them beyond their impasse to a final resolution in order to compose a settlement agreement.

Increasingly, even couples using a mediator hire separate attorneys to have in his or her back pocket. Often the spouse will meet with the attorney before the mediation begins to learn his rights from an attorney of his choosing. If questions arise during the mediation, the spouse can consult with his own lawyer. While having a lawyer or lawyers and a mediator adds to the cost of the divorce, the lawyer's role is far less than it would be in a divorce without a mediator, thereby further reducing costs.

Successful mediation takes more than one session. How long the process takes depends on the willingness of the parties to compromise. If one person will not budge in his or her position, the mediator will have to use all his or her resources to break down the barriers to compromise. This may be futile in the end, but if the couple is motivated to settle the case without litigation, eventually the mediator can help bring about compromise.

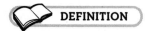 **DEFINITION**

Divorce **mediation** is a process whereby a neutral person—the mediator, who is usually a lawyer or social worker—works with the divorcing couple toward reaching a settlement agreement.

Say you want to keep the house and have primary custody of the children, but your spouse wants you to sell the house, split the sales proceeds, and have joint custody. There is a major challenge. You have a long way to go to reach an agreement. It's the mediator's job to find a practical solution that both parties can accept. At some point, the mediator will explain the laws regarding these issues and how a court might likely rule. Then it is up to the parties to decide if they can live with the court's idea of a resolution or if they are willing to modify their respective positions to reach a solution they both prefer.

Once an agreement is reached, each spouse brings the agreement to his or her own attorney for review. If the lawyers find no questions or problems with the document, one of the attorneys drafts the requisite paperwork for approval by the parties. If everyone is in accord, the settlement agreement is then submitted to the court for the judge to sign. Once it is entered into the court's records, it is finalized.

SILVER LININGS

Mediation is not binding. If you are not satisfied with the outcome of your mediation, you might have wasted some time and money, but you can start over by going to an attorney who can still attempt to resolve your matter without going to court. Of course, court remains an option.

Advantages of Mediation

For certain people, mediation is an appropriate way to reach an agreement. The best candidates are those who are willing to negotiate directly with their spouse to save money and heartache and get on with their lives. They are people who understand the value of avoiding expensive, heated litigation and are willing to give something up in order to settle quickly and as amicably as possible. Typically, they value the fact that, even in their darkest hour as a couple, they can sit down and talk face to face instead of interacting solely through their attorneys. Mediation usually takes place in a friendlier setting than legal meetings, although if there are hard feelings because of a betrayal, there can be considerable tension.

As a process, mediation is also more flexible than the legal protocols that guide lawyers and courts. For example, you can set the pace of mediation sessions to correspond with your own emotional and logistical needs. After you enter the legal system, deadlines and delays come with the territory, imposed not just by individual judges, but also by the system's mandate to "move things along," or more likely, slowed by the huge backlog in the courts.

Finally, mediation might sometimes work better, even for the most calculating among us. Because mediators usually meet with both spouses at once, it's easier during these sessions to grasp just where the other is coming from. After all, you cannot read body language or facial expressions when your only communication comes from a document from your lawyer. This might be a plus for those who can "just tell" when their spouse is bluffing or when he or she won't budge.

RED ALERT

If you do not know the value of assets in your marriage, including any pension or retirement accounts, a business, or your spouse's income, mediation is probably not for you. The reason: the mediator lacks any authority to force one of you to reveal assets to the other. An attorney lacks that authority, too, but he or she can go to a judge. The judge, in turn, can render a ruling requiring your spouse to reveal assets. The judge can penalize your spouse for refusing to cooperate or, worse, for lying. The mediator has no such power and does not give legal advice to either party.

When Mediation Works Best

Despite the advantages, mediation is not for everyone. The system works best when you and your spouse have mutually agreed you want a divorce, when each of you is fully informed of the other's assets and debts, and when, despite some disputes, you're both flexible and eager to work it out as amicably as you can.

Mediation also works best when you and your spouse are convinced of the mediator's impartiality. One lawyer tells us the most common reason clients give for abandoning mediation is the feeling that the mediator has begun to favor the other spouse.

Mediation also works best when there are no urgent needs that must be resolved with a judge's help. For example, if your spouse has cut off support and refuses to reinstate it, you can't afford the luxury of meeting once a week with a mediator to resolve the issue. You need a lawyer to race into court and ask a judge to order your spouse to resume supporting you now.

Finally, mediation works best when both individuals have had a relatively equal relationship. If one member of the couple has, historically, dominated the other, it may be more difficult for both to participate in the give-and-take of mediation.

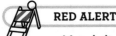

RED ALERT

Many believe that mediation is not a fair process for women. The reason given is that some men are able to bully the woman during the mediation process, and some mediators will not be strong enough to counter the bullying or apprise the woman of her rights under the law. If you're worried that your spouse may try to bully you during mediation, be sure the mediator is aware of your concerns. Alternatively, you might decide this process won't work for you.

When to Avoid Mediation

Take our "mediation-elimination" quiz. If you answer any of the following questions with a "no," mediation is not for you:

- Do we both want this divorce?

- Do I know what our assets and debts are?

- Are we communicating?

- Can we both be flexible?

Although wonderful in concept, mediation could be a disaster in certain situations. Even if you passed the "elimination quiz," take time to review the following list. As you consider your response to the questions, you might conclude that mediation is not for you:

- If you and your spouse are not talking, mediation sessions are not the time to start. Remember, the mediator is not a marriage counselor but rather a conflict resolution specialist whose job it is to help you address and resolve issues.

- If either you or your spouse, or both, harbor extreme feelings of anger, mediation probably won't work.

- If one of you does not want the divorce, mediation doesn't stand a chance.

- If you have secrets that impact your case, you should probably avoid mediation. Mediators do not have "attorney-client" privilege in many jurisdictions, so anything you tell the mediator can later come out in court.

- If your case is very simple, it might not pay to use a mediator because attorneys will still have to review the agreement. Remember, mediation is useful when there are unresolved issues between you and your spouse.

- Finally, if you're trying mediation but you feel the mediator is siding with your spouse, you should stop the process. If one of you has lost confidence, mediation is unlikely to be successful.

Choosing a Mediator

To find a mediator or another professional specializing in alternative dispute resolution, look for a community dispute resolution center, located in many areas, or a professional organization for alternative dispute resolution. Your local dispute resolution center may offer free mediation sessions as well as be able to give you names of trained divorce mediators.

Any mediator you hire should at least have a degree in social work, counseling, or psychology. It is helpful, but not imperative, that the mediator have a law degree as well. Even without a law degree, however, the mediator should be completely familiar with the divorce laws of your jurisdiction.

When interviewing the prospective mediator to see if he or she is right for you and your spouse, here are some questions you'll want answered:

1. Does the mediator know the law in your jurisdiction?

2. How long has he or she been practicing mediation?

3. How many cases has he or she handled?

4. How does he or she keep up with new developments in the law?

The prospective mediator should be able to answer your questions without sounding defensive.

Find out what and how the mediator charges before you hire one. You and your spouse should agree on how the mediator's fees will be paid. Will you each pay half the fee at the end of each session, or will one of you pay all of it and be reimbursed when the case is over and the assets are divided? Will one of you foot the bill with no reimbursement? If you cannot work that out with the mediator's help, mediation might not be for you.

Finally, ask for references—and call those references. The mediator might not be willing to give you the names of clients (and should not do so without the clients' prior consent), but the mediator should be able to give you the names of attorneys familiar with his or her work. After all, the mediator should be sending couples to attorneys to review any agreement before it is signed. If the mediator doesn't know any attorneys or can't give you any names, interview someone else. Sometimes it is useful to engage in a dual mediation process where there are two mediators, one a lawyer and one a psychologist. This raises the cost, but in the right case, it might be worth it.

 **RED ALERT**

What if one of you really likes the mediator you're thinking of and the other doesn't? Don't feel pressured. If you are not entirely comfortable, don't hire the mediator. If one of you is ambivalent, that will undermine the entire mediation effort. It's important that you are both confident that the mediator seems to be competent and fair.

Before choosing your mediator, fill out the candidate's credentials to decide whether a given mediator is for you.

Mediator Information

Mediator's name: _____

Address: _____

Date seen: _____

Mediator's education: _____

Mediator's experience: _____

Mediator's fees: _____

How fees will be paid: _____

Did I feel comfortable with the mediator? _____

Did the mediator seem to favor one of us over the other? _____

Was the mediator able to work out the payment of fees between us? _____

Does the mediator have an overall plan for our case? _____

Will the mediator draft an agreement if we come to one? _____

Mediation as a Process

What goes on behind closed doors in mediation?

A mediator will often start the process by asking you to write out your goals. You will be asked to anticipate such problem areas as custody or support. You might be asked to set forth your assets and liabilities in a sworn (notarized) statement, just as you would have done with an attorney. This gives everyone involved a clear idea of the issues and how far apart you really are.

The mediator will work with both of you to divide assets, allocate support, and resolve custody and visitation or any other disputes. The mediator should not advocate one side over the other but should help you both by noting where compromise might work and by coming up with new solutions.

 **SILVER LININGS**

Don't be your own worst enemy: if you can put any anger you have aside, you'll be in a better position to resolve the issues and reach a settlement you can both live with. The mediation process is set up to facilitate an agreement based on knowledge that only you and your spouse have about each other's temperaments, emotional state caused by the divorce, and finances. If you can see past the breakup to a solution and an end to the uncertainty, both parties might come away from the process with less damage than simply relying on the laws, as would be the case with opposing attorneys or in court.

If at any point during the process you don't like the way things are going, consult with an attorney. If you find yourself calling your lawyer more than once or twice, however, you might be better off stopping the mediation and just using the attorney. After all, why pay for two professionals?

After all the issues are resolved, the mediator will draft a written agreement and suggest that each of you have it reviewed by an attorney, who will make sure everything has been covered. For example, some people don't realize they're entitled to part of their spouse's pension or other employment benefits in many jurisdictions. Maybe the mediator overlooked this, or maybe you discussed it but decided to waive any right to the pension plan. Your lawyer should point out your rights and suggest that you pursue them or waive them in writing. The agreement is then ready for signing by the parties and then brought before the judge for signing.

Can you go through the mediation process without ever using a lawyer? Possibly. But if you had enough issues to see a mediator, you're probably better off spending a little more on an attorney to make sure everything is okay. This is especially true if your mediator is not a matrimonial attorney. You must make sure your divorce agreement follows the laws and guidelines of your jurisdiction and that you are not signing away a benefit that you will regret down the road.

If you dislike the result of your mediation, don't sign the agreement. Say that you and your spouse have just spent four months and $4,000 on mediation, but as the process nears an end, you feel uneasy. Perhaps you even think the agreement is being "shoved down your throat."

Maybe you began to think the mediator was siding with your spouse from the beginning, but you were afraid to say anything, or you think your spouse is "pulling a fast one."

If, after being as objective as possible, there is some legitimate basis to your feeling, do not sign the agreement. Seek advice from an attorney. On the other hand, if the real problem is that you're just not ready to end the marriage, or you still hold the faint glimmer of hope that the marriage can be saved, you need to discuss these feelings with a therapist. The truth might be that you'll never be ready to sign an agreement, no matter how fair.

If you are consciously or subconsciously subverting the negotiation process, don't take comfort in the thought that your spouse won't be able to get a divorce. You will simply be laying the groundwork for a litigated divorce. If you are in this situation, a consultation with a mental health professional might help you avoid the financial and emotional stress and lengthy time of going to court.

If You Think Your Spouse Is Lying

Based on your knowledge of your spouse, you may suspect he or she is covering up the truth about finances or other matters. How is it possible to know, and, if it's true, how is it possible to continue using mediation as the vehicle to settle your case?

In a litigated divorce, the process of discovery is supposed to reveal the assets of both parties. This is a mandatory process that yields evidence admissible in court. During mediation, however, discovery is not required. The divorcing couple relies on mutual trust that the other will tell the truth and bring in all documents showing financial status.

How can you make sure that your spouse is telling the truth? If you are suspicious, hire a forensic accountant to review the financial papers and books of your spouse, especially if you are not a financial expert. Not only will a professional be able to notice a deficiency, but the very fact that an accountant is scrutinizing your spouse's affairs will help to keep him or her honest during the negotiations.

Avoiding Old Patterns in Mediation

You may have heard that the patterns of interaction that typified your marriage will characterize your behavior as a couple during mediation. It is the job of a skillful mediator to help the couple break these destructive patterns. Accomplishing this doesn't mean the mediator is siding with one party or the other; instead, it is the only way that a fair settlement can be established.

Rebecca did not want to mediate her divorce with Michael, but he insisted she not hire an attorney and give mediation a chance. She hesitated for a long time, but finally gave in, as was usually the case in their marriage. Once at the mediator's office, Michael took center stage in presenting the "facts" to back up why he wanted a divorce and how the settlement should look. Rebecca disagreed with Michael's version of the "facts" but was reticent to speak up.

The mediator observed the pattern of interaction between the two and encouraged Rebecca to speak her mind. This skillful mediator simply would not allow Michael to gain the upper hand or let a subject drop without a full hearing from both Rebecca and Michael on all issues during the negotiation sessions. As a result, the mediator was able to facilitate a fair settlement.

All About Arbitration

Arbitration is sometimes confused with mediation, but it's really quite different. In arbitration, an individual—the arbitrator—hears your case outside the court system and makes a decision that usually cannot be appealed. As in a court of law, you and your spouse would generally be represented by a lawyer, and depending on the arbitrator, he or she might even insist that the rules of evidence in your jurisdiction be followed by the book.

 **DEFINITION**

> In **arbitration**, a case is decided by an official arbitrator who hears all evidence and makes a decision. Individuals are represented by attorneys. Unlike litigating in court, there are no appeals.

The arbitration itself usually takes place in an office around a conference table. In many ways, arbitration is like going to court but without the ability to appeal. The arbitrator's word is final.

Unlike lawyers, arbitrators do not make an effort to settle the case. They certainly do not do what mediators do—identify issues and then help you resolve them together. Instead, an arbitrator is more like a judge. You come to the table (with your lawyer), ready to present your side. The issues, whatever they might be, have already been determined by you and your lawyer. You must present the arbitrator with your position on those issues and argue your case as cogently as you can.

Given the restrictions, why would anyone ever choose to go into arbitration rather than to a judge? The reasons, for some, are compelling.

Expediency. Depending on where you live, it could take as long as a year to go before a judge, whereas an arbitrator might be readily available.

No need to appeal. You and your spouse might both feel that neither of you will appeal, no matter what the outcome. Maybe you have no more money or you simply can't withstand another round of litigation. Because you're not going to appeal, arbitration has no downside.

Privacy. Everything is private. Unlike a trial, in an arbitration proceeding, there is no public record of who said what or which records were put into evidence.

Cost. Arbitration might be cheaper than a trial. In some jurisdictions, trials do not take place day after day until they are finished. Rather, the judge might schedule one day for your case in January, one day in March, two days in April, and so on. You get the picture. Each time your lawyer has to refresh himself about your case, it costs you. Arbitrators, on the other hand, usually meet day after day until your case is fully heard. Your lawyer only has to prepare once.

Duration. Your case may have been in court (without being tried) for so long that you just want it over with, so you're more than willing to go to arbitration to save time.

After you and your spouse have agreed you want to have your case arbitrated, the lawyers usually pick the arbitrator. Often, arbitrators are retired judges or lawyers with an area of expertise, such as matrimonial law, and are thus quite competent. As with mediators, their fees must be paid by you and your spouse.

Collaborative Divorce

Collaborative law is a relatively new style of legal practice that aims to settle cases without going to court. If you need more protection than a mediator can offer but still want your divorce to be as amicable as possible, a "collaborative lawyer" may be for you.

According to the Collaborative Law Center of Cincinnati, OH, "Collaborative Law is representation without litigation. The goal of collaborative law is to offer lawyers and their clients a structured, nonadversarial alternative to an increasingly adversarial system of dispute resolution. It encourages mature, cooperative, and noncombative behavior and eliminates the option of litigation. By entering into a collaborative law participation agreement, lawyers and their clients commit to the lawyer serving as a negotiator, capable of representation toward settlement but not going to court.

Collaborative divorce has become increasingly popular and is international in scope. To find a collaborative divorce lawyer in your area, check out the website of the International Academy of Collaborative Professionals: www.collaborativepractice.com.

RED ALERT

Nothing in the collaborative law agreement precludes parties from litigating if the process breaks down, but if they choose this avenue, they will have to move ahead with new attorneys.

What Sets Collaborative Law Apart

How is collaborative law different from mediation? Mediation involves the use of a neutral third party to facilitate the negotiation and settlement of a dispute. Parties can always walk out of mediation and decide to litigate instead.

However, in collaborative law cases, lawyers and their clients will talk and negotiate without the assistance of a neutral third party, unless they find such an intervention would be useful. They are committed to continuing the dialogue until a satisfactory solution is reached, since litigation is not an option with these attorneys. Should the talks break down, the divorcing couple would be bound to find new counsel and start the process again. Even though litigation has been ruled out, clients remain protected in a way not possible in mediation. Whereas a mediator does not have attorney-client privilege, a collaborative lawyer never ceases to be the client's advocate, and privilege is maintained.

Is Collaborative Divorce for You?

How can you decide if collaborative divorce is right for you? Pauline Tesler, a California attorney and pioneering founder of collaborative law, offers some advice. "Selecting the dispute resolution process that best suits the couple's unique needs maximizes the likelihood of out-of-court settlement," Tesler states. "Choosing a process which is a bad fit can result in failed negotiations, anger, and a more adversarial divorce than might have been necessary."

RED ALERT

If you want the best deal possible no matter what the cost or emotional pain for others, the collaborative divorce model is not for you.

According to Tesler, "Mediation works best when both spouses share a basic trust in one another's honesty and are reasonably at peace with the fact of the divorce." Still, disparity— lopsided bargaining power or financial sophistication—can play havoc with the mediation process, with no guarantee that a neutral mediator will get it right.

In that instance, those hoping for an amicable divorce should consider collaborative law. Collaborative law "can help spouses arrive at creative settlements even when the problems are complex," Tesler says. "The settlement results can often be more creative than in other models, because neither lawyer succeeds in the job she or he was hired for unless both spouses' legitimate needs are met in the settlement."

The Least You Need to Know

- Mediation works best when both of you can communicate, when you know what assets and liabilities you have, you're both willing to be flexible, and you want the process to work.

- Mediators should have a degree in social work, counseling, or psychology, and possibly law. Even without a law degree, a mediator should be thoroughly familiar with the matrimonial laws of your jurisdiction.

- Any agreement decided with a mediator should still be reviewed by an attorney.

- Do not sign an agreement with which you feel uncomfortable, but be sure that your discomfort is rooted in logic, not emotion.

- Consider arbitration if you and your spouse would not have appealed a trial judge's decision anyway or if your case has dragged on due to a backlogged court.

- If you want individual representation and the comfort of attorney-client privilege, but you also want your divorce to be amicable, consider hiring a collaborative lawyer—as long as your soon-to-be ex will hire one, too.

Taking Your Case to Court

You and your spouse have tried for months, maybe even years, to settle your divorce on your own, but you've gotten nowhere. Your lawyer hasn't had any luck either. Finally, you've reached the end of the line: it's time to go to court.

Here Comes the Judge

Perhaps the most important person you'll deal with as you go to trial is the judge—just another human being, albeit one who has the power to make decisions for you and your spouse. In a small number of jurisdictions, your case might be tried by a jury, but if not, a judge will decide the outcome. As the decider (or "trier of fact," in court speak), the judge listens, takes notes, sometimes asks questions, and when the case is over, makes a decision. Because the judge is also the referee, he or she will set the schedule of the trial, make rulings when the lawyers disagree, and rap the gavel if the courtroom gets out of control. You might have one judge throughout the case or several different judges until trial, at which time you will have only one judge.

In This Chapter

- The role of the judge
- Understanding court speak: conferences, motions, and discovery
- The difference between family and civil court
- A word about military law
- Should you appeal?

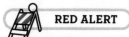 **RED ALERT**

If you attend a court matter, keep in mind that you will be in front of the judge who might eventually try your case. Do your best to make a good impression. Speak in a conversational tone and do not display emotion or make threats. Even if the current judge will not try your case, you stand a better chance of winning a request if the judge is happy with your demeanor.

In most jurisdictions, you must file an application to put an issue before a judge for a ruling. The application has to be made through a *motion* or *order to show cause.*

How Judges Resolve Issues

While those going through divorce await trial, they often find themselves unable to resolve even the most mundane issues on their own. When that happens, the judge on their case gets involved. For instance, Jake wanted to have his sons spend the last three weeks of the summer with him so that they could visit his sister and her family, who were in the United States for only a short time. Sara—the boys' mother—had already enrolled them in summer camp for those same weeks. Because Jake and Sara could not agree on a solution to this conflict, their lawyers were asked to intervene. Discussions between the lawyers also went nowhere.

Finally, Jake's lawyer asked for a ruling from the judge. Jake brought a brochure from the summer camp, showing three sessions. He had contacted the camp and told the judge that the first and second sessions still had room for his sons. Since the boys could attend the first and second sessions, they would be able to be with Jake and his sister for the last three weeks of the summer.

The judge immediately granted Jake his request. The cost to him? Less than $1,000 in legal fees. As an added bonus, he made a good impression on the judge (he had done his homework and had delivered his pitch calmly), whereas Sara seemed unreasonable and stressed. Not only would Jake get the boys when he wanted them, but he would also be walking into the upcoming trial with a reputation for reason, responsibility, and calmness.

Remember, if you have the same issue as Jake but lack an attorney, you may, depending on your jurisdiction, benefit from filing an application with the court as a *pro se* to make the same request. If you do, be sure you have gotten as much legal guidance as possible beforehand—especially if your spouse has legal representation.

We suggest that if you have limited resources, you save them for a situation like this. If you are purchasing legal services à la carte, there is no better way to spend your limited resources than in pursuit of extra time with your children. And there is no question that such legal input will help you in the end.

How to Impress the Judge

Given the fact that your judge might be determining your fate and, if you have children, theirs too, making a good impression is vital. To make sure that you score points with this powerful figure, study the following helpful tips for appropriate behavior whenever you have occasion to be before your judge:

Remain composed. Avoid gesticulating wildly with your hands. The judge might not remember the issues raised up until the trial, but if you had made a spectacle of yourself when before him, he might well remember that. Sometimes, it's hard to maintain control when you know your spouse is lying, but you have to do it.

Speak only when appropriate. If your lawyer is present, it's best that you follow accepted courtroom protocol and not speak at all unless your lawyer instructs you to or the judge asks you a question directly. If you think your lawyer is missing an issue, nudge her gently and ask if you can speak to her for a minute. You can also write a note and push it over to your lawyer.

Be prepared. If you are a *pro se* litigant, be sure you have learned as much as possible about procedure and expectations before stepping into the court.

Going Through the Motions

Sometimes you cannot wait until the trial to resolve certain conflicts, and your attorney will have to make a request, usually in writing, for a court ruling on a matter within a period of days (a *motion*) or on an emergency basis (an *order to show cause*). If you want to obtain immediate, temporary support until the trial commences, temporary custody of the children, a visitation schedule, lawyer's fees, expert's fees, or any other temporary relief, these are the tools to use—although costly.

 **DEFINITION**

> A **motion** is a request made of a judge by a **movant** (the person who makes the motion) while an action is pending or at trial. Motions can be made in writing for the court to consider, or orally, such as at trial. In matrimonial cases, motions are typically made for temporary support, temporary custody, visitation rights, or to enjoin someone from taking money or property. A *motion* may also be called an **order to show cause,** if it's brought under emergency circumstances where the court must act quickly to resolve the issue.

Filing a motion is like a tennis game, except paperwork—instead of a ball—flies back and forth. Say your spouse has stopped paying the mortgage on the marital residence. He has moved out, and he thinks you should pay for it because you're living there, but you don't want to use up your limited savings. It's been four months since he last paid the mortgage, and you're getting nasty letters from the bank. What do you do? Your lawyer will probably draft a motion asking the judge to immediately order your spouse to pay the back due mortgage and continue to make monthly payments. The motion will include your sworn statement, explaining that the mortgage has not been paid. Your lawyer will probably include the bank letters you've received as exhibits for the judge to see. Once your paperwork is completed, your lawyer sends a copy of the papers to your spouse's lawyer before giving the motion to the judge.

If you do not have an attorney, try to get help with the protocol for writing a motion from the court clerk. Many jurisdictions now provide plentiful help with such issues for *pro se* litigants in family court. There are even forms for common requests of the court. Some jurisdictions make the forms available for download from their websites.

After you or your attorney files the motion, your spouse or spouse's attorney has the chance to answer. The answer will be in the form of a sworn, signed statement opposing your motion. Maybe your husband will say he gave you the money to pay the mortgage each month, but you spent it on a vacation. He might include canceled checks as exhibits. If he wants additional relief, such as an order directing you to pay the utilities on the house, he can ask for that as well. That's called a *cross-motion.*

If he has a lawyer, the lawyer will take care of it. If he does not have an attorney, he will be drafting the cross-motion himself, probably with the help of a court clerk.

You then have the chance to respond to both his response to your motion—maybe those checks were used for food—and his cross-motion. Some states will allow him to respond to your response to the cross-motion. All the paperwork eventually goes to the judge, who makes a decision. Expect the process to be limited to the movant's application, the *cross-movant's* response, and the movant's reply—anything more requires special permission from the court.

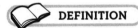 **DEFINITION**

A **cross-motion** is a counter request made of a judge in reaction to a motion made by the opposing party. The party filing the cross-motion is the **cross-movant.**

In some jurisdictions, even with all this paperwork, you or your attorneys still must appear in court to present oral arguments to the judge. This is just the type of legal ping-pong that runs the meter up on legal fees. You can well imagine that by the time all is said and done, the person paying a full-service attorney could have taken a trip to the U.S. Open instead of paying legal fees in his or her own tennis match.

The Discovery Zone

Before your case can go to trial, you will go through the process of *discovery.* Here, you and your spouse, generally working through your attorneys, exchange information that might be important to your case. In some jurisdictions, discovery is limited to financial and custody issues. In other places, the discovery can involve issues of physical and mental health, especially if these issues were part of the grounds for divorce.

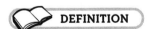 **DEFINITION**

Discovery is the act of revealing information so both parties are fully informed of facts before trial. Discovery can pertain to custody matters or finances or to one's physical or mental condition when those issues are relevant, such as when a spouse claims an inability to work due to an injury. Depending on the jurisdiction, other areas may be discoverable as well. Discovery methods include depositions, answering interrogatories, producing documents, and undergoing a physical.

How does discovery work? It's like a scavenger hunt. Your attorney will receive a list (usually long) from your spouse's attorney, setting out all the information that lawyer wants—bank statements, credit card slips, cancelled checks, loan applications, credit card applications, deeds, wills, names of anyone with whom you own property; the list is limited only by the lawyer's imagination and the local law.

What if you don't have the materials requested? Unfortunately, your spouse probably won't believe you. You could end up before a judge, with your spouse's lawyer claiming you're hiding information and your lawyer explaining that you no longer have it. A judge will then rule for or against you.

Discovery is not limited to the production of written materials. You could also be *deposed*—obligated to answer questions under oath in front of a stenographer, your spouse, and his lawyer. You could be served with extensive written questions, which you are obligated to answer truthfully.

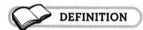 **DEFINITION**

A **deposition** involves answering questions under oath. In matrimonial matters, a deposition usually centers on a party's finances and is conducted in a lawyer's office or in the courthouse, but a judge will not be present. In some jurisdictions, the grounds for divorce may also be the subject of the deposition. A stenographer takes down everything that is said and later types it up for review by the parties and their attorneys. Once final, this deposition transcript can be used at trial to impeach your credibility or to prove a fact in the case.

Discovery could also involve a physical examination by a medical doctor (if, for example, the issue is your ability to work), a blood test (if the issue is paternity), and even a psychological examination (particularly if custody is at issue or you claim you need support because you have psychological problems).

A judge need not be involved in discovery if the lawyers agree on a schedule and stick to it, and if they agree on what is to be disclosed. However, if one side doesn't agree on what is to be disclosed, then the decision will rest with the judge.

Your Day in Court

Judges generally try to help you resolve your case before the trial date, but that is often simply impossible. If, after months and even years of negotiations, conferences, and motions, you and your spouse or ex-spouse still have not reached an agreement, your last recourse is to have a trial. The trial gives the judge the opportunity to hear both parties' wish lists, substantiated by volumes of documents, possibly witnesses, and any other information the contenders think will persuade the judge in their favor.

 **RED ALERT**

While a *pro se* litigant is certainly entitled to step in and take deposition as well as conduct discovery, we do not advise it. In general, if you have enough money or property at stake to require these steps, you should dig in and hire an attorney to help you out. If there is enough at stake, it may well be worth a short-term loan.

After the judge ponders all the relevant information, she will make her decision. Because the judge has heard all the evidence and witnesses, a decision made by the judge at the trial's conclusion is taken very seriously by the powers that be. This decision should put an end to motions and conferences called for modifying temporary orders or changes in visitation schedules without a change in circumstance. Everyone has spent a lot of time, money, and effort at the trial, and asking for subsequent modification might not do you much good, unless there's been a substantial change in circumstances that would warrant modification after the fact.

Your trial will be very much like those you've seen on television and in movies. If you are the plaintiff, or petitioner—the spouse who started the action—your lawyer presents your case first. He will probably call you to the witness stand, where you will be sworn in and asked to take a seat. After your lawyer has finished asking you questions (direct examination), your spouse's lawyer has the opportunity to ask you questions (cross-examination). Your lawyer has the right to object to improper questions, so give her time to do that before answering. It's also a good idea to take a moment before you answer to collect your thoughts.

After the cross-examination, your lawyer can ask you questions again; maybe your spouse's lawyer interrupted you while you were trying to explain something. Your lawyer can now give you the chance to present your explanation (your re-direct examination).

After your re-direct examination, there can be a re-cross-examination. The questioning can go back and forth for as long as the judge will allow it. When there are no more questions for you, your lawyer can call a witness to the stand on your behalf, and the whole process starts all over again.

After you have presented all your witnesses (in divorce cases, it's often just you, your spouse, possibly your child's *guardian ad litem*, the court-appointed psychiatric evaluator, and expert witnesses such as an appraiser of real property or of a business), your side "rests." It is now your spouse's turn to present his witnesses. The same questioning occurs, only the roles are reversed. Your spouse's lawyer conducts the direct questioning, and your lawyer cross-examines the witness.

 **DEFINITION**

A **guardian *ad litem*** is a person, often a lawyer, but in some states a psychologist or social worker, selected by the judge and assigned to represent "the best interests" of the children. Some jurisdictions do not have guardians *ad litem*.

After your spouse (in this case, the defendant) presents her witnesses, your lawyer can call witnesses to refute what's been said (called rebuttal witnesses). After you've called your rebuttal witnesses, your spouse can do the same.

It is the rare *pro se* litigant who has enough skill and experience to question an expert witness hired by the other side. When both sides have rested, the judge might allow each attorney (or if there are no attorneys, the spouses themselves) to make a short, closing speech. Alternatively, he might ask that memoranda be submitted to him by a certain deadline. Sometime later, he makes his decision, usually in writing.

If your trial was by jury, the jury decides the outcome after all the witnesses have testified, closing speeches have been made, and the judge has instructed the jurors about their responsibilities.

Some judges might give you a bench (oral) decision at the end of your motion or trial, as though you had a jury. (You or your lawyer should be able to find out, before the trial, if your judge makes bench decisions.)

Trials can be as short as half a day or as long as several months (although that would be unusual for a divorce trial). The length of a trial depends on the number of witnesses, how long each examination takes, and what motions are made during the course of the trial. The emotional and financial costs rapidly add up.

Judicial Bias

Do judges "play favorites" with lawyers? The answer is, probably not, but who knows? We like to think justice is blind, but there are some realities, too. In some jurisdictions, the same judges tend to hear matrimonial cases, and the same lawyers tend to appear before them. Does that mean they're all buddies, and you had better find the lawyer the judge likes best? No. Cases are decided on their merits. It does mean, however, that if you've hired a well-respected attorney, the judge has probably already observed him at work and trusts his or her integrity.

While the presumption of joint custody or the awarding of joint custody where parents agree has become increasingly popular, this chapter on divorce by trial assumes you and your spouse are at odds on this issue.

Do some judges favor mothers over fathers in custody disputes? The answer to that question is probably "yes," although that is likely moderating. There's really no way to know for sure. Even though custody determinations are supposed to be gender neutral, the reality for many fathers is that, traditionally, they have been the parent to go off to work while the mother stays home. Even if the mother does work, she is the one who probably did most of the child-care. It follows that the mother has spent more time with the children, the main criterion for custody. Many judges also work under the assumption that young children (seven and under) belong with their mothers, even though there is no law to support this premise. This said, times have changed quite a bit over the last 10 years, and facts should prevail in a trial.

Will a judge ever admit to a bias? No. But most lawyers will tell you that if you're a father seeking custody, and you have not chosen to put your career on hold to raise the kids, you'll probably need a good reason why the mother should not have custody. Should you throw in the towel? Consult with an attorney first. If you have limited funds, this may be the time to spend some of it on legal advice or representation. As we've said, many jurisdictions now have some sort of joint custody (joint legal, or both legal and physical custody) preference. Even in jurisdictions with a sole custody preference, parenting time has become more flexible and generous for the noncustodial parent.

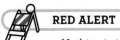 **RED ALERT**

Nothing irritates a court more than a manipulative litigant. Keep this in mind when the tears are about to flow, unless they're for real.

What about other biases? Years on the bench, of course, can make one skeptical. Some judges have heard umpteen tales of the business that fails, miraculously, right before the divorce action, and a few years of seasoning means that they've seen the couple who spent $100,000 a year while reporting income of $20,000 and even less. Does this mean you're doomed if your business really has taken a bad turn, or you had no idea what your spouse reported as income? No, but when you appear before a judge, you must be thoroughly prepared to prove your case.

SILVER LININGS

Although the issues being decided at your trial are extremely important and will affect you profoundly, this is not a criminal trial. No one is going to be sentenced to jail (unless this is a trial for contempt of court—a deliberate failure to make support payments, for example). Matrimonial judges might get annoyed at your bad behavior or obvious lies, but they are used to the deep feelings divorcing spouses have and are generally sympathetic and patient.

When You're the Witness

As much as you might wish the witness seat would open up and swallow you, you will need to deal with the opposing attorney the best you can. (If your spouse is *pro se* and questions you himself, his lack of experience could be advantageous to your case.) What can you do when you're looking at a lawyer, but you feel as if you're peering into the mouth of a shark? Some pointers:

- Take your time before answering questions. Think before you speak, and give your lawyer time to object to the question.

- Do not let the lawyer get you riled. Control your emotions.

- If you feel faint, tell the judge you need a break. Just be sure not to interrupt anyone else, unless it's an emergency.

- If there's water nearby, pour yourself a cup or ask the judge for some. Do not be shy about making these requests.

- Keep shaky hands inside the witness box so the lawyer won't know what effect he's having on you.

- Remember to look at the judge and, if appropriate, at your lawyer, in addition to the lawyer who is questioning you.

- Don't be afraid to cry if your emotions have clearly reached the boiling point. At this time, the judge will probably call a recess, and you'll have a chance to pull yourself together.

Traps You Can Avoid

A trial should be about the pursuit of truth and justice, not about who used what gimmick to "win." However, you can do things to help your case:

- Visit the courthouse before the day of trial, when a trial is in progress, if possible. You'll feel better knowing you're not stepping into uncharted territory.

- Tell your lawyer everything. It will be much worse for you if your lawyer hears about something for the first time while you're being cross-examined.

- Dress appropriately. Our picks: conservative blouse and skirt, suit, or dress for women; suit and tie for men.

- Leave expensive jewelry at home, unless you're trying to prove that your extravagant marital lifestyle included such trinkets.

- Be sure to bring all the documents needed. Pack them the night before. Bring paper, or ask your lawyer to bring an extra legal pad for you to take or write notes.

- Pause before answering any questions. Give yourself time to think and give your lawyer time to object.

- If you don't understand a question, tell the lawyer you do not understand, and ask that it be repeated.

- If your trial involves a jury, look at the jurors when you answer questions, but do not stare at any one juror. You don't want to make any juror feel uncomfortable.

- Be aware that when your side is presenting its case, you're probably going to feel great. During the presentation of your spouse's case, you'll probably feel miserable.

- During the trial, get plenty of rest at night.

- When the trial is over, try to put it out of your mind. You might keep thinking about what you should have said differently. Try to forget it.

Common Mistakes You Must Not Make

The following points might seem obvious in the calm of your living room while reading this book, but under the stress of the trial, for your sake, they must be subjected to memory:

- Do not make faces, ever. If your wife lies like a rug, do not roll your eyes or shake your head.

- Do not speak out in court. It may be tempting, but the judge will view outbursts negatively.

- Follow your attorney's instincts. This is not a good time for the camp to be divided. You can clarify your attorney's actions during a break.

- Do not flirt with, excessively smile at, or in any way try to engage the judge or a juror.

- If your trial is by jury, never speak to a juror while the trial is in progress.

- Do not argue with your spouse's lawyer. If you're too angry to speak, wait or take a sip of water before continuing to testify.

- Avoid sarcasm.

- Avoid crossing your arms while you're on the witness stand.

- Don't doodle. The judge or jurors might notice, and it will look as though you just don't care.

- Don't talk to your spouse in court without good reason (scheduling the children, for example). Usually, there's just too much emotion for communication.

Family Court vs. Civil Court

Whether you go to family court is largely dependent on what jurisdiction you live in and how far you have gotten in your case. In some places, you have to go to civil court if you want a divorce. In others, all family-related matters may be handled in family court.

In general, family court might be a little more relaxed because many more people handle their own cases without a lawyer. The good news is that the courtrooms, whether by design or through lack of funding, might be much smaller than a "regular courtroom" and might feel less intimidating. The bad news is that while you wait for your case to be called, infants might be screaming all around you, and, depending on where you live, many cases might be ahead of yours. Civil court, on the other hand, tends to be quieter, less congested, and more professional.

Despite these outward differences, how the trial proceeds depends more on the judge than the courthouse. Some judges are very strict about the rules of evidence; others are more liberal. Some judges are very formal, requiring you to rise when they enter the courtroom. Others are more relaxed.

Military Law

As with most family law in recent times, if you're in the military, it's important to be aware of the latest in military law. The American Bar Association's Military Committee has an informative website to get you started: apps.americanbar.org/dch/committee.cfm?com=FL115277.

In the end, though, you will be best served to hire a lawyer who specializes in this field.

For military spouses who live overseas, even serving the divorce papers has obstacles, as there may be restrictions imposed by the hosting country. If you are located in the United States, the base may not be close to your spouse. Getting to a trial can be difficult in these situations as well. Determining which jurisdiction's laws should prevail poses another hurdle for military couples.

Child support, custody, visitation, medical expenses, pension, disability, survivor benefits, and other financial issues also have their unique slant because of the special circumstances of being in the military.

To repeat: military family law is often very complicated, depending on which country you come from. Service members are well advised to hire a specialist in the field.

Should You Appeal?

You've gone to trial and the judge or jury has made a decision, but you're not happy. Should you appeal? As with so much in life, the answer is, "It depends."

If the issue is critically important to you, and your lawyer thinks you have a reasonable shot at getting a reversal, and you can afford it, and you have the emotional fortitude to continue, you probably should appeal.

On the other hand, if the issue is critically important to you, but your lawyer says you have virtually no chance of winning, and you'd need to mortgage your share of the house, you probably shouldn't appeal. An appeal is expensive not only because your attorney has to do legal research and then write a brief, but also because you usually need to furnish the appellate court with copies of the entire *record below*—the evidence admitted in the case—as well as the transcript of the trial. Depending on how many days the trial lasted, that alone could cost many thousands of dollars. Then, you usually need to supply the appeals court with several copies of the record below, the transcript, and the brief—adding hundreds of dollars more to your costs in photocopy fees. (Some jurisdictions have procedures whereby you can save money on the transcript or photocopying fees if you meet certain low-income requirements.)

To make matters worse, in some jurisdictions, the appellate courts are so backlogged that your appeal might not be decided for more than a year.

Can you do an appeal yourself? If you're a lawyer, maybe. However, it would be very hard for a layperson to do the legal research, and you would still be faced with combing your files to produce the record below (the evidence admitted in your case), the transcript, and photo-copying costs.

When you consider whether to appeal, listen to your attorney and your head. As much as you might want to, this is not the time to vote with your heart.

The Least You Need to Know

- The judge is the final decision-maker if you and your spouse have not been able to come to an agreement.
- Motions tend to be expensive because lawyers have to put a lot of time into them. Settle whatever you can with your spouse to avoid having to make a motion.
- Always control your emotions in court. This includes your facial expressions and body language.
- Pause before answering questions. Give your lawyer time to object and give yourself time to answer correctly.
- If you or your spouse is in the military, consult a lawyer who specializes in military divorce law.
- Consider the chances of success and the expense involved before you decide to appeal.

When Divorce Turns Vicious

There's high-conflict divorce, and there's higher-conflict divorce. We've covered high-conflict divorce in Chapter 12, on litigation—where such scenarios generally play out. If one spouse has been unfaithful and deceptive during the marriage, it is difficult for the wronged spouse to agree to an amicable divorce. This can lead to anger and resentment. Anger and resentment can turn to belligerence, which in turn angers the other spouse. Before you know it, neither party will cooperate with the other, and the divorcing couple is headed for protracted litigation.

Why protracted? Both people tend to dig in their heels on issues of importance to them. Add to that the huge backlog in the court system, and you're in for the long haul. Sometimes it's the system itself that finally wears you down until you both yell, "Uncle!"

In This Chapter

- Escalating conflict
- How to obtain an order of protection
- The limitations of court-ordered protection
- How to use the resources of the legal system to reduce conflict
- Why stalking happens and laws that can protect you

Especially during the early years of a separation, fresh wounds from a betrayal or nonstop fighting during the marriage can generate such intense heat that neither person can be in the same room with the other. When children are an issue, things can get really nasty. (In Chapter 23, we discuss how harmful high-conflict situations are for the children and steps to mitigate the damaging effects on them.)

A custody battle can cause both parents to engage in extreme and hostile behavior never before seen by the other spouse. In some cases, a third party must be involved to help the children go from one parent to the next. Rude or aggressive behavior by one parent toward the other in front of the children is all too common in high-conflict divorce, and it is incumbent on both parents to walk away from situations where their "buttons" are being pushed.

 **RED ALERT**

If you have been abusing your spouse or children, you must stop and seek help. Often abusers have been victims themselves.

Yet more conflict may arise when a spouse is completely unwilling to let go. Buckle your seat belt: when one spouse wants the divorce and the other opposes it, conflict can be extreme.

If you are the spouse who won't let go, our advice is simply to move on. By dragging out the proceedings, you are merely postponing the inevitable at enormous cost, not just emotionally, but also financially as you and your spouse dribble away your savings on legal fees.

If you are the partner who wants the divorce, step back and give your partner some time and space to get used to the idea. Pull back on significant legal action for a month or two.

Major legal battles are bad enough, but it gets worse—much worse. One partner may have a genuine personality disorder or suffer mental illness. Now the situation can become dangerous.

Sometimes the fighting is just a continuation of a long-standing abusive relationship. A spouse who has been battered for years finally has the courage to make a break. Other times, a rejected spouse goes beyond what would be normal anger and retribution into pathological behaviors that can lead to violence and even death.

The remainder of this chapter briefly touches on the issues involved with this extreme situation.

The Nightmare Begins

You've heard divorce horror stories, but you never imagined yours could be in this category. Now it looks as if your worst nightmare is coming true. Your spouse just won't leave you alone. He hangs out near your office and leers at you when you leave. Or, she calls your new love interest on the phone in the middle of the night and mutters obscenities. Your one-time partner has become an actual threat to your physical safety, maybe even entering your apartment without your permission and against your will.

Whatever harassment you might be experiencing, if you haven't yet hired an attorney, now is the time. If you think you don't have the funds, contact the Legal Aid Society, its equivalent in your area, or your local Bar Association, which may list lawyers who work *pro bono* (with little to no pay) or other resources.

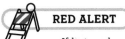 **RED ALERT**

> If being abused is already part of your existence, trying to separate or divorce your abusive spouse can be like poking a bees' nest. Be proactive and take the necessary steps *now* to get the legal protection you need. If you think you are in imminent danger, contact the police and go to a local abuse shelter. As hard as it may seem, you must break the habit of accepting your spouse back into your life. Take this moment to free yourself so you can live an independent and secure life. A psychotherapist can help you to overcome destructive patterns.

Harassment

Denise couldn't deal with Jack's leaving her. He was her entire life, or so she imagined. She couldn't live without him, and she told him so—over and over, in every form of communication possible. She called him night and day, both at home and at work. She sent him text messages and emails and even called his friends to tell them what a so-and-so he was, yet how much she needed him. Jack could not escape her attempts to get at him. He was sleepless. He was afraid to go anywhere he thought she might be—restaurants they had frequented, the supermarket, the cleaners, movie theaters, and more. He dreaded stepping out of his office and apartment buildings for fear she would be waiting for him. In effect, he was under attack. Clearly, he was dealing with a woman who had gone beyond the normal reaction of being rejected. What were his options?

Order of Protection

Every year millions of people–mostly women, but some men–experience domestic abuse, especially if they are in the process of trying to separate from their spouse.

In 1994 Congress passed the Violence Against Women Act. One of the most powerful parts of this Act was mandating the "full faith and credit of protection orders," so that an order issued in one jurisdiction is enforceable in any jurisdiction anywhere in the United States and its territories and tribal areas. These orders have protected the vast majority of victims and helped them gain a sense of security and independence. Courts are also able to order supervised visitation during separation or divorce.

On June 6, 2013, the European Union passed an EU-wide protection order for survivors of domestic abuse, affecting all member nations. The European law is effective even when traveling across borders. For more information, visit the UN Women website: unwomen. org/2013/06/eu-wide-protection-for-victims-of-domestic-violence-becomes-law/.

If you have been victimized by your spouse, the first step toward protecting your rights and forcing your spouse to keep a distance is to obtain an *order of protection* (sometimes called a restraining order). This is a document signed by a judge that prohibits your spouse from having contact with you.

Judges don't always grant requests for orders of protection. You must usually provide evidence showing that you have been or could be victimized by your spouse. If you have been beaten in the past, photographs of injuries, police reports, and hospital or doctor's reports concerning your injuries will help you present your case. Orders of protection can be issued for other offenses, including harassment, stalking, interference with personal liberty, intimidation of a dependent, neglect, and willful deprivation.

While an order of protection has helped many women and men, because enforcement by local authorities can be uneven, it's not foolproof. In the United States, some states do not afford the same protective order to gay and lesbian victims of domestic abuse. Visit the American Bar Association's website (americanbar.org/content/dam/aba/migrated/domviol/ pdfs/CPO_Protections_for_LGBT_Victims_7_08.authcheckdam.pdf) for more information, and check your state's laws on this matter if this applies to you.

 **DEFINITION**

An **order of protection**—which can only be filed against a current or former family member by blood or marriage, family or household members, or other like relationship, depending on the jurisdiction—is an order directing one spouse to refrain from abusing, harassing, or even contacting the other, among other restraints. Violation of an order of protection can result in arrest and imprisonment.

Typically, an order of protection may compel your spouse to stay a certain distance from you, or it may prohibit your spouse from contacting, harassing, menacing, endangering, or in any way bothering you. In most jurisdictions, you can obtain an order of protection yourself by going to court (often the family court or criminal court) even if you and your spouse have not yet filed for divorce. If you have filed for divorce, the court where you filed usually has the authority to issue an order of protection, and in many states, criminal court judges have that power as well.

You can also obtain a temporary restraining order—a stop-gap order until a trial begins—against the use of property, the changing of beneficiaries on insurance policies, or the removal of your children from the jurisdiction. Although violations of these orders will not usually result in arrest and imprisonment, it is important to have these restraints in place as an incentive for spouses to refrain from such activities.

Typically, you can get an *ex parte* temporary order of protection. *Ex parte* means that you (or you and your lawyer) have gone to court without first notifying your spouse. Depending on the situation presented to the judge, the order might have a time limit in days or weeks after which you must return to court. Your spouse and his or her lawyer will have been notified in advance that he or she should be present. At this meeting, the judge will listen to each of you and decide whether to issue another order of protection, usually for a longer period of time.

 RED ALERT

Under no circumstances should you give the order or a copy of the order to your spouse. Instead, the sheriff's office or a process server will serve it. When you return to court on the assigned date (the return date), you are required to present proof, usually a sworn statement by the server that your spouse has been personally served with the initial order. Your sworn statement will not be accepted as proof. Remember, your spouse may react violently when served, so leave this job to the professionals.

Serving the Order

The order of protection can be served by a police officer, sheriff, or licensed process server. An officer of the law is usually available at the courthouse. Process servers often have offices near the courthouse, or you can find one online. Be sure to give the server the order of protection with a photograph of your spouse. Even if the local police will not serve the order of protection for you, you should still bring or send a copy to your local precinct so that the police have it on record.

The person who serves the order of protection must sign a sworn statement detailing when and where he served the order and how he knew the person who received the order was your spouse. You or your attorney will then bring the sworn statement to court on the day you are scheduled to be in court, thus documenting to the judge that your spouse received notification of the court date.

The conflict, anger, and violence that can accompany some extreme cases during and after divorce must be dealt with swiftly. If your spouse becomes violent, this is not a time to try to settle your case or work out your problems with a marriage counselor or mediator. Pull out all stops. This situation calls for the intervention of the authorities—your lawyer, the police, victim specialists, the district attorney's office, and the courts.

 RED ALERT

If you are being stalked or followed, the first thing you should do is contact your local police. If you suspect that you are being stalked, don't hesitate to get advice and help from local victim specialists to design a plan of action.

The Least You Need to Know

- Call the police if your spouse is harassing you, even if you do not have an order of protection.
- If necessary, get an order of protection. Always file the order of protection with your local police and keep a copy with you at all times.
- If you or your children are in immediate danger, go to a local shelter.
- If violence is a pattern in your home, teach your children how to dial the police emergency number, and have a plan for where they can go to be safe.
- All 50 states in the United States now have laws against domestic violence that are enforceable in every other jurisdiction. The European Union has enacted a law protecting victims of domestic violence that is enforceable in every member nation.

Paying the Bill

If you're going through a divorce, you might be hard-pressed to think of anything worse than the breakup of your marriage—until you get your lawyer's bill. Why are lawyers so expensive, and how do they charge for services rendered? This chapter uncovers the mystery behind the fees associated with hiring a divorce attorney.

Why Is Legal Representation So Costly?

All lawyers do is talk, right? And don't they say talk is cheap? Not when there's a Juris Doctorate after the person's name.

From the lawyer's perspective, as with any business, the fee incorporates their overhead: office rent, staff, and anything else a business needs. Added to that, lawyers are recouping their high cost of education. Then there's the profit motive. Lawyers charge what the traffic will bear. As one honest

In This Chapter

- Understanding divorce lawyers' fees
- How you can save money on your legal fees
- Negotiating a retainer agreement
- Determining whether your attorney's charges are legitimate

lawyer told us, put simply, moneyed clients are ready and willing to pay these high fees, and there are enough moneyed clients around to keep lawyers from having to worry about lack of business. Rates vary, depending on the size of the firm and the location, but be prepared to pay more than you'd like for a full-service law firm.

 **SILVER LININGS**

> Some competent attorneys are willing to work out a payment plan in advance. It is to the attorney's advantage to make bill payment as painless as possible. Many attorneys never collect the fully invoiced amount. If you and your attorney are willing to work out a payment plan, the attorney is more likely to collect his fees, a win-win situation.

How Matrimonial Lawyers Charge

Many lawyers charge an hourly rate and bill you for every hour worked. If Paula Smith's rate is $250 an hour, and she does 10 hours of work for you, you'll get a bill for $2,500. It can be pretty straightforward. If you are hiring your lawyer à la carte, you'll pay as you go.

Most full-service lawyers, on the other hand, want some payment up front. This fee is called a retainer. The amount will vary, depending on where you live, your specific case, and the lawyer's hourly rate. In the New York City area, some matrimonial attorneys charge as much as a $15,000 to $25,000 retainer. While fees vary in other U.S. states and countries around the globe, the down payment is never cheap—and it could be a drop in the bucket. You'll probably spend much more than this if you have a protracted case.

After you pay the retainer, your lawyer subtracts her hourly rate from what you've paid for each hour worked until the case is over or until she depletes your retainer, whichever happens first. When the hours charged for work on your case has depleted your retainer, you'll start getting bills. Some lawyers will want a new retainer; others might simply bill you on a weekly or monthly basis.

Wait a minute, you might think. Doesn't the hourly billing rate encourage the lawyer to drag out my case to earn more money? Although this might seem an easy ploy, within the profession it is considered unethical for a lawyer to deliberately drag out ("churn," as lawyers say) a case. Another deterrent is that when a case drags on, lawyers can lose clients, or clients will not be able to afford to continue paying. It's possible that the lawyer won't collect everything he's owed. Whatever he doesn't get paid is written off and, in effect, reduces his hourly rate. On the other hand, if the lawyer finishes her work within the amount of time covered by the retainer, she gets her full hourly rate and comes out ahead.

Does that mean you don't have to pay your bill? No. However, it does mean if ethics don't stop a lawyer from dragging out a case, the practical realities of collection will.

In matrimonial law, it is very hard to predict how much time your lawyer will have to spend on your case. If you and your spouse have agreed on everything up front—and this may be your biggest incentive to do just that—the lawyer won't have to do much more than draft the legal documents, make sure you understand them, get them to the other lawyer, and submit them to the court. If you and your spouse are at war, a lot of time will be spent on your case, and you can end up spending an astronomical sum of money.

Before You Put Your Money Down

One of the most important things to understand as you enter a financial relationship with your matrimonial attorney is the retainer. If you pay a retainer, the first thing you will do is sign a *retainer agreement*. Remember, any agreement regarding your retainer must be in writing and should always provide for a refund if the fees are not used up.

 **DEFINITION**

A **retainer agreement** is a contract signed by an attorney and client setting forth the billing arrangement to be instituted between the lawyer and the client.

The agreement should also stipulate what happens when the retainer is used up. Will you have to pay another lump sum, or will you be billed on a monthly or weekly basis? When it comes to your retainer, make sure that all the ground rules are spelled out first.

A reputable attorney will not only have no problem putting the retainer agreement in writing but also will ask you to take the agreement home and study it before signing it. You should be invited to call and ask any questions you have. As eager as you might be to sign the retainer and write out a check, hold back until you read the agreement and thoroughly understand what it says.

 **RED ALERT**

Never sign any agreement in which you use your house as collateral. Legal fees add up quickly with a full-service attorney, especially if you go to trial or your spouse repeatedly takes you to court to try to change orders from a judge. You could be in the unfortunate situation of losing your house if your cash runs out.

At a minimum, your retainer agreement should establish the amount of money you are paying up front and should stipulate hourly rates for the lawyer as well as others who might be assisting in your case, including paralegals and junior attorneys.

The agreement should also outline how you will pay for out-of-pocket expenses such as process servers and court fees. Maybe those expenses will come out of your retainer, or maybe you'll have to pay them in addition to your retainer. Find out now.

A retainer agreement should explain how often you will be billed. Are you going to get a bill only when the retainer is used up, or will you be kept informed with a statement each month as the retainer dwindles?

What happens if you don't pay your bill? Does the lawyer have an automatic right to abandon your case? Does he or she have an obligation to work out a payment plan with you? Are you being asked to guarantee payment with collateral, such as your house? Watch out for any lawyer who demands security in the form of something you cannot afford to lose.

Usually, you will be asked to countersign the retainer agreement and send it back to the lawyer with the retainer check.

Here's a sample retainer agreement. Keep in mind that each attorney's agreement will vary.

Elayne Kesselman, Esq.

Retainer Agreement

October 9, 2013

PERSONAL AND CONFIDENTIAL

John Doe, New York, New York

Re: Doe v. Doe

Dear Mr. Doe:

I appreciate your retaining me to represent you in connection with your matrimonial situation, and I write this letter in order to confirm our understanding regarding the financial arrangements between us with regard to that work.

As an initial retainer, you have agreed to pay, and I have agreed to accept, $10,000. Applied against this fee shall be my hourly billing rate. The rate presently applicable to my services is $500.00 per hour. Because of mounting costs, it may be necessary from time to time for the applicable time charges to be increased, and I will notify you in advance of any such increase. You will be billed on or about the first day of each month for services rendered during the preceding month.

You will not be billed for any time spent discussing your bill.

I do not anticipate having anyone else work on your case, but should another attorney assist me in this matter, I will notify you of that in advance and of that attorney's billing rate.

You will also be charged separately for any out-of-pocket disbursements (such as court costs, messenger service, postage, service of papers, experts, and so on) that are incurred on your behalf. In addition, you may be asked to pay certain disbursements directly to the vendor or provider of services involved (such as appraisers, process servers, transcripts of depositions or court proceedings, and the like), and you agree to do so upon my request. I will advise you of any such costs in advance of incurring the same.

If your retainer is used up, and work remains to be done on your case, you will be billed on a monthly basis, and you agree to pay the amount due for services rendered and disbursements incurred within thirty (30) days from receipt of the bill. In the event of your failure to make prompt and timely payment of a bill, and should we fail to agree on suitable alternative arrangements for such payment, I reserve the right to cease work on your matter and, if I am in the midst of litigation, to seek permission from the court to withdraw from your case. Should a dispute arise between us concerning the payment of attorney's fees in the sum of $5,000 or greater, you may seek to have the dispute resolved through arbitration, which shall be binding upon you and me. I shall provide you with information concerning fee arbitration in the event of such a dispute or upon your request.

You will be provided with copies of all correspondence and documents relating to your case, and you shall be kept apprised of the status of your case. You have the right to cancel this agreement at any time. Services rendered through the date of such cancellation and not yet billed will be billed to you upon such cancellation, and payment shall be due within thirty (30) days of receipt of the final bill.

I look forward to working with you and ask if the contents of this letter accurately reflect our understanding, that you please sign the enclosed copy and return it to me.

Very truly yours,

_____Elayne Kesselman

EK:ek   CONSENTED AND AGREED TO:

Enc.   _____   John Doe

Who Pays for What?

The assumption that the man has to pay all the legal bills is no longer true. Often, the spouse with the deeper pockets has to pay some or all the legal fees. In many cases, where the assets are going to be equally divided, the pockets are equally deep, and wives are shocked to learn that their share of the legal fees must come out of their share of the assets.

If a lawyer assures you that he will only collect what he can get from your spouse, have that put in writing. Most lawyers will not make that promise because they stand a chance of never getting paid. A reputable attorney will explain that payment will be due even if your spouse does not pay.

Sometimes, early in a case, a judge will order the wealthier spouse to pay temporary legal fees on behalf of the other spouse. By the time the case is over, however, both sides usually end up paying something.

 YOU CAN DO IT!

If you have a moderate income, give serious thought to being reasonable in a divorce settlement—you could save enormous sums in legal fees. How much in legal fees is it worth to get the sterling silver wedding present that cost $5,000? Is it worth $4,000 in legal fees? It could easily cost that. For your own sake, put your anger and hurt aside and save yourself some money and aggravation. (We like to advise heading for the racquetball or tennis court immediately after a divorce settlement meeting and putting a face on that ball!)

Tips for Keeping Fees Under Control

We can't emphasize enough the importance of being vigilant about how and when you spend your hard-earned money on legal fees. Self-restraint is the order of the day. Here are some tips from the trenches of divorce. You may say, "I don't have the patience for all this detail," but take it from us, you will save thousands of dollars if you follow these guidelines:

Hire a lawyer whose billing rate is manageable for you. This may mean finding a lawyer who is willing to create a reasonable payment plan. For example, the lawyer will agree to be paid at the rate of $500 a month for however long it takes you to pay the bill.

Hire a lawyer who is willing to unbundle his services. Paying as you go for specific issues will be less expensive than full coverage.

Ask to receive a detailed bill every month. The bill should describe services rendered and disbursements paid. Tell your lawyer you want this even if your retainer is not yet used up.

Ask to be notified in advance of any major work to be done on your behalf. Typically, you and your lawyer have developed the plan of action, but it is possible your attorney might be ready to make a motion that you think unnecessary.

Ask for an estimate of the disbursements in advance. You don't have to be told about every postage stamp being billed to you, but your lawyer should tell you about messenger services or court stenographers (deposition or trial transcripts can cost thousands of dollars).

Keep a record of the time you spend with your attorney. This applies to both time spent on the phone and time spent in person. When you get your bill, check it against your personal records.

Watch out for suspicious charges. We know of one instance in which two attorneys representing opposing sides in a divorce case met to reach a settlement. After the meeting, they went out to dinner together. One of the lawyers had the audacity to charge his client for the time spent at dinner and for the dinner itself! Needless to say, the outraged client agreed to pay only for the time spent on his case. Then, he changed attorneys.

Ask whether you will be charged a minimum for phone calls and what that charge will be. You should get this information before signing a retainer. Some lawyers charge a 15-minute minimum under the theory that your call has taken them away from other work and they need time to "get back into it." Others will charge a minimum of five minutes. Still others will only charge the actual time spent on the phone. If there is a 15-minute minimum, save your questions for one longer call rather than several short calls.

Be aware that lawyers charge for all time spent on your case. This includes reading and answering your emails and text messages, so resist the urge for sharing every thought.

If you've gone to a firm with many attorneys, ask whether an attorney with a lower billing rate is able to do some of the work on your case. However, make it clear that for certain work—negotiations, for instance, or the actual trial—you want the attorney you hired.

If more than one attorney will be working on your case, find out before you sign the retainer how double services will be billed. If two attorneys are discussing your case, are you going to be billed at their total hourly rate or only at the higher attorney's rate?

Find out what you will be billed for photocopying. If possible, photocopy whatever you can yourself.

Ask your attorney to use delivery services and express mail only when necessary. These charges can add up quickly.

Organize materials your attorney wants in the way she needs them to be organized. For example, if your attorney sends you a list of 20 documents demanded by your spouse's counsel, organize the records by year and category in separate folders. Your lawyer might want to change what you've done a little, but the cost will be far less than it would have been had you brought in a shopping bag full of receipts.

Don't engage your attorney in aimless phone calls. For example, don't start bad-mouthing your spouse, your spouse's attorney, the system, or the judge. Do not make small talk or discuss anything irrelevant to your case. You might feel better after venting, but you won't when you get your bill.

 **RED ALERT**

> Can the divorcing couple use the same lawyer? It's possible, but it's not a good idea, no matter how friendly the divorce may be. Later, one of you might claim you didn't understand what you signed or that the lawyer or the deal was really one-sided. When claims of unfairness arise, judges usually don't like situations where there was only one lawyer. If your case is simple, both spouses might represent themselves in negotiating a basic settlement; then they might hire a single attorney to draft it.

Are Your Lawyer's Charges Legitimate?

It's often hard to tell whether the amount of time your lawyer spent working for you was "legitimate." After all, you weren't there, and you're not a lawyer, so how are you supposed to know whether the charges are correct?

Although you can't keep track of every microsecond, you can keep an eye on things. First, always ask your lawyer to discuss the amount of time and cost that will be incurred for a project your lawyer has in mind before he begins that project. Maybe your lawyer wants to make a motion asking the judge to order your spouse not to call the kids during dinner. The motion might cost $5,000. You could ask the lawyer whether he can call your spouse's lawyer first or send a letter about the problem. In fact, many states require the attorneys to certify that they attempted to resolve the issues with their adversaries before filing motions with the court.

Check your bills carefully. Sometimes law offices, like any business, can make a human error and charge for work not done on your behalf. If a lawyer tells you he has to be in court on your case and might have to sit there for three hours before the judge calls your case, ask whether he can do anyone else's work while he's there and not charge you for the waiting time. Some lawyers do just that and then "double bill"—bill you and the other person. An honest attorney won't do that, but it doesn't hurt to ask.

What if you're just not sure whether you're being treated fairly? You should probably reevaluate your relationship with your lawyer. If you think he or she is deliberately cheating, you may not want that individual involved in your case.

Getting the Most for Your Money

Hourly rates depend on a lawyer's experience and education as well as the market itself. In a major urban setting, such as Los Angeles, lawyers often charge $300 to $700 an hour. In smaller cities, equally competent lawyers might only charge $250 an hour because no one will pay more.

If you hire an attorney from a major law firm, chances are that the rates will be higher than those of a solo practitioner or a small law firm. The larger firm has more overhead, which adds to the bill. However, if the attorney at the larger firm is more competent than the attorney at the small firm, it might be worth the higher fees because he can cut the case shorter by virtue of his experience. This is not to say that small firms and solo practitioners are, on the whole, less experienced. It depends on the attorney.

Attorneys charge within a range of the current market rate in your area. Whether the fee is at the top, middle, or bottom of the range is not necessarily reflective of his or her skill. It's better to get references in order to know the quality of a candidate. An expensive, high-profile lawyer might be just the one, you're thinking, to bully your spouse into settling. Maybe so, particularly if your spouse is a person who is impressed by names, but it's a ploy that rarely pays off. In fact, if you hire a well-known lawyer, they are usually quite busy, and your case might get lost in the shuffle. The attorney's ability, integrity, and attention to your case—not his or her fee—is most important.

The Least You Need to Know

- Make sure you can afford your attorney, and work out a suitable payment plan before you hire him or her.
- Put your fee arrangement in writing. Unearned retainer fees should be refundable to you.
- Ask your attorney to let you know in advance the cost of anticipated legal work or third-party expenses, such as process servers, delivery services, or court stenographers.
- Keep a record of time spent with your attorney.
- Do not be impressed by hourly rates. High rates may indicate a lawyer who's too busy to call you back.

CHAPTER 15

Closing the Book on Your Case

It's finally over, or at least you think it is. You've been to court and had a trial, or you've signed a settlement agreement. You're done, right?

Probably not. Depending on where you live, your lawyer (or your spouse's lawyer) most likely must draft a document known as the *judgment of divorce* or *decree of dissolution*. If your case has been decided by a judge after trial, the judgment of divorce usually refers to everything the judge wrote in his decision. If you and your spouse settled your case, the judgment of divorce might include provisions on custody, child support, division of property, visitation schedule, or other issues; it might also simply refer to your settlement agreement with the assertion that all its provisions are deemed to be included.

In This Chapter

- When the divorce decree goes into effect
- When you can collect pension, Social Security, and other benefits
- How remarriage can affect the divorce decree
- When a spouse does not comply with the decree
- When it's really over

 **DEFINITION**

A **judgment of divorce** is a written document that states that a husband and wife are divorced. In some jurisdictions, this may be called a **decree of dissolution.** Typically, lawyers draft the judgment of divorce for the judge to review and sign.

If you and your spouse simply bought a "divorce kit," a collection of printed forms necessary to obtain a divorce, it probably includes a judgment of divorce. You'll need to fill in the relevant information and then submit the judgment to the proper court.

When the Judgment Is Final

After the judge signs the judgment of divorce and any record is made of that signing, the divorce is usually effective. (In some jurisdictions, recording in a record book the date on which the judge signed the judgment of divorce is called *entering the judgment.*) In some places, the judgment of divorce might be deemed effective even before it is entered. Either way—whether the judgment has to be entered or merely signed—for better or worse, you're single again.

You can usually get a copy of the judgment of divorce from the court or from your lawyer. It's a good idea to get a certified copy of the judgment of divorce (a photocopy with a stamp from a court official stating that the document has been compared with the original and is the same). There is usually a fee for this service. Also, depending on where you live, you might need identification to be allowed to look at your divorce file, so be sure to bring some identification to the courthouse. This document will be necessary to prove you're divorced for any purpose, whether financial or legal, going forward. For example, if you would like to remarry, you will need to prove you're divorced.

After the Judgment Has Been Entered

When your lawyer (or your spouse's lawyer) has the judgment of divorce, he'll send it to your spouse's lawyer (or vice versa). This isn't just a courtesy to let him know you're divorced; it starts the clock running during which an appeal can be filed. If you and your spouse settled your case, in some jurisdictions there can't be an appeal, but your lawyer will send the copy anyway. If a judge tried your case, either one of you could appeal, but the clock doesn't start running until the actual judgment or decree is signed. Some jurisdictions are more lenient and stop the clock from running till the date that the court clerk serves the judgment on the parties or their counsel, or when one lawyer sends the judgment of divorce to the other, with notification of when it was entered.

But no matter where you get your divorce, it is very important to determine when the clock starts ticking and when it stops, because once that time is up, you cannot ask the court to extend it or relieve you from your default if you did not file your notice of appeal on time.

If you and your spouse handled the case yourselves, make sure that you both get a copy of the judgment of divorce. If you're no longer talking, have a friend mail your spouse a copy of the judgment with notification of when it was entered and ask the friend to sign a notarized statement that he has mailed it. This is your proof that you had the judgment sent to your spouse.

Your Benefits

Your settlement agreement or decision by the judge should include getting the part of your spouse's Social Security, retirement, survivor, or disability benefits that you are entitled to.

When will you receive your benefits? Usually, you receive them when your ex-spouse does or at the earliest possible time he could have received them. For example, some retirement plans allow employees to take out money when they turn 55, even if they are still working. The plan might allow ex-spouses who have been awarded part of the plan to do the same. Every plan is different.

You probably won't get these benefits right after the divorce. To get your part of your spouse's Social Security, survivor, or disability benefits, the Social Security Administration will usually need a certified copy of your judgment of divorce and any agreement in order to process your claim. In the case of pension benefits, your lawyer (or your spouse's lawyer) will usually have to draft an order (either a qualified domestic relations order [QDRO] or a court order acceptable for processing [COAP,] depending on the kind of plan you're dealing with) at the same time he drafts your judgment of divorce. The order (QDRO or COAP) explains when you'll get your pension benefits. The judge then signs it, while your case is fresh in everyone's mind, and your lawyer sends a copy to your spouse's pension-plan administrator. Notify the plan administrator if you move, and as the time draws nearer for you to receive your benefit, contact the plan administrator (the address should be in the order) to find out what information it needs to process your claim.

Changing Your Last Name

In some jurisdictions, the judgment of divorce will include a paragraph giving a wife the right to resume her maiden or birth name or take another name entirely. Government offices usually require that you show them a certified copy of the judgment of divorce before they'll issue documents in your maiden, or other, name.

For the most part, however, you can simply start using the name you now want to be called. For some, it's the maiden name. For others, it might be the name from a prior marriage. Many women who have children retain their ex-husband's family name until their children are out of school. Although divorce is common now, they'd rather not flag their status, and some find it easier, from a practical point of view, to have the same last name as their school-aged child.

Modifying the Divorce Decree

Modification of a divorce decree is complicated, and you will need your attorney's involvement. In some jurisdictions, it's easier to get a decree modified if you had a trial and a judge decided your case than if you and your spouse settled.

When Bobby Kingston was 4 years old, his parents divorced and signed an agreement including all financial issues as they related to Bobby until he turned 21. Unfortunately, no mention was made of who would pay for Bobby's college. When Bobby turned 17, his mother, Irene, tried to get Bobby's father, Joe, to help pay for college. Joe refused to pay. Irene hired an attorney, who made a motion asking the judge to order Joe to pay for college. The judge refused, saying Irene had the chance to ask Joe to pay college tuition when she signed the agreement 13 years earlier. The judge protected the settlement agreement.

If, on the other hand, a judge had decided the case between Bobby's parents after a trial, Irene would have had a good chance of getting the tuition paid by Joe. Because the trial took place when Bobby was only 4 years old, the judge would probably not have made a decision on college tuition. After all, what if the child doesn't want to go to college? Because tuition might not have been considered by a judge when Bobby was 4, Irene's request would seem reasonable to a judge 13 years later.

 **RED ALERT**

A growing number of jurisdictions don't distinguish between tried cases and settled ones when it comes to subsequent modification. Rationale: courts prefer not to punish less aggressive litigants (i.e., those willing to settle) by denying relief at a later date when the facts warrant it.

What if you notice a mistake in your divorce decree right after you get it? It will probably be easy to modify if the mistake is clerical, such as an incorrect date. It will be harder to modify if there is a dispute between you and your spouse over what is correct.

For example, it is not a clerical error if your lawyer forgot to include in the judgment of divorce your wish to be with your children on Mother's Day. Your lawyer can try to have the decree modified. Judges will usually agree to a modification if both sides agree to it.

How Remarriage Alters Things

If your case was settled, your agreement probably took into account the possibility of remarriage. For example, if your ex is paying you maintenance and the agreement says that stops if you remarry, you can be sure your ex will comply with that part of the agreement! If your ex's lawyer forgot to put in that provision, your ex might have to go to court to be allowed to stop paying maintenance, and he might not win.

On the other hand, the law in your state might affect what happens if you remarry. For example, the law might provide that support automatically stops on remarriage. Your ex does not have to go to court to have this change made; the law has made it for him.

Can you keep your remarriage a secret? Of course you can, but that's not a good idea. Most agreements require you to notify your ex-spouse (or your lawyer, who will notify his lawyer) about a change that affects the deal. If you don't have an agreement and you're collecting maintenance, the law probably provides that it stop on remarriage. Eventually, you would have to give back the money you kept. If for some reason your case went back to a judge, your actions would work against you.

When Your Second Marriage Ends

What if you get divorced from your second spouse? Does your first spouse have to resume paying you? Not usually. The same applies to any benefit you gave up when you remarried. A second divorce does not bring your first spouse back into the picture, so be sure that you want to give up your entitlements before you tie the knot a second time.

Remarriage after a divorce has the most impact on the person who was the breadwinner in the first marriage. If you're the breadwinner, suddenly you're contributing to two households, not just to your former household and your own expenses. Your new spouse might resent the money that's going to your ex or your children. He or she may also resent the time you spend with your children or the time they spend with the two of you. This resentment can put a great deal of strain on your new marriage. Before remarrying, consider the responsibilities you have to your ex and your children, and think about how those responsibilities might impact your new relationship.

RED ALERT

When negotiating your settlement agreement, if you are the spouse who might pay alimony, consider adding a clause to the agreement stating that you no longer have to pay alimony if your ex-spouse remarries or dies—the latter event is important for tax purposes. As always, see a tax professional before agreeing to the terms of a divorce settlement.

What If You Lose Your Job?

If your case was settled and not tried and you lose your job, you might still be obligated to pay whatever you were paying while you were employed, depending on the laws of your state. Why? You (or your lawyer) had the opportunity to include in your agreement a provision calling for reduction of maintenance or child support should you lose your job.

Might a judge give you a reduction anyway? Possibly, but it would be easier if your case had been decided at trial, where the judge would address only what was before him, not what may or may not happen. In some jurisdictions, unforeseeable events might provide a basis for changing an agreement. Also, in some jurisdictions, if your children's economic needs are not being met, a judge might be more likely to review and possibly change the agreement. It is essential that the paying spouse go to court immediately for the modification. Generally, spousal support continues to accrue unless you obtain an order modifying it, and child support definitely does.

When Your Ex Does Not Comply

Enforcement of the decree is difficult, if not impossible, without the help of a lawyer. Some lawyers specialize in collections, and others won't touch it. Before you incur the cost of trying to chase your spouse to collect money, ask yourself:

Does my ex-spouse have the money or income for me to collect? If the answer is "no," you might be wasting your time and money trying to collect what he owes you.

Are there any other assets that the judge will allow me to collect? A car, home, boat? If so, how much will it cost me to collect against those assets, and how long will it take? Again, it simply might not be worth it.

Has my ex-spouse put assets in someone else's name? If so, you might run into serious collection problems. Or, if you can prove your ex did this, sue the third party and try to recover the assets from him or her.

If you're dealing with the collection of child support or spousal support, try having your state support enforcement agency work with you to collect from your ex. (Read on!)

 SILVER LININGS

> If you have problems collecting the child support ordered by court or put into your settlement agreement, it is a crime, and you do have recourse. Your ex-spouse's wages can be garnished, or you can contact your jurisdiction's child support enforcement agency. If you are a U.S. citizen, you can contact the Federal Office of Child Support Enforcement (acf.hhs.gov/programs/css) or the National Child Support Enforcement Association (ncsea.org). Internationally, the Hague Maintenance Convention Agreement sets up a worldwide system for recovering child support and maintenance. It also provides free legal aid for international child support cases.

What if money isn't the issue? The problem is that your ex-spouse has custody of the children but refuses to send you their school reports.

If you still have a lawyer, you can ask that he or she call your ex's lawyer about the problem. Sometimes a phone call is all it takes. If lawyers are no longer in the picture (or never were), you can try writing a letter to your ex. It might not do any good, but at least you'll be making a record of the problem should you later decide to pursue the issue in court. (First, make a copy of the letter. Unless your agreement requires you to do so, you don't have to send it by certified mail. Some people don't pick up certified letters.)

Of course, some problems with compliance must be handled by a judge. A woman lived in Missouri, but her daughter flew to New York every summer to visit her father, in accordance with the parties' separation agreement. At the end of one summer, the father refused to send the daughter home. He claimed his daughter's stepfather spanked her. The judge ruled that the child should not be spanked by anyone except a parent, but that she should be returned to her mother in Missouri.

Saying Good-Bye to Your Lawyer

Once the divorce is final, and the time for appeals has expired, your lawyer is no longer your lawyer. Technically, the case is over, and any new problems that might arise can be addressed by any lawyer you hire to work for you. Will lawyers help if there are problems after the divorce decree is final? That depends. Some will assist and bill you for the work. Others will tell you they can no longer handle your case. They might be too busy, or they might not like your ex-spouse's lawyer, or they simply do not want to be involved anymore. Still others might take a call or two from you without asking for payment.

In some jurisdictions, a lawyer must take formal steps to withdraw from your representation after the case is completed. Family law matters are often ongoing because of support payments or later division of assets, so someone must be "of record" to receive service of process in the event that there is a reason later to go to court. When your lawyer withdraws, the person of record is you, by default, and your address must be on file with the court.

For those who tapped the full-service option, the months or years of dependency on a lawyer are at an end. Indeed, once the judgment of divorce is final, some people feel lost. Others feel angry that the lawyer who won them a big award and earned thousands of dollars on their case is not willing to help them collect it.

It might be hard for you to accept that lawyers are simply in the business of providing legal services. Don't take it personally if your lawyer says good-bye. It is time for you to move on to your own, independent life.

The Least You Need to Know

- Be sure that your spouse has received a copy of the final judgment of divorce with the date of its entry. Have a friend mail a copy if need be, and then sign a notarized statement that she mailed it. Include the date of mailing and the address where it was sent.

- Entitlement to Social Security, pension plan, and retirement benefits should all be addressed at trial or during negotiations. Don't wait until after the judgment of divorce is final to discuss your ability to collect against your spouse's benefits.

- In some jurisdictions, it is more difficult to modify a judgment of divorce that was the result of negotiations than it is to modify one that was the result of a trial.

- Before you hire a lawyer to collect unpaid moneys, ask yourself whether you have a reasonable chance of collecting, how much it will cost you to collect, and, if you have children, whether re-engaging in battle might negatively affect them.

- Your lawyer is technically off your case once the judgment of divorce is final.

Same-Sex Divorce

The new century, host to so much change and invention, has opened its eyes to a human reality long swept under the rug: gay people, like straight ones, have a basic need for connection, family, security, and recognition. They need to be at a loved one's side at end of life, and they want to share their love and attachment–and home—as openly as anyone else in the world.

In light of these changing attitudes, it only makes sense that same-sex marriage and its approximate cousin, legal civil union, have been enabled and embraced in nations around the world. In fact, increasing acceptance and legalization of unions between same-sex couples represents one of the largest revolutions in marriage in the last 200 years.

In This Chapter

- Same-sex marriage and civil unions in the United States and elsewhere
- The difficulties of same-sex divorce
- Navigating divorce as a same-sex couple

Same-Sex Marriage and Civil Union: A Global Trend

As of this writing in 2013, 15 nations around the world have legalized same sex marriage, including Argentina, Belgium, Brazil, Canada, Denmark, France, Iceland, the Netherlands, New Zealand, Norway, Portugal, Spain, South Africa, Sweden, and Uruguay. In Mexico and the United States, many jurisdictions now allow the practice. By 2014, same-sex marriage will be legal in England and Wales. The trend is picking up steam, with laws or bills proposed or about to be enacted in Germany, Ireland, and Finland in Europe, as well as Taiwan and Nepal.

Same-Sex Marriage in the United States

As of this writing, more than 30 states define marriage as the union between a man and a woman, according to the United States Conference of State Legislatures. But there are constant updates, easily accessible at the Conference website (ncsl.org/issues-research/human-services/same-sex-marriage-overview.aspx).

On the other hand, same-sex marriage is legal in California, Connecticut, Delaware, Iowa, Maine, Maryland, Massachusetts, Minnesota, New Hampshire, New York, Rhode Island, Vermont, Washington, and the District of Columbia. There are also five Native American tribal organizations that now allow same-sex marriage. *Civil unions* are allowed in Colorado, Hawaii, Illinois, and New Jersey. In Colorado, couples in a civil union have the same rights, benefits, protections, and responsibilities as married couples under Colorado law.

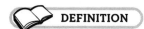 **DEFINITION**

> A **civil union** (also referred to as a *registered partnership* or a *civil partnership,* among other terms) is a legally recognized form of partnership just short of marriage. The labels as well as the rules differ from one jurisdiction to the next. People enter civil unions because they confer certain legal rights, benefits, and responsibilities unavailable simply by living together. Both gay and heterosexual couples may enter civil unions in some jurisdictions. As with same-sex marriage, civil unions are not automatically recognized by all jurisdictions.

Change in the United States is often an incremental affair. As we go to press, some states that had permitted only civil unions in the past now allow same-sex marriage. And legalization of ties to natural birth or adoptive children is increasingly common for same-sex spouses as well.

In June 2013, the U.S. Supreme Court overturned Section 3 of the Defense of Marriage Act (DOMA), which excluded married same-sex couples from federal programs, protections, and responsibilities, including healthcare, retirement, and tax benefits, as well as green cards for same-sex immigrant spouses. Section 2, which allows discrimination against same-sex couples married in other states, still stands. (This ruling does not apply to civil unions.) By declaring Section 3 of DOMA unconstitutional, the court effectively required the federal government to recognize same-sex marriage in those states that permit it, and cleared the way for married same-sex couples to receive the same federal benefits as heterosexual married couples in their states.

Federal agencies and departments are in the process of changing their policies to reflect the Supreme Court ruling. In August of 2013, a federal court ruling made it possible for same-sex veteran spouses to get benefits, such as health and survivor benefits, and the Department of Defense will grant full benefits to all married active duty troops. The effects of the ruling will continue to ripple throughout the federal government.

Some local federal judges are now weighing the implications of the Supreme Court ruling on Section 3 of DOMA on same-sex marriage issues. In new cases, some are now leaning toward favoring a request by a same-sex couple against a state's discriminatory statute. As an example, soon after the Supreme Court ruling, a federal judge in Michigan refused to disallow a trial by a lesbian couple to adopt each other's children, paving the way for the possibility of striking down a state law preventing same-sex marriage.

A Gauntlet of Laws and Rules

The rules applied to same-sex marriage and civil unions can be highly idiosyncratic from one jurisdiction to the next—not just across borders but within a country as well. Where same-sex marriage exists, it confers the same rights as heterosexual marriage to the couple involved. But when the same-sex couple moves to another jurisdiction, those rights might be altered or upended in full.

It is even more complicated when the legal bond is not marriage but a civil union. In that case, a jurisdiction might recognize the union only if it has been forged under laws and guidelines similar to its own.

Indeed, same-sex couples who relocate may find themselves subject to a Byzantine nexus of regulations determining what rights they have or not. In short, they must navigate what attorneys call *conflict of laws*—the rules that dictate which legal system or jurisdiction applies to any given dispute. Usually conflict of laws is an international concept, applying across national borders. But when it comes to same-sex marriage and civil unions, the rules can change radically from within a country, from one jurisdiction to the next. In large countries with many jurisdictions, such as the United States, Canada, and Australia, figuring out which law prevails can prove especially complex when dealing with property ownership, parenting, adoption, and the other hot buttons of family law.

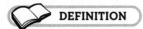

DEFINITION

Conflict of law rules attempt to determine which law will apply in a particular situation when there is a difference between the laws of two or more jurisdictions with some connection to a case. The conflicting legal rules may be from the laws of different countries, U.S. federal law, or the laws of U.S. states.

The issues these couples face while married range from property ownership to parenting, including adoption. Even *in vitro* fertilization may be regulated differently for same-sex couples, depending on where they live. An August 15, 2013, article in *The Telegraph* reported that the National Institute for Health and Clinical Excellence in the United Kingdom will now pay for *in vitro* fertilization for same-sex couples as they do for heterosexual couples. But if the legal conflicts are challenging for same-sex marriages, they become even more complex when it comes to same-sex divorce.

The Same-Sex Divorce Trap

People being people, wherever there is marriage there will be divorce—and same-sex couples are hardly exceptions to the rule. The increased legalization of same-sex marriage and the strengthening of rights of couples in civil unions mean that concomitant laws for divorce must catch up.

In 2013, *Time Magazine* ran a story about the U.S. state of Minnesota, which had approved same-sex marriage only to find, a week later, a backlog of such couples already applying for divorce. In its largesse, Minnesota had opted to recognize any marriage or civil union entered into anywhere else in the United States or the world, which made it possible for same-sex couples married elsewhere to divorce in Minnesota, too. In fact, the first same-sex couple to divorce in Minnesota had actually married in Canada. Under Minnesota law, the couple benefited from the same rules of parental support, alimony, and property division as anyone in the queue.

The simplicity of the system in Minnesota may explain why same-sex couples are flocking there, forming their exit line around the block. The rights conferred to traditional couples as a matter of course—joint parenting plans, alimony, fair property division—help pave the way for new, separate lives.

Alternatively, building new lives may be difficult to impossible when jurisdictions lack any clear path for these couples to divorce. For example, imagine a couple from Florida, where same-sex marriage is outlawed, travels to New York, which has legalized same-sex marriage. If the couple then goes home to Florida, divorce would be impossible. To sever their ties, they would have to move back to New York and live there for a year—or follow the divorce bandwagon to Minnesota and its open rules. Indeed, when same-sex couples are denied divorce by their home jurisdiction, the only alternative to ending the union may be a costly civil suit. However, while a civil suit may determine child support or ownership of the family home, it cannot sever the marital bond. For that final step, only divorce will do.

 **RED ALERT**

If you marry in one jurisdiction and move to another, neither may permit you to divorce, leaving you in limbo. The new jurisdiction may lack provisions for same-sex marriage, *de facto* blocking the path to legal divorce. The old jurisdiction may have a residency requirement of a year or more.

Navigating Divorce as a Same-Sex Couple

The Supreme Court ruling striking down Section 3 of DOMA may ease the path for same-sex divorce in the United States. After all, if it is illegal to deny a marriage exists, then jurisdictions now refusing to process the divorce may ultimately be forced to relent. Yet "may" is the operative word. The ruling is so new that its net impact on divorce may take years to clarify.

The State of Texas will be one of the first to take this issue head on. Two cases coming before the Texas Supreme Court will decide whether same-sex couples who are legally married in other states can get a divorce in Texas. The Texas couples married in Massachusetts, where same-sex marriage is legal. They are now applying for divorce in their home state. The Texas Attorney General is arguing that the Supreme Court ruling allows states to determine their own marriage laws and that Texas does not, therefore, have to recognize same-sex divorce. The lawyers for the couples interpret the ruling to mean states have to treat all couples equally. If the Texas Supreme Court can deny divorce to a same-sex couple married out of state, the couples argue that the state ban on same-sex marriage is illegal.

Canadian same-sex couples, on the other hand, have a leg up. Canada legalized same-sex marriage across the country by enacting the Civil Marriage Act on July 20, 2005, which defines marriage as gender-neutral, but since Canada had a national divorce law that did not address same-sex couples, it had been impossible for same-sex couples to divorce. After a successful legal challenge, legislation was passed correcting this problem. Section 8 of the Civil Marriage Act amended the Divorce Act to permit same-sex divorce. In June 2013, Parliament passed a law (Bill C-32) allowing nonresident same-sex couples to divorce in Canada.

The bottom line for same-sex couple divorce is that rules are being designed and enforced almost on the fly. The U.S. state of Colorado ruled that as of May 1, 2013, same-sex couples who married in another state can get a divorce in Colorado if they are residents. In August of 2013, Rhode Island legalized both marriage and divorce for same sex couples. Prior to this new law, residents of Rhode Island who had married in a state where same-sex marriage was legal were not able to divorce in Rhode Island. Instead, they had to return to a state where same-sex marriage was legal in order to divorce, such as Massachusetts. This was especially problematic because many of these states have residency requirements, creating a major obstacle. In Massachusetts, the residency requirement is 12 months.

The best thing you can do while laws are being reworked for the new reality is to be proactive in your paperwork and keep up with changes in the law. Lambda Legal (lambdalegal.org) provides ongoing information for United States citizens.

 **SILVER LININGS**

> Even when jurisdictions remain officially closed to same-sex divorce, judges have granted them quietly to couples. But these acts have often been a favor granted by a judge, going far beyond the requirements of current law.

To deal with the complexities, same-sex couples are advised to keep their eyes wide open, creating as much legal scaffolding around the marriage as they can. Then, should the marriage end, they will have a stronger case to present in court.

At the very least, same-sex couples should take a few basic precautions:

Hire an experienced lawyer. Find an attorney who is an expert in same-sex marriage and divorce or at least up to date with local and national laws. As we've emphasized, the laws are too complex and fast moving to be able to handle this yourself. If you want to pursue a same-sex divorce, paying an expert to show you the ropes could save time and thousands of dollars up the road.

Plan ahead. If you are not yet married, strongly consider having a prenuptial agreement and an estate-planning document. In case your marriage doesn't work out, these documents can help protect your property and assets.

Think before moving. Before relocating for a job, consider not just salary but also the marriage and divorce laws for same-sex couples in the new locale as well as the state in which you married.

Protect your custody rights. If you share children, make sure that nonbiological parents have gone through the legal adoption process. If the same-sex couple lives in a jurisdiction where this kind of adoption is not allowed, parents who want their rights respected at all cost might be able to adopt in another district.

If you are in a same-sex relationship and would like to get married or divorced, you might feel like Indiana Jones in *The Temple of Doom,* fighting the tangles of the Indian jungle to uncover the mystical stone. But as same-sex marriage becomes a cultural fixture, roadblocks to same-sex divorce should fall away. The signs are promising. Progress has been faster than anyone could have imagined. There is now a clearer path to a unified system of laws—some legislated jurisdiction by jurisdiction and some nationally. Divorce will always be a dirge, but ultimately, same-sex splits will be no more daunting or complicated than splits of the heterosexual kind.

The Least You Need to Know

- The rules applied to same-sex marriage and civil union can be highly idiosyncratic from one jurisdiction to the next—not just across borders but within a country as well.

- For heterosexual couples, marriage and divorce laws can shift across jurisdictions, but the shifts are regulated and known in advance. Laws for same-sex divorce are constantly changing. If you are thinking about divorce, be sure to hire an attorney who specializes in or is very familiar with same-sex family law.

- The striking down of Section 3 of the Defense of Marriage Act in the United States has changed the landscape for marriage and probably divorce for same-sex couples going forward. Watch for changes in your local laws as well as rulings by local federal judges.

- Same-sex couples must create as much legal scaffolding and paperwork around the marriage as they can. Prenups and estate-planning documents are absolute requirements. These documents can strengthen your case for requesting an equitable divorce decree.

CHAPTER 17

Divorce in Europe

Gone are the days when divorce was the province of Hollywood moguls or the jet-setting elite. Today, people of all economic brackets in virtually all sovereign states worldwide have laws permitting divorce (except for Vatican City and the Philippines, where a pending bill may usher in the practice any day).

While we would love to give you specific information on divorce around the world, it would go well beyond the scope of this book. Instead, we offer readers some basic facts on marriage and divorce in Europe, with its myriad languages, cultures, and terrains, as a more circumscribed example of the global scene.

The European continent has put forth some of the most sophisticated and nuanced divorce laws in the world. Yet even in Europe, those nations steeped in Catholic influence have been latecomers to the game. Divorce wasn't legal in Italy until 1970, and it wasn't allowed in Portugal until 1975. Spain legalized divorce in 1981 and Ireland in 1996. Malta, a strongly Catholic nation, didn't pass its divorce law until 2011.

In This Chapter

- Marriage in the European Union
- Navigating European divorce laws
- How to file for divorce as an international couple

Marriage in the European Union

Europe is comprised of countries that are members and nonmembers of the European Union (EU), an affiliation of nations formed on November 1, 1993. Twenty-eight European countries are now members of the EU (see table below), and eight more are candidates or potential candidates. The EU was formed to improve the working relationship of its members, improve trade, and facilitate the mobility of Europeans. Some 200,000 to 300,000 people move from one country to another either for temporary or permanent work or to cement new relationships in marriage, among other reasons.

European Countries: Members, Candidates, and Nonmembers of the European Union

Members	Candidates	Nonmembers
Austria	Iceland	Andorra*
Belgium	Montenegro	Azerbaijan
Bulgaria	Serbia	Belarus
Croatia	Macedonia	Georgia
Cyprus	Turkey	Kazakhstan
Czech Republic	Albania (potential)	Liechtenstein*
Denmark	Bosnia and Herzegovina (potential)	Moldova
Estonia	Kosovo (potential)	Monaco*
Finland		Norway
France		Russia
Germany		San Marino*
Greece		Switzerland
Hungary		Ukraine
Ireland		Vatican City
Italy		
Latvia		
Lithuania		
Luxembourg		
Malta		

Members	Candidates	Nonmembers
Netherlands		
Poland		
Portugal		
Romania		
Slovakia		
Slovenia		
Spain		
Sweden		
United Kingdom		

Represented by larger EU members

No matter what legal system European couples follow, they will find matrimonial laws deal with the same general terrain through rules that govern:

- Property, parental roles, and regulation of the family name.

- The relationship between religious and civil marriage. (Only some nations recognize religious marriage as legally binding.)

- Requirements for marriage, covering such aspects as residency and same-sex marriage.

Same-Sex Marriage in Europe

As of this writing same-sex couples can marry in Belgium, Denmark, France, the Netherlands, Portugal, Spain, and Sweden. These marriages may not be recognized in other European nations, so check before you move.

Some European countries also allow registered partnerships and de facto unions, which offer officially recognized partnerships just short of marriage. Each country has its own rules to govern these partnerships, which may or may not be recognized by other countries.

Jacques and Marcel married in France, where same-sex marriage is legal. A few months after their honeymoon, Jacques was offered a job in Germany, and the couple decided to move there together. To their dismay, soon after arriving in Germany they discovered that their marriage was not recognized there. The good news was that in Germany their marriage falls under the German Life Partnership Act, where they have a registered partnership. The registered partnership gives them almost the same rights as marriage. There is an effort by the Federal Constitutional Court of Germany to increasingly promote equal rights for same-sex couples through its rulings.

RED ALERT

If you and your spouse are from different countries, or if you are living in a country other than the one where you are a citizen, register your marriage at the consular office of your country of origin. If you will be moving to another country in the European Union, be sure to check which laws apply to your marriage, as this can affect your rights and obligations, including the matrimonial property regime. Ask the authorities in both countries about the formalities needed for your marriage to be valid, such as any registration or publication requirements.

Choosing Your Marital Property Regime

When a couple decides to tie the knot in most of continental Europe, one of the first decisions they must make is to choose how their financial relations and property will be organized from the beginning of a marriage to its end. Most countries offer a range of *matrimonial property regimes* that do just that. If no selection is made up front, the couple will, by default, be choosing the country's statutory regime. In some countries, if a couple has a prenuptial agreement, it will take precedence over the matrimonial regime. Other nations, like England and Wales, have no marital property regime.

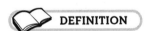

DEFINITION

Matrimonial property regimes are the sets of legal rules defining spouses' financial relationships resulting from their marriage, both with each other and with third parties, in particular their creditors. When couples divorce, the regime is dissolved. Marital regimes differ across countries. They range widely on a spectrum from community property regimes, in which most property is communal, to separate property regimes, where property is individually owned.

Matrimonial property regimes generally fall into three broad categories, but there are variations across nations:

Community property regime: Marital property acquired during the marriage, except for gifts or inheritances in most places, is owned jointly by both spouses and divided upon divorce, annulment, or death.

Deferred community property regime: Property acquired during the course of the marriage by either party is separate property during the marriage but deemed to be the property of both parties on the breakdown of the marriage. Net gains or losses are usually divided 50-50 upon divorce.

Separate property regime: All property acquired either before or after marriage remains the property of the individual.

European Divorce Laws in Selected Countries

Each European nation has its own distinct divorce laws. These national laws apply to couples in their native country as long as they live there. However, for those who move or marry across borders, the EU has adopted alternate regulations for these citizens of member states to help govern divorce.

Divorce laws within European countries address the usual issues that come with the dissolution of a marriage: determining grounds for the divorce, property division, resolving child custody and time sharing, and allocating spousal support, if warranted in a particular case.

From the liberal Scandinavian nations to the more conservative nations, such as Italy and Malta, divorce laws reflect the culture, history, and religious values of the country involved.

In a tour of the continent, we present a sampling of European divorce laws in brief.

France

Like most continental European countries, France requires couples to choose a matrimonial regime to govern the division of their property and finances, unless a prenuptial agreement has been set up instead. The *notaire* (a public officer authorized to oversee and draw up contracts and other official acts) can also help tailor a suitable regime.

There are three common matrimonial regimes to choose from in France. If the couple wants to pool their assets and liabilities, they choose a universal community of assets regime (*communauté universelle*). They can keep their property separate in a separation of property regime (*séparation de biens pure et simple*), but the family home can't be sold unless both parties agree, even if only one spouse has title to the home. Another choice is the dividing property after marriage regime, also known as a deferred community property regime (*participation aux acquêts*). If they don't choose any regime, by default they will be working under a regime of community of assets reduced to property acquired after marriage (*régime légal de communauté réduite aux acquêts*).

If the marriage doesn't work out, and the spouses decide to go their separate ways, they will be able to divorce on the following grounds:

Mutual consent by either or both parties. The notaire is the first official to handle the application for divorce if the parties have worked out an agreement. The couple must submit a draft contract to the notaire or judge that includes how they plan to divide their assets, provide for the children, determine custody and time sharing, and other relevant issues. The notaire can help them figure out the division of property.

On the grounds of irretrievable breakdown of the marriage. The judge makes sure that both parties agree that their marriage has broken down, issues the divorce, and rules on the consequences.

Irrevocable damage to the conjugal bond by separation for more than two years. Only one spouse is allowed to apply for the divorce. The judge issues the divorce and decides on the consequences.

On the grounds of fault, contested divorce. The judge issues the divorce and rules on the consequences. An effort is made to encourage the spouses to come to an agreement by choosing one of the other kinds of divorce.

In the absence of mutual agreement, the judge tries to get the couple to negotiate and reconcile before the hearing. He issues a temporary ruling on financial matters, custody and support of the children, establishes the separate residences, decides who lives in the marital home, and assigns a notaire to draw up the dissolution of the marital regime, among other things.

Financial support is issued as a cash sum paid in the form of an annuity or annuity and cash.

Parents in France are jointly responsible for their under-aged children's maintenance and education whether the couple is married, divorced, or separated. Custody may go to one parent if the judge determines that is in the best interests of the child.

Germany

In Germany, if the couple doesn't select a marital property regime, their marriage will be governed by the statutory, or default, marital property regime, which is the community of accrued gains (*Zugewinngemeinschaft*). This statute lasts from the beginning of the marriage to the day the divorce petition is served on a spouse. Under this statute, the assets, minus liabilities of each spouse at the time the divorce papers are served, will be calculated. Then the assets of each at the beginning of the marriage, including any inheritance or donations, are added. The difference between them—the accrued gains—will be divided equally between the spouses.

The couple can choose an alternate marital property regime in a marriage contract, such as a separate property regime (*Gütertrennung*) or community property (*Gütergemeinschaft*).

In Germany, a breakdown of the marriage is the only grounds for divorce. Germany does not recognize fault. The law permits dissolution of marriage if the spouses have been separated for one year, so long as both apply for a divorce or the respondent agrees to divorce. After a separation of at least three years, the marriage is deemed to have broken down.

Custody in Germany is presumed to be shared unless one parent requests sole custody and the court agrees. Child support is shared by the parents in accordance with their financial means. Maintenance may be provided to a spouse who does not work full time because of child care or is for other reasons unable to work.

Italy

Italy passed its first divorce law in 1970. The strong Catholic tradition in Italy had been a formidable foe of the law. Ending a marriage in Italy remains a long and expensive process.

There are two types of marital regimes in Italy: the community property regime (*comunità dei beni*), which is the statutory regime, and the separate property regime (*separazione dei beni*). The communal property includes all goods acquired together or separately during the marriage except for personal goods, businesses managed by one or both spouses, and profits of a business. The separate property regime can be chosen before or after marriage by agreement signed by a notary.

Italian lawmakers, having resisted passing a divorce law for so long, made it especially difficult for couples to officially end their marriage. For divorce Italian style, a three-year legal separation is a prerequisite. Grounds for divorce include:

- If one spouse committed a serious offense and was incarcerated for over 15 years for crimes such as murder or attempted murder of the spouse's children.

- Incest or sexual violence.

- An unconsummated marriage.

- If a non-native spouse married someone else abroad.

- If a spouse had sex change surgery.

- A legal separation for at least three years.

- Annulment.

Marital property is divided by the court, which also awards custody to one parent or jointly—whichever is in the best interests of the child—and determines child support. Maintenance to a former spouse is ordered if that spouse does not have sufficient means of financial support.

The Netherlands

Unless there is a prenuptial agreement, the financial assets of the couple, including what was acquired prior to the marriage, are considered general community of goods and property (*algemene gemeenschap van goederen en onroerend goed*) except for inheritance, which is governed by the will of the deceased.

Either spouse can file for divorce. The grounds must be an irreparable breakdown of the marriage. Assets and liabilities are divided equally upon divorce. As of January 1, 2012, the owner of the matrimonial home will be able to claim the net increase in its value plus amount invested.

As to custody, the presumption is joint custody, with sole custody being awarded to one parent only in exceptional cases. The couple may choose a different arrangement either in a prenuptial agreement or upon divorce.

England and Wales

Matrimonial property regimes do not exist in England or Wales. Instead, the courts have wide discretion to determine distribution of the property, including any payments made to a spouse and other financial matters, depending on the state of affairs of the individual spouses. The goal is to have a fair distribution of assets and income.

To get a divorce in England and Wales, a petition must be filed with the County Court proving that the marriage has irretrievably broken down. Grounds for divorce, which must be proven with evidence, include one or more of the following faults:

- Adultery.

- Unreasonable behavior creating intolerable living conditions.

- Desertion for a period of two years before applying for divorce.

- Consensual separation for two years prior to applying for divorce.

- Nonconsensual separation for five years prior to divorce. The petitioner must show that he or she can no longer live with the spouse.

If the court agrees that the qualifications are met, the district judge will grant an interim decree of divorce. The petitioner must file for a permanent (absolute) decree after 6 weeks and before 12 months. If he or she misses the deadlines, he or she will have to submit an explanation for the delay.

A plan for the arrangements of any children must be submitted to the courts before the decree absolute, the legal document that ends the marriage, is made permanent. Both spouses have parental responsibility for the children.

England and Wales are planning to simplify and help reduce the cost of divorce by providing a formula for division of property online. The goal is to make it easier for couples to settle their divorce by using the formula provided to come up with a fair distribution of their assets.

Divorce Across Borders

Helen and Philippe, a German-French couple, were living in Germany. Philippe had to move to France for work. After a few months, he decided to remain in France, but Helen didn't want to move to France to be with him. They agreed to file for divorce in Germany. Since the last place they lived together was Germany, where Helen still resided, the divorce was legal.

Figuring out the jurisdiction for divorce if you and your spouse are from different countries or have moved to another country is like taking a back road trip without a GPS. It can be so complicated that in some cases you may need to hire a lawyer to sort it out.

The substantial differences in laws prompted the European Union to harmonize the conflicts of laws so that couples who are from different countries or who move from the country where they married could have an easier path to ending their marriage.

If the divorce is contentious, there may even be the added temptation for each spouse to push to have the divorce in the jurisdiction that's most favorable to him or her. Doing so can amount to huge differences in property awards. Until recently, the laws of the jurisdiction where the petition is filed first prevailed and may still in certain cases. (England, with laws more favorable to wives, is known as the "go-to" country for women.)

This rush to court, also called *forum shopping,* helps one spouse get a jump-start by filing for divorce first, thus preventing the other spouse from filing elsewhere. The practice is just one of the reasons the European Union was eager to end uncertainty and confusion by establishing a procedure for cross-border couples who want to end their marriages.

 **DEFINITION**

Rush to court or **forum shopping** is an attempt to find the jurisdiction with the most favorable laws for you. It is the consequence of a rule that gave "first mover advantage" to the spouse who filed for divorce first in the jurisdiction of his or her choice.

Here is a good example of why the rush to court is problematic. A couple married in France under the marital property regime of separate property (séparation de biens). The wife filed for divorce in England and the husband in France on the same morning. The French court ruled that the wife was the first to file. A substantial amount of assets were in question. The English court awarded the wife millions of pounds. Had the husband been first to file, the marital property regime would have only given the wife a fraction of what she received by order of the English court.

 **RED ALERT**

When two or more countries are involved, the law that applies to your divorce may not necessarily be the law where you file for divorce. Because of conflicting laws in the European Union, you may have to ask a lawyer.

European Union Regulations to Aid International Couples

An enormous effort has been made by some members of the European Union to prevent the chaos of divorcing for international couples. On December 20, 2010, the EU established the European Union Divorce Law Pact, also referred to as the Rome III Regulation. Rome III allows international couples to select the law that would apply to their case in advance. If the spouses cannot agree, judges have a common formula to decide the laws that apply.

The regulation took effect on June 21, 2012, for the original 14 countries signing the Pact: Austria, Belgium, Bulgaria, France, Germany, Hungary, Italy, Latvia, Luxembourg, Malta, Portugal, Romania, Slovenia, and Spain. Lithuania has since joined.

Not all members of the European Union signed the Pact, preferring to have their own laws prevail. The accompanying table lists the countries that signed or did not sign the Pact.

Signatories to Rome III Regulation as of July 2013

Members of the European Union That Did Not Sign the Pact	Members That Signed the Pact
Croatia	Austria
Cyprus	Belgium
Czech Republic	Bulgaria
Denmark	France
Estonia	Germany
Finland	Hungary
Greece	Italy
Ireland	Latvia
Netherlands	Lithuania
Poland	Luxembourg
Romania	Malta
Slovakia	Portugal
Sweden	Romania
United Kingdom	Slovenia
	Spain

Divorcing couples from countries joining in can choose where to file for divorce but must follow clear-cut rules.

The Rome III protects the weaker spouse and children during the divorce process by providing more certainty and clarity. Under the agreement, if you are an international divorcing couple, you may choose the law under which to divorce. You can file a request to divorce in a country where:

- You and your spouse live.

- You last lived, if one of you still lives there.

- One of you lives, if you file a joint application.

- Your spouse lives.

- You live, if you have lived there at least six months immediately before filing and are a national of that country, or at least one year if you are not a national.

- Both you and your spouse are nationals.

The court where you first file for divorce is the court that will have jurisdiction. With the exception of Denmark, a divorce in one European Union country is recognized in another.

For more information, check the European Union website: europa.eu/youreurope/citizens/family/couple/divorce-separation/index_en.htm.

As more countries join the European Union and Europeans become even more mobile, nations not yet embracing the pact are beginning to reconsider.

If you're in a cross-border marriage or are living in a country not of your origin, or if you and your spouse are living apart in different countries, it's best to get legal advice from a lawyer who specializes in cross-border family law.

Enforcing Support Decisions

The European Union is helping families of divorce by passing regulations to enforce divorce decisions such as spousal and child support. The rules, which are binding on member states, stipulate the jurisdiction where claims for maintenance can be made and say that, with some exceptions, maintenance awarded in one member state must be recognized by the others.

The new regulations now allow disputing spouses to apply to the courts of any member state, and they stipulate that each member nation must appoint a central authority to enforce maintenance awards.

For more details on the new maintenance regulation, visit the official website of the European Union at europa.eu/legislation_summaries/justice_freedom_security/judicial_cooperation_in_civil_matters/jl0024_en.htm.

 **SILVER LININGS**

In 2011, the European Parliament stepped up to protect victims of domestic violence by stipulating that each member nation must respect an order of protection from any other member. Then in 2013, the European Union Ministers of Justice established a Europe-wide protection law that aims to stop human trafficking, sexual abuse, and sexual exploitation of children. This law is applicable to all members of the EU.

The Least You Need to Know

- Each country in the European Union has its own laws governing marriage, including the rights and obligations of the spouses, the relationship between religious and civil marriage, and the requirements to get married.

- Same-sex couples can marry in Belgium, Denmark, France, the Netherlands, Portugal, Spain, and Sweden, but such marriages may not be recognized in other European Union countries in every case.

- The European Union has enacted the European Union Divorce Law Pact, or Rome III Regulation, giving international couples the right to select which law should apply to their divorce.

- Because of the complications involved with international marriage and divorce, getting advice from a specialized lawyer can prevent future problems.

- The European Union has passed regulations that apply to all member states to enforce marriage, divorce decisions, and orders of protection of any member state. It has also passed a European Union law protecting victims of violence, including human trafficking, sexual abuse, and sexual exploitation of children.

The Economics of Divorce

When we're young and idealistic, it's difficult to understand how mere money—or lack of it—could cause conflict in a marriage, let alone destroy it. As we go through life, however, the importance of money looms large. Even in the best of marriages, a lack of money can cause tension as working parents burn the candle at both ends attending to their relationship, their children, and the bills. If money causes such dissension in marriage, it's only natural that during divorce it may become the white-fanged monster that destroys any remaining civility.

In Part 3, we help you navigate the financial minefields that can turn even the friendliest of divorces into a battle. We explain how to negotiate effectively and protect your interests, how to land on your feet despite the financial hit, and how to mitigate financial fallout such as bankruptcy or credit card debt.

Dividing It Up

Division of assets can be an unpleasant and expensive aspect of divorce, especially when strong emotions are at play. Consider the unhappy wife who hires movers the weekend her husband is out of town. They haul away all the furniture and put it in storage. It's not the fairest way to divide the spoils of a marriage, and it's not the most cost-effective, either. She pays big bucks to the movers and her lawyer, who faces the unenviable task of explaining to a judge what her imprudent client has done. The woman's actions also place a significant emotional impediment in the way of settlement. In this chapter we'll explore ways to make dividing your property as fair and painless as possible.

In This Chapter

- Simple, low-conflict techniques for dividing your assets as fairly as possible
- How to look out for your interests when dividing money, property, and debt
- How your jurisdiction defines your family's wealth
- What to do if your spouse files for bankruptcy or transfers assets

The Art and Science of Division

If you can't just take the money and run, how should you go about fairly splitting the accumulated possessions of your life together?

Depending on what you have, the job can be easy. You can go around the house and simply take turns choosing what you want. Whoever chooses first during the first round will choose second during the second round and so on. This worked for a friend of ours—until her husband went up to the attic and selected an antique lamp she'd forgotten about. But she swallowed her protest and went on with the process, and she's glad she did. This game of round-robin might sound childish, but if it works for you, go for it! It's better than paying your lawyers hundreds of dollars an hour to do the same thing.

Many people divide furnishings and other items in the home, including collectibles, by listing everything and then taking turns choosing from the list. The key is establishing ground rules. If sets (sterling, bedroom, dining room) are not to be broken up, for instance, then you might decide to allow each person to choose three items per turn, not one. Write each person's name after the chosen items. Then, when it's time for one or both of you to move out, each one receives the items allocated on the list.

Variations in Laws

What do you need to know and do? First, you must familiarize yourself with your local laws because the laws governing the division of property vary, depending on where you live. Lawyers use legislation (the local statutes or codes), court rules, and case law (decisions from cases decided by judges) as a guide to what would happen in your case should you end up in front of a judge. Based on these laws, your lawyer should have a pretty good idea of where the chips would fall if your case went to court. If your lawyer (full-service or limited) is doing the job, he or she will use that knowledge to work out a fair distribution of what you've acquired. If you are purchasing your legal services à la carte, this is one area where a consultation will pay off.

Courts generally divide property (and debt) according to the rules of three different regimes, or legal constructs, adhered to by different jurisdictions. The regimes include the community marital property regime, the equitable distribution regime, and the separate property regime.

In simple terms, the community property regime assumes that a married couple owns all assets and debts equally, except for separate property acquired by inheritance or prior to the marriage; under this regime, property is divided accordingly upon divorce. The equitable distribution regime assumes that property and debt will be divided "fairly" upon divorce—the meaning of the word "fairly" to be determined by courts. The separate property regime assumes each spouse owns his or her own property, free and clear of the other.

Of course, application of the rules can be far more complex in practice and vary from jurisdiction to jurisdiction around the world. Within the United States, the European Union, Canada, and Australia, among other nations, these schemes can be adjusted, nuanced, or combined. And courts can weigh in on the schemes before they are actually applied. Some jurisdictions will add the value of household work and childcare, for example, as part of the marital contribution, and others will not. In some cases, the increase in value of the property during the marriage is also divided.

Things get tricky when couples move from one jurisdiction to another. To cut costs, you can check with a certified public accountant as to how these laws apply to you; otherwise, you'll have to ask your attorney.

More on Community Property

The idea of community property—property acquired during a marriage and shared equally—was handed down from Mexican law, which itself originated with Spanish law. Perhaps that explains why, in the United States, the regime is most common in the western states. Yet the concept varies from place to place. In the United States, community property does not include property acquired before the marriage, by gift, or bequest. In the Netherlands, on the other hand, possessions and debt are considered community property even if acquired before marriage.

When distributing assets in the wake of a divorce, community property jurisdictions presume that husband and wife jointly own all money earned by either party from the beginning of the marriage until the end of "the community," generally determined by the date someone physically moves out of the marital residence—with an intent to end the marriage—or when the couple signs an agreement stating their intention to end "the community" of their marriage. The rules concerning when a marriage or "the community" ends vary widely. In addition, property bought with community money during the marriage is owned equally by both the wife and husband, no matter who purchased it.

What is true for money and property, however, is also true for debt; from credit card bills to loans, any debt assumed before the date of marital separation is the responsibility of both spouses in equal measure.

Equitable Distribution Jurisdictions

Jurisdictions in the United States that are not community property states are called common-law states. These states adhere to the equitable distribution scheme. Here the court considers a range of factors when dividing property, such as the length of your marriage, amount and sources of income, liabilities, the contribution to the marriage of each spouse, the nature of the property, the responsibilities each of you had in the marriage, whether you have children and who they are going to live with, your health, your education, your noneconomic contribution to the marriage, vocational skills, employability, and your estate, among other things. In a long marriage, the likelihood of a 50-50 division of assets is much greater than in a brief one.

Separate Property Jurisdictions

England, Scotland, and Australia, among other jurisdictions, use a separate property matrimonial regime, in which each spouse owns his or her own property throughout marriage. In practice, at the time of divorce, the court can exert a heavy hand in weighing the needs of the parties and distributing the assets as it deems best. Some courts consider the value of household work in the total assets.

Taking Inventory

After you've determined the ground rules under which your property will be divided, it's time to take a full accounting of your assets.

Unfortunately, for most people married more than a couple of years, complexity rules. The game of round-robin, described earlier, is a lovely exercise in forgiveness, but many of us own more than furniture, china, and knick-knacks. There's a pension, a savings account, an account for the kids' college tuition, and some paintings that aren't worth much now, but you never know.

How do you work it out? The first step is, again, a detailed list of all your assets. Your master list must include all the assets you have accumulated during the course of your marriage. Include the date the asset was acquired. (If you can't remember but you know it was acquired during the marriage, that's good enough.) Make sure to note the cost (if you can recall) and what you think it's worth now. Also, note to whom it belongs—you, your spouse, or both. Remember, under community property regimes even if one spouse bought it, if it was bought during the marriage, it belongs to both of you.

Furniture, Cars, the Small Stuff, and the Cash

According to financial planner Carol Ann Wilson, furniture and personal belongings are valued at "garage sale" value in divorce. So it's up to you and your spouse to pick through your possessions and divide them up according to who is more attached to which item, making trades as you go along.

In the wake of divorce, many people like to start from scratch and leave the furniture behind. Our friend Lisa, for instance, didn't take a single sheet or towel from the family home following her divorce. Her sudden liberation signaled, for her, a chance to reinvent herself. All her new possessions, in the context of her new life, became symbols of her personal growth as well as her release from marital pain.

For others, the possessions accumulated during a lifetime represent luxury or comfort; association with a former spouse is not an issue. For those who end things amicably, dividing the furniture and cars should present little problem. Just set values for your belongings, and then divide them according to value. If one item, such as the car, is worth more than all the furniture, the spouse who keeps the car will have to pay the difference out of the cash that you will be dividing. Personal assets, such as tools used to repair the house or for gardening, should remain with the spouse who used them the most—or the one who "keeps" the home or garden.

Who Gets the House?

If you have children, the spouse who has primary custody usually remains in the house with the children, unless you and your spouse can't afford it. If there are no children, you and your spouse can also work together to decide what to do with the house. The easiest solution is to sell the house and divide the proceeds. However, one of you may be more attached to the house than the other. In this case, you will, of course, need to have it appraised. You might each hire a real estate appraiser to value the house and then take the average of the two values. If you both trust and like the same person, you might decide to save money and hire one person.

The current equity in your house is usually stated on your monthly mortgage bill. Or, you can calculate the equity by subtracting the mortgage from its assessed value. What's left, the equity, is what you will negotiate with your spouse if one of you decides to keep the house.

If you think you might sell the house, review the following considerations before placing your home on the market:

Finding new housing. Will either of you be able to find comparable or sufficient housing at a lower monthly cost? Remember, mortgage payments are often tax-deductible, rent usually is not. You might be better off paying a higher monthly mortgage than a slightly lower rent. However, when insurance and taxes are figured in, renting might be cheaper, although this all depends on the housing market.

Renovating. Does the house require significant work? Will a renovation make it more marketable, and if so, do you have the funds to pay for the work? If not, you might decide to hold onto the house for now—even if you rent it to someone else—and sell it later.

Moving. Will a move be so disruptive to the children that keeping the house is important, even in the face of financial sacrifice?

Finally, consider consulting a tax professional to help you determine your best option.

When You Keep the House

Suppose you have custody of your child and have decided to stay in the house until your youngest child turns 19 and has been out on his own for a year. Assuming you and your spouse are working this out (rather than letting a judge decide for you), you can make whatever arrangements you both like.

We recommend that the spouse who pays the mortgage from the time of the divorce until the house is sold gets a credit from the net sale proceeds (gross proceeds less outstanding mortgage, broker's fees, and so on) to the extent the principal of the mortgage was reduced while he or she lived there and paid the mortgage (with his or her own income or assets). But do adjust for any mortgage deduction for tax purposes. However, if the remaining spouse is paying the mortgage with support from the other spouse, it might be fairer to simply agree to divide the net proceeds with no credit to the remaining spouse for his or her mortgage payments.

Likewise, credit any spouse who has paid for home improvements following divorce and prior to the sale so that these cash outlays are included when calculating the net proceeds of the sale.

Decide now how you're going to handle the sale of the house when the time comes. If you are going to sell the house right after the divorce, start looking for a real estate agent you can live with, and learn about the market in your area.

SILVER LININGS

Remember, if you and your spouse can work together in a businesslike manner, you'll be much better off in the long run. Create ground rules that work for both of you. Perhaps you want to agree to a credit equal to only a percentage of the amount of the mortgage paid off. After all, whoever stayed in the house had the benefit of its use. Lastly, to maximize the money in your pockets when the home is sold, make sure you get tax advice before you sign any binding document.

Finally, anyone who's bought or sold real estate understands that the tax issues can be substantial. If you plan to keep the house in the family after the split, you should consult a tax attorney or accountant about the ramifications of keeping your interest in the home and leaving your name on the deed, even if you'll be living elsewhere. The last thing you want to discover, 20 years down the road, is that you're liable for capital gains taxes you never dreamed of.

If you haven't included it in your settlement agreement, now is the time to decide who will pay the capital gains tax on the profits from the sale of your house or how to share the bill. Will you split it 50-50? Divide it in the same proportion as the proceeds of the sale? You might get a larger share of the net proceeds if you made the mortgage payments, but you might then have to bear the larger share of the taxes as well. Your accountant is a good resource. Make an appointment before finalizing the deal with your spouse.

Dividing the Family Business

If you and your spouse share a family business, dividing it may be an especially contentious task. The first step is to gather the documentation of share ownership. A reputable business appraiser should determine the value of the business. Your respective accountants and legal advisors will have to consider the tax consequences for each of you and how division of the shares of the business fits into the overall divorce settlement. The advisors will take into account the value each spouse contributed to the business, both through loans or outright capital and the activity of each spouse, whether there was a prenuptial agreement that addressed the formation of a business or other agreements regarding the business, as well as any alimony included in the divorce agreement.

The three most common ways to handle the division of a family business are selling the business and dividing the assets, one spouse can sell all shares to the other either with cash or by trading another asset, or, if they're on good terms, the spouses can continue the business relationship after the divorce. The choice depends on how they get along, the value of the business, and how each person feels about being involved in the business.

Leave No Stone Unturned

When dividing the spoils of a life spent together, make sure you account for all the financial elements, including retirement and employee benefits, taxes, and debt. Here are some tips:

Pensions and other retirement plans. In some jurisdictions, pensions and other retirement accounts can be divided between you and your spouse, even though only one of you earned it, since marriage is most commonly viewed as a partnership. Pensions are often divided 50-50 from the date of your marriage until the date you separated, started a divorce action, or actually became divorced. Check your local laws or ask your attorney.

Tax liability. Be sure to decide in advance how you will handle any audits of jointly filed tax returns. If a deficiency is found, will the spouse whose income was underreported or who took too many deductions shoulder the tax debt? If it's impossible to figure out or prove who's to blame, do you each pay half the debt? Although the spouse who didn't work might be appalled at such an idea, if you both enjoyed the money when it was earned, at least in the United States, then you were also both responsible for paying. (Check your laws for other countries.)

On the other hand, if you had no idea what your ex was up to as far as taxes are concerned, you might not be liable under the theory you were an innocent spouse. But if you've received a "deficiency" notice from the IRS about a joint income tax return, you will need the assistance of a tax lawyer.

Debt. Debt is a joint burden in most places. Judges will divide debt just as they divide assets. Although the lion's share of the debt might go to the spouse with the significantly larger income, an individual who has managed to avoid paying bills during the marriage might be saddled with large loan payments after divorce, providing that individual has the income or assets to make the payments. To know if this applies to you, check the laws in your jurisdiction or ask your attorney.

It's essential that you subtract debt from savings before you divide stocks, bonds, or cash. If the debt is larger than the savings, or you don't want to deplete savings to pay off the debt, you must still divide the debt. You can divide it any way that seems fair. If one of you spent too much despite the protests of the other (maybe that's part of the reason you're divorcing), an arrangement might be for the "spender" to pay the debt, unless he or she used the money to pay family expenses. In this case the debt might be shared equally.

RED ALERT

Consider paying off all the credit card debt with available cash. This will both decrease the amount of dollars owed and secure the credit history of both parties. A late payment by either party on a jointly held card will be reported on both parties' credit reports. If your spouse is accumulating unreasonable credit card debt, both of your credit ratings will take a hit. In this case, cancel the joint card and get your own as soon as possible.

To protect your interests and arrive at a fair solution, make a list of your debt, when it was incurred, who incurred it, and why. Write down the monthly payment due, and then think about who should and can pay it. If this is giving you a headache, as a last resort, ask for accounting or legal advice. It will cost you money, but it might save you money in the end.

Watch Out for Ploys to Avoid Payment

Among those planning a divorce for a while, you occasionally find the wise guy who comes up with some clever strategy to hide money or other assets from the family. Keep this in mind—but don't be paranoid. On the remote chance that this is your spouse, your lawyer can usually recover the missing assets.

Bankruptcy

To avoid payment to an ex, some people will go so far as to file for personal bankruptcy in the middle of their case. Bankruptcy laws in some jurisdictions are based on income and require the filer to submit to credit counseling before applying for bankruptcy, among other obligations. If this problem comes up, consult an attorney, since the issue is quite complex.

Illegal Transfers

Another devious way the moneyed spouse might try to reduce the amount of assets declared during a divorce action is to transfer assets to a friend or family member. The spouse will then claim that he or she no longer has these assets. The lawyer for the recipient spouse has to then prove the transfer was made to deprive that spouse. If the transfer is about to happen, the recipient's lawyer can go to court to try to block the transfer. To substantiate this claim, the lawyer has to prove to the judge why he thinks the property is about to be transferred and what property or money is involved.

Marion Dupont came from a wealthy family, from which she inherited several properties after she married Andrew Billings. After three years of marriage, Marion met a man with "more intelligence and energy than Andrew could ever hope to have." After she broke the news to Andrew and filed for divorce, she began transferring the titles of her property to her sister. Andrew was clever enough to suspect Marion would do something sneaky, so he hired a private investigator. The PI did his homework and was able to provide proof that Marion was in the process of transferring the titles. Andrew's lawyer then brought this to the attention of their judge and was able to block the transfer.

Although the property would not likely be distributed to the husband because it was inherited, this asset might affect the determination of total equitable distribution, if that's the financial regime in your jurisdiction. In general, it's better not to transfer assets just before divorce simply because judges don't like it.

Gather Your Financial Information

With the help of financial analyst Ted Beecher, we've developed a series of worksheets to help you move toward financial settlement and cut the best deal you can. In the end, whether you plan to settle or litigate, you will need to document your assets and your debts. The sooner you compile these documents, the better off you'll be.

In addition, the very act of compiling your financial information will help you work through the process: you will find out what your true financial position is, get a sense of what you can really ask for, and try to imagine what kind of counterproposal you are likely to get from your spouse.

Just as important, by filling out these worksheets, you will come face to face with the likely gap between your position and that of your spouse. You will be better able to support your position in settlement negotiations or in court once you are familiar with these details. It's this simple: the more prepared you are, the more likely you will be to come out ahead.

The information in these worksheets is similar to what you will need to present in any court-ordered financial affidavit. By organizing this material in advance, you will save time and legal fees.

A Basic List to Get Started

This first list is intended to give you a sense of the assets owned by you and your spouse as separate property and what you own jointly. Start by listing each of your assets and the net value of each item.

List of Assets and Their Values

ASSET	JOINT PROPERTY	HUSBAND'S SEPARATE PROPERTY	WIFE'S SEPARATE PROPERTY
House			
Business			
Car			
Savings			
Checking			
Brokerage			
Pension			
IRA or 401(k)			
CD			
Furniture			
Jewelry			
Other			
TOTAL:			

Details About Your Residence

Identify the value, expenses, and plans for your home or apartment, if you own it. This will help in your negotiations and preparing for your future.

Fair market value (FMV) _____

Current mortgage amount _____

Monthly payments, including utilities and rent or maintenance _____

What did you pay for the house? _____

Will the house be sold now or later? _____

If the house is not sold, who will live in it? _____

Details About Your Assets

Gather this information, and add it to the financial affidavit in the next section.

Annuities _____

Checking accounts, bank accounts, CDs,
savings accounts, and so on _____

Stocks, bonds, mutual funds, limited partnerships _____

Real estate (in addition to the primary residence,
other rentals, vacation properties, and timeshares) _____

IRAs, 401(k), 403(b), pension, deferred
compensation, etc. _____

Unpaid bonuses and noncash compensation,
such as company car and paid lunches _____

Defined benefit plan (you will need details for later) _____

Life insurance cash value _____

Personal possessions _____

Antiques and collectibles _____

Debts (credit cards, loans, personal debt, and so on) _____

Make sure you have sample paycheck stubs and tax returns for the last three years as well.

Prepare for Your Financial Affidavit

The final step is to make a list of all the information you'll need to fill out a financial affidavit or written statement confirmed by oath. Courts typically require most of this information before they will hear your case. Financial affidavits are not necessarily the same in every jurisdiction, but items included in the following list are the most common. Some of the information provided in the financial affidavit may be used to calculate child and spousal support as well as the division of assets and debt. It will be to your advantage to have all this information filed in a single, safe place as soon as possible.

Complete the worksheet that follows, and use the information from the preceding sections where necessary. Keep in mind that all policies, such as medical or life insurance policies, should have the policy number listed as well. You'll need the policy itself and any other related documents. Your bank and brokerage account name and account number should be included, and you'll need a copy of the most recent statement(s).

 ## INCOME AND EMPLOYMENT INFORMATION

Job title   _____

Primary employer   _____

Hours per week   _____

Income

Monthly payroll   _____

Monthly payroll deductions

      Exemptions claimed   _____

      Federal income tax   _____

      Social Security   _____

      Medicare   _____

      State or local income tax   _____

      Health insurance premium   _____

      Dental insurance premium   _____

      401(k) contributions   _____

      Total payroll deductions   _____

Net monthly payroll income   _____

Income from other sources   _____

Deductions from income from other sources,
including legitimate business expenses   _____

Net monthly income from other sources   _____

Net monthly income from all sources   _____

Net monthly income of children   _____

Monthly income of other spouse   _____

Income reported on last tax return   _____

Assets

Real estate, including location, market value, outstanding mortgage, net equity, and a list of all furniture:

_____

_____

_____

_____

Motor vehicles, including year and make, market value, outstanding loans, and net equity:

_____

_____

_____

_____

Bank accounts, including name of bank and current balance:

_____

_____

_____

_____

Stocks, bonds, and mutual funds. Include stock or bond name, shares or par, and the market value for each position or holding:

_____

_____

_____

_____

Life insurance. List the company name, the policy number, the owner's name, the insured's name, the beneficiary's name, the face value, and the cash surrender value:

_____

_____

_____

_____

Pension, profit sharing, and retirement plans. For each plan, list the plan name, the participant, and the value:

_____

_____

_____

_____

Total Assets   _____

Expenses

Housing

     Rent   _____

     First mortgage   _____

     Second mortgage   _____

     Homeowner's fee   _____

     Subtotal   _____

Utilities

     Gas and electric   _____

     Cell phone   _____

     Landline   _____

     Water and sewer   _____

     Trash collection   _____

Cable/internet _____

Subtotal _____

Food

Grocery items _____

Restaurant _____

Subtotal _____

Medical (after insurance)

Doctor _____

Dentist _____

Prescriptions _____

Therapy _____

Subtotal _____

Insurance

Car insurance _____

Life insurance _____

Health insurance _____

Dental insurance _____

Homeowner's insurance _____

Subtotal _____

Transportation

Vehicle 1

Payment _____

Fuel _____

Repair and maintenance _____

Insurance _____

Parking   _____

Subtotal   _____

Vehicle 2

Payment   _____

Fuel   _____

Repair and maintenance   _____

Insurance   _____

Parking   _____

Subtotal   _____

Clothing

Clothing   _____

Laundry   _____

Subtotal   _____

Expenses for Children

Childcare   _____

Education   _____

School   _____

Lunches   _____

Extracurricular activities   _____

Subtotal   _____

Miscellaneous Expenses for Each Spouse

Tuition   _____

Books and fees   _____

Recreation   _____

Entertainment   _____

Hobbies   _____

Membership in clubs   _____

Miscellaneous   _____

Gifts   _____

Hair/nail care   _____

Books/newspapers   _____

Donations   _____

Other   _____

Subtotal   _____

Total Monthly Expenses for You   _____

Total Monthly Expenses for Your Spouse   _____

Total Monthly Expenses for Your Child(ren)   _____

Total Expenses for All Family Members   _____

Estimate the monthly expenses for each adult separately and all the children together by dividing the total living expenses accordingly. Tack on the expenses specific to the children and each adult. For example, add the food, housing, and clothing monthly expenses for the children as well as childcare, extracurricular activities, school, etc. Do the same for each adult. This information will be used to calculate how much money is needed to cover expenses for each family member.

Settlement Software

After you have recorded important financial information, what should you do with it? Clearly, dividing your debts and assets and predicting the outcome of that deal into the future is a task more complex than most of us can handle. To help you—and your accountant—crunch the numbers, there are a number of family law software programs on the market. If you're interested in doing your own settlement comparison, search the internet for a software package that works for you.

In addition to software that delivers a comprehensive financial settlement, online calculators are available that cover the various financial aspects of divorce. There are many free divorce calculators specific to your own jurisdiction. Some are even available at your jurisdiction's official courts or government website.

If you have significant assets, your best bet is to consult a certified financial planner or perhaps even a financial advisor specializing in divorce. There are so many quirks, loopholes, and pitfalls that it takes an experienced pro to navigate them all.

The Least You Need to Know

- Your financial matrimonial regime—whether community property, equitable distribution, or separate property—will determine how a court treats the distribution of your property during the divorce process.
- Dividing the small stuff can be less painful if you do a round-robin list of who wants what.
- Get your finances in order by filling out a list and finding all the required paperwork.
- When dividing assets, it's in your best interest to work out a division that you both think is fair.
- If left up to a judge, debt will be allocated based not only on who incurred it, but also on what was bought and taking into account both of your incomes.
- Before selling your house, be sure that is the wisest financial course of action; factor in the tax implications.

Inheritance, Wills, and Other Estate Issues

This chapter will explain how to protect your own wealth in the event of an impending divorce. The divorce laws regarding estate issues, including inheritance and wills, are determined by country and jurisdiction. Most jurisdictions consider inheritance prior to marriage as separate property; the more the date of an inheritance precedes the date of a marriage, the more protected that inheritance will be. Once married, it's important to update or redraft your will to reflect how you would like to dispose of your assets in light of your new relationship. Keeping your will up to date will prevent future problems should your marriage take a turn for the worse.

In This Chapter

- What happens to property you owned before you got married?
- How are assets inherited during a marriage handled?
- When one spouse dies before the divorce is final
- The role of the will in divorce

Inherited Money and Personal Property

Whether you reside in an equitable distribution, community property, or separate property jurisdiction, the rules and guidelines are not always clear-cut. Depending on where you reside and your situation, you may need tax and estate experts to guide you through.

For instance, what about property you had before you got married? In theory, it's not usually considered marital property, providing it's been kept in your name alone, but there are many loopholes and complications. What if the property has increased in value during the marriage? What if you have taken a mortgage on it and, with your spouse, paid the mortgage off? What if the property has been renovated? You need to talk to your attorney. Depending on where you live and what was done to increase the value of the property, part or even all of the property might be subject to distribution.

Likewise, property inherited during a marriage is most often said to belong to the heir, alone, as long as it hasn't been sold and the proceeds pooled in a joint account. Yet, once a property is sold, it's difficult to prove that money has remained untangled and aloof, unless it's placed in your individual account.

On the surface, things could not be clearer than the community property state of Texas, where all property is divided into two categories: separate property or community property. Under Texas law, separate property includes anything the individual owned prior to the marriage, anything he inherited during marriage, and any payment accrued in a lawsuit as the result of personal injury, except any recovery for loss of earning capacity during marriage.

Community property in Texas is everything acquired during the marriage aside from separate property. It doesn't matter if just one spouse holds the title to a car or is named on a credit card; if it was obtained during the marriage, the asset or debt belongs to both.

In a Texas divorce, the court can only divide the community property and does not have the power to divide separate property. But it isn't that simple. You have to prove the property is truly separate by tracing it with documents from the moment it was acquired to the present time. If separate assets somehow become commingled over time, it will be considered community property no matter how you acquired it. For instance, if inherited cash has been deposited into a joint account or any account with money that might be considered community property (for example, salary), the "separate money" becomes subject to the joint management of the spouses, unless they sign an agreement to the contrary.

Despite some of the loopholes, in Texas, ownership of one spouse's separate property cannot, in general, be awarded to the other spouse.

SILVER LININGS

In most jurisdictions, if you have inherited property before or during your marriage, the inheritance is your own separate property as long as you open a bank account solely for the inherited property. Make sure not to mingle any other assets with this account. Since this is not the case in all jurisdictions, check with your attorney to learn about local law.

This is not true in Connecticut, which is not merely an equitable distribution state—but what is called an "all-property equitable distribution state" (jud.ct.gov/lawlib/Notebooks/Pathfinders/EquitableDistribution.pdf). Connecticut law spells out the situation clearly: "At the time of entering a decree annulling or dissolving a marriage or for legal separation … the Superior Court may assign to either the husband or wife all or any part of the estate of the other." In Connecticut, it would be possible for a spouse to receive at dissolution a large percentage of an inheritance that the other party received a few days before the marriage dissolution action was filed, even though that party made no contribution to the acquisition, preservation, or appreciation of that inherited property.

England considers an inheritance to be part of the family "pot," although there is judicial discretion based on family income and assets and whether the inheritance was before or during the marriage. So once again, it is very important to check the laws of your jurisdiction or ask you lawyer about how inheritance is treated in the event of divorce.

When a Spouse Dies Before Divorce Is Final

Donna and Jonathan, both divorced, met on a cruise to Alaska and less than a year later tied the knot. It was a second marriage for each. Both in their mid-forties, they had children from first marriages but expected none this time around. Six years later, their relationship was in shambles, and after attempting to reconcile, they realized their marriage had come to an end. Jonathan filed for divorce, alleging that Donna had been involved in numerous affairs and was unusually cruel.

As it turned out, Jonathan, an entrepreneur, had accumulated significant personal wealth a few years before meeting Donna. With so much money at stake, each hired a full-service attorney. Because Jonathan wanted to give Donna as little of his personal wealth as possible, the case inched toward trial. In the equitable distribution state of New York, Donna knew the bulk of the assets were Jonathan's separate property, but she felt she could do better in court than through negotiation, given the offers made by Jonathan's attorney.

Then, in a shock to everyone, Jonathan was killed in a car accident the week before the trial was to begin. In line with the law, the divorce action was halted at once and Donna, still Jonathan's wife, became executor of his will. A relatively young man, Jonathan hadn't bothered to change his will prior to the divorce action; after all, once the divorce was finalized, the will would be null and void.

But with Jonathan now dead and the will unchanged, Jonathan's intent to keep the bulk of his money and leave his estate to his children from his first marriage could not be fulfilled. The will had bequeathed to Donna far more than she could ever have hoped for in court, even under the most favorable of circumstances.

Furious, Jonathan's children sought legal advice, but were told to back off. They could not successfully contest the enormous inheritance to Donna because they simply had no grounds.

In most instances, of course, the distribution of property is protected by wills. But when it comes to divorce, confusion about wills and inheritance abounds. The widespread lack of knowledge leaves many divorcing people in the lurch—and because they haven't attended to the technicalities, they could unwittingly leave hard-earned assets to a soon-to-be-former spouse, with children from a prior marriage out of luck.

 **RED ALERT**

If you think your marriage might be in trouble, and you're mulling divorce as a real possibility, re-evaluate the designated heirs in your will or rewrite your entire will. Discuss your circumstances with your estate attorney as soon as possible to prevent your spouse from inheriting your estate should you not outlive the divorce process.

Writing in the *CPA Journal,* Louis Skroka, a Minneola, New York, attorney specializing in complex divorce and related matrimonial matters, describes the problems that can result when one spouse dies before the divorce has been finalized in New York State: "Without insight and planning, unanticipated consequences will almost certainly result if one of the spouses dies unexpectedly during the transition period. It is crucial to take necessary precautions in order to prevent the problems that may occur," Skroka says.

The reality, in a nutshell, is that "a marriage endures until a judge executes a final judgment of divorce, regardless of the length of separation, lack of communication, or bitterness of allegations," Skroka says. Thus, when a spouse dies in the midst of a divorce, the parties are still legally married, and the divorce action automatically stops. The court loses jurisdiction to decide the marital status of these individuals, and also the right to decide property issues arising out of that status. As a result, the decedent's estate plan and prior will prevail. The law states that the surviving spouse is entitled to whatever bequests are described in the will and whatever accounts or assets for which she is the named beneficiary.

"As soon as a divorce decree is signed, the provisions of a will leaving property to the now-divorced spouse become null and void, and the will is construed as if the divorced spouse predeceased the survivor," Skroka explains. "But until a judge's signature is affixed to the final decree, the marriage lasts, and so does the effectiveness of the will." The same is true of any trusts and beneficiary assignments for life insurance policies and bank accounts.

 **RED ALERT**

Even after a divorce settlement or trial is over, the deceased spouse's will prevails until the judge signs the divorce decree.

If the deceased spouse's estate plan was generous to the soon-to-be ex, and if it was left unchanged with the expectation that divorce itself would take care of it, the surviving partner would come into a windfall. The children from a prior marriage—the intended beneficiaries—would have few grounds on which to protest the will.

On the other hand, if the will was changed to disinherit the surviving spouse prior to divorce, that individual could mount a legal fight and might well prevail. "A spouse, including a nearly divorced one, is protected by law from being disinherited," Skroka says. "A surviving spouse may 'elect' against the estate and receive the *elective share,* which is the greater of one-third of the net estate or $50,000." In addition, the spouse is entitled to other assets not even part of the probate of the will: pension plan, profit-sharing accounts, and the like.

In short, the surviving spouse, whether as a beneficiary or an *elector,* stands to inherit far more than might have been the case had he or she been subject to the equitable distribution of the divorce. There is just one caveat: at least in New York, the surviving spouse cannot become an elector in the estate if he or she has abandoned or otherwise failed to care for the deceased spouse, despite an ability to do so. What does this mean? The law defines abandonment as leaving the marital home without any intention of returning and without the consent of the other spouse. In one pivotal case in New York State, says Skroka, "the husband was found to have lost his right to an elective share [of the estate] when he moved out of the marital residence several years before the wife's death and never paid any rent despite the fact that she was evicted."

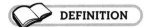 **DEFINITION**

An **elective share,** in some jurisdictions in the United States, entitles a spouse to receive a portion of the deceased spouse's estate, usually one-third, depending on the state law. This is intended to prevent disinheritance of a spouse. With this right, a spouse who was disinherited in a will, the *elector*, can challenge the will. Specific conditions apply, depending on the state.

Given all the twists and turns in the law and all the nuances, anyone dealing with significant property or wealth would do well to consult a knowledgeable attorney as soon as possible. Do not do anything until your situation has been analyzed under a legal microscope.

"When an individual wants to disinherit a spouse, a new will should be prepared and all beneficiary accounts should be changed to eliminate the spouse," Skroka says. "To maximize the chances of prevailing in an elective share contest (in New York, at least), the individual should develop a case for abandonment or lack of support against the other spouse, and include such claims in any action for divorce or separation. Often, such specific planning is not done."

 YOU CAN DO IT!

In some jurisdictions, such as New York State, a spouse who has left the marital home or has not supported the dying spouse may lose their right to receive part of the estate. To completely disinherit a spouse, a new will should be drawn and signed and proof of abandonment established. For the spouse who seeks the inheritance, stay in the home and take care of your sick spouse.

As for the spouse to be disinherited, the advice is the opposite. If you believe you're entitled to all or a portion of the estate because you have shared a good part of your life with your spouse and played a supportive role, then put aside any animosity you might be feeling that caused you to seek a divorce. Try to remember the good times for both of your sakes, if possible, near the end of life. By abandoning your spouse at this time, you could be unknowingly relinquishing any rights you have to his or her estate.

The Least You Need to Know

- Property that you brought into the marriage is considered yours going out in most places; but your spouse may be eligible for a portion of any increase in its value.

- Inherited property is viewed differently from one jurisdiction to the next. Be sure to check the laws governing your particular situation.

- If a spouse dies before the divorce is final, the estate is distributed as it would have been had the marriage stayed intact.

- A disinherited spouse can contest a new will. It's best to spell out in the will why you're drafting a new one.

- When drafting your marital settlement agreement, insert explicit mutual waivers relinquishing rights to receive anything from the other's retirement accounts, insurance policies, and employment plans in the future, except for those rights outlined in your agreement.

- Make sure you change beneficiary designation on qualified retirement benefits like pensions and other retirement accounts, and the like, as well as life insurance policies, as soon as the law permits.

Spousal Support

Long after the ink is dry on your judgment of divorce, you might still be writing checks to your ex. These payments are called alimony, spousal support, or maintenance, depending on the jurisdiction.

Maybe the payments haven't begun. You're not divorced yet, but you want some idea of what this breakup is going to cost you. Or perhaps you need to know how much money you can expect to receive so you can start to rebuild your life.

Maintenance Basics

Whatever your situation, you must first understand what *maintenance* (or *alimony*) is exactly, when it is appropriate, and how the general rules applying to maintenance will determine what happens to you.

In This Chapter

- What is maintenance and when is it appropriate?
- The rules governing spousal maintenance
- How to get the best deal for yourself
- When altered life circumstances affect what you receive or what you pay

Maintenance is financial support that one spouse provides to the other after divorce or legal separation. Maintenance is guided by the laws and precedents of the jurisdiction where you live.

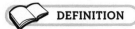 **DEFINITION**

> **Maintenance,** or **alimony,** refers to payments made by one spouse to the other to assist with the support of the recipient spouse. The duration of payments is usually correlated to the length of the marriage and the financial circumstances of the spouse who receives the maintenance. Either the court or your settlement will determine the amount. Maintenance may also terminate upon remarriage or cohabitation of the supported spouse.

Some of the factors considered by a court, depending on the jurisdiction, in awarding maintenance are …

- Duration of the marriage
- Marital fault in fault jurisdictions
- Standard of living
- Status as custodial parent
- Other local statutes

Maintenance payments in the United States are usually tax deductible for the paying spouse and taxable for the recipient spouse. (See irs.gov/publications/p17/ch18.html for more tax information.)

In Europe, each member nation maintains its own laws governing maintenance and spousal support. These laws are recognized and enforceable in all member states of the European Union under Council Regulation (EC) no. 4/2009. See Chapter 17 for more details.

What's Fair? Coming Up with a Number

Maintenance awards have changed over the years because of increased participation of women in the workforce. Courts are now addressing this societal change by assuming that women are able to support themselves—even if they will need to retrain—and allowing fewer years of maintenance. Also, since men now sometimes stay at home and care for the children part time or full time, they might also be awarded maintenance.

How do you know how much maintenance to pay or to demand? There are well-established parameters. In general, courts look at the following factors to determine the maintenance. It follows, of course, that you and your lawyers, when trying to settle your case out of court, will look at these factors as well:

Your income. Is there sufficient money to enable both of you to enjoy the same lifestyle, or are you both going to have to cut back?

The length of the marriage. The longer the marriage, the stronger the claim for support.

Your ages. Younger people are thought to be better able to find work. Older people nearing retirement might be unable to pay support for a long period of time.

Social Security. This might be an issue if either of you is close to retirement age. In a marriage of more than 10 years, if the nonworking spouse does not remarry, at retirement age, he or she will be able to receive benefits based on the ex's Social Security record.

Your health. Is one of you ill and unable to work? That could affect how much will be paid and for how long it will be paid.

Job sacrifices. Did you give up a good position because your spouse had to relocate for her job? Maybe you never used your degree because you worked as a bookkeeper in your husband's business. Whether your sacrifice was obvious or subtle, it could affect the duration of your support award.

Education and job skills. The sooner you can find work, the shorter the duration of your support.

Where the children will reside. If they're going to live with you, and that shortens the time you can spend working each day, you might be entitled to more maintenance than if the children were living with your spouse or if you had no children.

Independent income sources. Maybe you have a trust or other source of income. You never touched it during the marriage because you planned to leave it all to your children. Now its existence could affect the amount of support you'll receive or have to pay.

Distribution of other assets. If you and your spouse accumulated a lot during the marriage that will be split, you might not be entitled to any maintenance. Let's say your wife built up her medical practice while you were married, and now she has to pay you half its value of $350,000. Depending on where you live, the receipt of that lump sum could reduce additional support payments.

Marital fault. In some jurisdictions, the reason for the breakup of your marriage could affect the duration and amount of support.

Tax implications. If you have to pay taxes on what you receive, you might need a larger amount than if you do not have to pay taxes on the payment.

Standard of living. In many jurisdictions, the idea of maintaining the same lifestyle (assuming it was based on fully reported income) is part of the alimony statute and is a goal, although it may not be reached.

While judges and lawyers look at these factors to determine how much maintenance one of you should pay the other, the single most important factor is, of course, how much money there is to go around.

YOU CAN DO IT!

Here's a word to the wise: take that job. Don't turn down a job for fear it will lower your maintenance settlement. If it's a good job with the possibility of advancement, you'll be better off taking it than depending on maintenance payments that are likely to fall short of your needs. In fact, a judge might just look at your lack of employment and, instead of increasing payments to you, simply declare you *underemployed*—that is, earning less money than you're capable of, and imputing or attributing the dollar difference to you anyway!

How much maintenance can you reasonably expect? We've all heard the notion, bandied about on TV and in the movies, that maintenance should enable the receiving spouse to continue to live "*in the style to which he or she has become accustomed.*" Well, in a perfect world, it'd work out that way. But the reality in many cases is that the income used to support one household simply isn't enough to support two, at least not at the same level as before.

It is, in short, impossible to state any rule about how much you should expect to pay or receive. Unless you are wealthy, you should expect to cut back a bit, create and stick to a realistic budget, and consider going to work or working more.

YOU CAN DO IT!

When negotiating, start by asking for more than you either need or expect to get. Then, during negotiations, be willing to give up what you don't mind losing.

Getting the Best Deal

When negotiating for maintenance, be sure to look at the big picture. For instance, Ann Parsons didn't want to sell her house under any circumstances. Her lawyer told her that if her case were decided by a judge, the judge would order the house sold and would order her husband to pay her support. Ann's husband had a checkered job history, although he was well paid when he did work. Ann decided that rather than take any support, she would keep the house and get a job to pay the bills.

It wouldn't have been the right deal for everyone, but for Ann, it was. She decided what she really wanted was the house and looked at the big picture. She couldn't rely on her husband to pay her support, and the house would give her income when and if she was ever ready to sell it.

All situations are different, of course, and negotiating the terms of maintenance will vary from one couple to the next. However, as you go about cutting your own deal, make sure to follow these general guidelines:

Know what you want. The deft negotiator will first figure out what he or she really wants and will cast a cold eye on the reality of the situation. Do you want to stay home with the kids or go back to work? Do you want the house or your share of the cash from its sale? Will your spouse be responsible enough to meet his or her obligations? Don't hold out for promises you know your spouse probably will not live up to.

Determine your expenses. If you decide you want support above all else, you must determine your expenses, including recurring expenses and one-time costs due to the divorce. Will you have to move and have all of the expenses of fixing up a new place? Or are you staying put, but you need some replacement furniture?

Make a detailed list of one-time and recurring expenses. Then, make a list of all income and savings. Look at your checks and credit card bills from the previous 12 months and get an average of your monthly expenses. Realize that you might need to use some of the savings for your one-time expenses.

Come up with a number. After you determine the monthly expenses, calculate your shortfall. Is the shortfall a sum you can realistically expect to receive from your spouse? If so, great. (Remember, you might have to pay taxes on the money, so subtract that from your spouse's payments.)

Refine your budget. If you know your spouse can't pay much, look at your list again. Is there any place where you can compromise? Is there any way you can add to your income?

Negotiate. You don't have to be Donald Trump to know that, when making a deal, you never present your bottom-line figure right away. Maybe you've played enough mind games with your spouse to last a lifetime, but you must play one more to get a fair shake. Start high (or low if you're the one who has to pay), and gradually move down (or up).

If you're going to pay, avoid a deal that requires you to reveal your income every year. If you do have to reveal your income, make sure it's a mutual obligation, so you can see what your ex is making, too!

Set limits. If you're paying, make sure that the duration of the alimony has a limited time-frame, and make sure you can afford to pay or accept what you're about to agree to. However guilty, angry, or in love with someone else you might be, do not agree to something you cannot afford.

Hire a professional. Consider using a lawyer to negotiate maintenance. Even if you and your spouse have worked out everything, this area is usually so fraught with emotion, you're better off leaving that to a professional. If you have allocated limited funds for unbundled legal services, consider spending some of them here.

A Word of Warning

Make sure that maintenance payments do not end when a child comes of age. In general, the U.S. Internal Revenue Service will view such payments as disguised child support and might disallow the tax deduction for them. (Other countries may have different laws.) That is because the recipient spouse does not have to count that money as income (though the paying spouse can't deduct the payment from his or her taxable income). Although this might be good for the recipient, who now won't be taxed on the support, it is bad for the paying partner, who will now be unable to deduct the payments from his or her income. It can wreak havoc on a deal.

 YOU CAN DO IT!

If possible, arrange spousal support through mediation or settlement, not litigation. This will provide both parties with the most flexibility in getting what they deem most important from the arrangement.

In addition, reworking an agreement after it's been in place for a while can present a sticky problem because the IRS might go back to recharacterize what is taxable and what is not taxable. Presumably, the receiving spouse has been paying the taxes. You would now have to amend your returns and seek a refund. It is better to draft your agreement correctly the first time.

When Circumstances Change

We all know that life is a roller coaster. One moment, you're flying high, on top of the world; the next, your world has been shattered into a thousand bits. Economies can crumble; companies can fold; real estate values can soar or plummet based on world events or the fates.

The roller coaster is one reason why it might be best, in some places, to see a judge when negotiating maintenance. In a few jurisdictions, if a judge decides your case, you will have an easier time changing a support award than if you and your spouse sign off on the payment in a separate agreement.

Why is that? According to the law in certain jurisdictions, when you sign an agreement, judges will assume that you thought of all the possible things that might happen in the future and that you accounted for them in the agreement. For example, if you were to pay support at the rate of $300 a week for five years, the agreement could have provided that if you lost your job, you would no longer have to make payments. If you didn't provide for that and you do lose your job, you can ask a judge to allow you to stop making the payments—but the judge might point out that you had your chance to include that in the agreement, and now it's just too late.

When a judge decides your case after a trial, on the other hand, he or she does not account for future possibilities. The decision is based solely upon what the judge has heard in court. Therefore, if you or your spouse loses a job in the future, you'll have an easier time, in this case, convincing the judge to make a change than if you had signed an agreement.

Bottom line? Try to account for all possibilities when you sign an agreement, and always consult with an attorney.

 SILVER LININGS

> Despite the security of those monthly support checks, it may be the best thing for the receiving spouse when the period of spousal support is over and the maintenance ends. At that point, both partners are economically independent and, with the umbilical cord cut, can go their own ways. Such separation affords a true sense of closure—often not possible, even after divorce, when financial strings persist.

The Least You Need to Know

- Spousal support (also called maintenance or alimony) is based on a number of factors, as opposed to child support, which is usually based on a fixed percentage of your income, the children's needs, or a combination of the two.

- Spousal support is usually included in the receiving spouse's income for tax purposes and is tax deductible from the paying spouse's income in the United States.

- When negotiating, never reveal your bottom line in the beginning. Think about what you really want before you start.

- In some states, it is easier to change support that a judge ordered than it is to change an amount you agreed to pay or accepted in a negotiated settlement, so be sure that you consider all possibilities before you sign an agreement. Better still, consult an attorney.

Child Support

Let's face it. Raising kids is expensive. Medical expenses alone can account for a huge portion of the budget in the United States. Add to that clothes, food, a home to accommodate the kids, child care, computers, smartphones, activities, and lessons—the list goes on and on. Married couples combine their resources to cover these costs, but the expenses don't end just because you're separated or divorced.

When parents live apart and custody resides with one parent, the parent who lives with the children the least, the noncustodial parent, pays his or her share of the children's expenses to the parent who lives with the children the most, the custodial parent, unless there is a 50/50 shared-time arrangement. This payment is called child support. The parent with whom the child primarily resides is presumed to pay his or her share of the expenses directly to the child.

In This Chapter

- Understanding child support
- Figuring out what's fair
- Dealing with deadbeat parents
- Paying for your child's insurance and healthcare

In almost all cases, the amount paid is based on the relative incomes of the parents and the needs of the child, maintaining the same lifestyle as if the family had remained intact.

If the parents have joint physical custody, where the child spends about 30 to 50 percent of her time at both homes (virtually equal), child support usually is adjusted.

A Closer Look at Child Support Guidelines

In most jurisdictions and countries, the factors that are considered when issuing guidelines for child support are the income of the parents, typical expenses for a child, the number of children, medical expenses, and shared parenting time offsets. Many jurisdictions have the guidelines, formulas, and calculators available online, so check the website of your local government or court system to find out the guidelines for your situation.

Income can be defined in the very broadest way—to include not only wages, but also assets, such as stocks or a pension, government benefits, or regular, annual gifts from family members—or it can be defined in a narrow way, limited only to earned income.

For the purpose of calculating income for the paying parent (to determine the amount of child support to be paid), the law usually provides for deductions to be taken from the income, and those deductions vary, depending on location. Federal, state, and local taxes, mandatory retirement contributions, union dues, and health insurance, as well as payments already being made on behalf of other children and spouses from prior relationships are among the common deductions in the United States. Each country has its own formula.

In most cases, your net income (what's left after the allowed deductions) becomes the money from which you pay your child support obligation. Different jurisdictions use different methods to allocate child support payments between parents. Most use percentages, and the percentage usually increases with each additional child you have.

Parents receiving public assistance usually can exclude that income from the calculation. For these parents, there might be special guidelines for child support. On the other end of the income scale, jurisdictions may change the method of calculating child support if the parents are in a high-income bracket.

In addition to child support, parents are often required to maintain health insurance if there is no national insurance for the children and sometimes life insurance to guarantee the child support in the event of a parent's death. In most places, parents are also required to pay for child care, minus any child-care expense tax credit the other (typically, custodial) parent might receive.

Child Support in Sole and Shared Custody Arrangements

Let's look at an example of how child support is determined in New York State. (For European countries, please refer to Chapter 17.)

Unless the parents agree otherwise, New York State assumes a child will live primarily with one of his parents, as opposed to both parents sharing physical custody after the divorce.

The State of New York's child support guidelines state:

- "The gross income of each parent is determined and the incomes are combined;

- The combined parental income is multiplied by the appropriate child support percentage—17 percent for one child, 25 percent for two children, 29 percent for three children, 31 percent for four children, and not less than 35 percent for five or more children;

- This figure is the basic child support obligation, which is then divided between the parents on a pro-rata basis, according to the amount of their respective incomes;

- Additional amounts to be paid for child care, medical care not covered by health insurance, and educational expenses are determined by the court and added to the basic child support obligation; and,

- The noncustodial parent is ordered to pay his/her share to the custodial parent— sometimes called the 'parent of primary residence.'"

The amount of child support calculated in accordance with the (New York) guidelines is presumed to be the correct amount. "Either parent can offer evidence that this amount is not correct, and the court has the authority to decide whether the guidelines amount is unjust or inappropriate," the guidelines state. "If the court orders a different amount than the basic support obligation according to the guidelines, the court must set forth its reasons for doing so in writing. Either party can object to the findings of the court."

YOU CAN DO IT!

Many jurisdictions now make payment of child support easy by allowing you to pay through their websites. Search on the internet for your state or other jurisdiction and country and add *child support* to the criteria.

Here is an example of how such calculations might work in New York, New York. The following is taken from the Child Support Standards Chart of April 1, 2013, prepared by the New York State Office of Temporary and Disability Assistance/ Division of Child Support Enforcement:

Basic Child Support Guidelines Worksheet

The following worksheet applies to noncustodial parents only:

1. Annual income*   1. _____

2. Approximate basic child support obligation**:   2. _____

3. Subtract line 2 from line 1:   3. _____

   a. If line 3 is equal to or greater than $15,512 (the 2013 self-support reserve), enter the line 2 amount on line 7 below. No further calculations are necessary.

   b. If line 3 is less than $15,512 (the self support reserve) but greater than or equal to $11,490 (the poverty level), proceed to step 4.

   c. If line 3 is less than 11,490 (the 2013 poverty level), enter $300 on line 7.

4. Annual income (copy from line 1)   4. _____

5. Self support reserve   5. _____

6. Subtract line 5 from line 4   6. _____

Enter on line 7 the greater of $600 or the amount on line 6.

7. Approximate child support obligation   7. _____

Income includes gross total income as reported in the most recent federal income tax return.

**The basic child support payment includes the amount resulting from multiplying the noncustodial parent's income by the appropriate child support percentage, then adding the noncustodial parent's share of cash medical support obligations, educational, and child care expenses where appropriate.*

Where the total combined parental income of both parents exceeds $136,000, as of January 31, 2012, the law permits, but does not require, the use of the Child Support Percentages in calculating the child support obligation on the income above $136,000.

Many jurisdictions have laws that presume it's best if parents have joint or shared legal custody of their children after a divorce. The basic premise of both parents sharing in the care and maintenance of the child guides the child support guidelines. Again, the relative income of each parent with consideration of the time the parent cares for the child is the underlying basis for the support formula.

Direct vs. Indirect Child Support

Child support comes in two flavors—direct and indirect. Child support is when one parent pays support to the other parent directly on a regular basis—every week, every other week, or every month. Indirect child support, on the other hand, involves payments made to third parties for expenses such as school tuition, camp, lessons, after-school activities, and healthcare costs.

Whether you are the custodial parent or are involved in a joint custodial arrangement, if your ex has been ordered to pay child support, you might wonder whether you're better off receiving a larger amount of direct support and paying the third parties yourself or letting your former spouse make those payments and getting less direct support. Conceptually, it is nearly always better to receive sufficient funds directly. It's about more than money; it is a question of control. When you write the check to the school or camp yourself, the decision-making is in your hands. Yet the subject warrants a bit more thought.

 **SILVER LININGS**

> If you are the parent paying child support, you can negotiate a smaller amount of maintenance, also known as spousal support, in return for a larger child support payment. Bear in mind that your child support obligation, depending on the ages of your children, can last for many more years than maintenance. Alternatively, if your children are teens when you divorce, child support may end while alimony can go on and on. Remember, too, that there's no tax deduction for child support, whereas maintenance is usually tax deductible

If you are the parent receiving funds, choosing to receive direct or indirect support has its pros and cons:

Pros	Cons
If your former spouse pays the third party directly, and those expenses increase, he or she will pay the increase.	If what you receive includes amounts to be paid to the third parties, and the costs of those third-party expenses rise, you might have to bear the increase.
Some former spouses will be more reliable if they are paying third-party expenses directly because they feel more involved in their children's lives.	Some spouses will be less reliable if they are obligated to pay the third-party expenses. You will have to chase your former spouse for payment while the third parties are hounding you.

If you are the parent making the payments, choosing to pay direct or indirect support has its pros and cons as well:

Pros	Cons
If you're obligated to figure third-party expenses into your direct payments, your former spouse will probably bear the cost of the increase.	If you pay the third parties, you'll bear the cost of any increases.
You might feel more in control and more directly involved with your children if you pay third-party expenses.	If you give your former spouse money to pay third parties, and he or she doesn't make the payments, the third parties might chase you.

How do you decide whether direct or indirect support is right for you? If a judge decides your case after a trial, you'll have no choice; whatever the judge decides goes. If you're settling your case, on the other hand, you can compromise. If your former spouse is the non-custodial parent (or a custody partner with greater income) and is reliable, you're probably better off having him or her pay the expenses directly to the third party to avoid responsibility for increases in big-ticket items, such as school tuition. If your former spouse is unreliable or disagrees with you about signing up your child for an activity, you're better off receiving more child support and paying these extra costs yourself. The point of child support is to enable the child to enjoy the lifestyle of the wealthier parent. If that has a benefit to the ex, so be it.

One of the most frequent questions lawyers get from their noncustodial clients is "Why can't I pay child support directly to my child?" (So what if the child is two years old!) "Why can't I set up an account so I know the money is being used for the kids?" The real question being asked is, "Isn't my spouse the one benefiting from the child support?"

The truth is, your ex is benefiting, to a degree. If your former spouse pays the rent with child support, of course, he or she is also benefiting. The same goes for the utilities, internet, and even food. Let's face it, your ex isn't going to buy steak for the kids and hamburger for himself or herself.

What's Fair?

If you and your spouse believe you can reach a settlement, how do you determine what's in your child's best interest but also fair to both of you? It's not easy, but you can do it.

To Settle or Not to Settle?

Since almost all jurisdictions have formulas for determining child support, there is little mystery about the outcome if you were to have a judge decide. If you are the custodial parent and your spouse isn't willing to use the standard guidelines during negotiation, why should you settle? Most of the time, of course, you shouldn't. But there are exceptions. The following are some important reasons for agreeing to less child support than the guidelines might otherwise allow:

More certainty. Most parents will pay what they can afford and especially what they have agreed to pay. In contrast, when they fall hopelessly behind or a judge orders them to pay more than they can afford, they often default, and, if your ex lacks a job or assets, it can be a lot harder to collect.

Add-ons. If you agree to a child support figure that is less than the formula, you might be able to get your spouse to add on other items. Maybe the law doesn't obligate a parent to pay for after-school activities, camp, or even college. You might be willing to accept less child support than the formula provides if your spouse will pick up some of these items.

Exception to the formula. Remember, hardship provisions to the law usually make the formula inapplicable. If your spouse demonstrates to a judge that hardships exist, the judge might not apply the formula. If you might be in this situation, negotiation might be in your best interest.

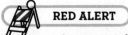 **RED ALERT**

In most jurisdictions, you cannot just agree to change child support informally, with your ex. Instead, you must go to court to obtain an order modifying the amount of support. Otherwise, your support obligation continues to accrue and is enforceable under the law.

Likewise, if you are the noncustodial parent, negotiating child support might be best for you because:

- Your spouse might agree to less than the guidelines allow.

- You have more say over what your financial needs are and can tailor the agreement to your situation.

- You can modify the agreement to state that if your income decreases by a certain amount, your child support payments can be reduced accordingly.

Duration of Child Support

Child support should terminate at the age your child is considered emancipated under your jurisdiction's laws. In some places, that means age 18; in others, age 21 or more.

Other events can terminate child support as well—the child's entry into the military, assumption of full-time employment, or marriage before the age of emancipation. If the child moves in with the noncustodial parent on a permanent basis, child support also should stop. (You might want to negotiate a sum the former custodial parent will have to pay you in that case.)

If you and your spouse agree, child support can extend beyond the age of emancipation. For example, if in your state the emancipation age is 18, but you want your spouse to continue to pay child support until your child graduates from college, you could try to negotiate a provision stipulating that child support continue for as long as the child is a full-time undergraduate student, but in no event beyond the age of 21 or 22, whenever the child graduates in due course.

 **RED ALERT**

If your child support agreement includes a mechanism to increase child support without returning to court, consider a similar mechanism to decrease child support in the event of a financial setback, such as a job loss or a reduction in income. If you are the parent paying child support, you might want a provision that reduces it by a third or half when the children are in camp or away at college. But beware, you'll have to formalize each decrease by way of court order, or your "official" child support obligation will remain as it was per the last court decree.

What Should the Child Support Figure Be?

How do you go about determining exactly how much child support you should pay or receive if you are negotiating an agreement that deviates from the guidelines? Keep in mind that the court is unlikely to allow you to give (or receive, depending on your position) less than what is provided in the guidelines, unless you persuade the judge it's appropriate to deviate from those guidelines in your case.

To ascertain a fair amount of child support without using the formula, it is best to figure out a monthly budget for the children. Household expenses, such as mortgage or rent, food, and utilities, can be allocated one half to the children and one half to the parent, or they can be allocated one part each among all the children in the household and the parent. Clothing costs for the year should be added up and divided by 12, as should camp, extracurricular activities, birthday party gifts, and similar items that are paid only once or twice a year.

After you and your spouse have worked out a budget, you can determine the total contribution for each of you. You should agree on a mechanism for calculating future cost-of-living increases for this payment. You can base your formula on the cost-of-living increase as determined by your local department of agriculture or other indices, or if you prefer, you can base it on increases in your incomes. Because most people prefer not to reveal their income each year, it's common to base such payment increases on outside, objective criteria.

Take All Expenses into Account

If your child is a toddler, it's difficult to think about what college will cost or who will pay for it years down the road. If a judge is going to try your case and you have young children, you'll probably have to return to court when the child is a junior or senior in high school to have the judge address the issue of who will pay for college. If you want to settle all the issues now, however, a provision that often works is this: you and your spouse simply agree now to pay half of what it would cost to send your child to the most appropriate school in your local college system. Any excess amounts (say your child gets into Harvard) will be paid by the parent or parents who can afford it. This way, both parents have a minimum obligation.

What about the First Communion, the Bar Mitzvah, the Sweet Sixteen party, the first car? If you negotiate an agreement, anything goes. If your case goes to court, judges may or may not address those types of expenses.

If you want to be ready for anything, figure some of the following expenses into your agreement now:

- Babysitter and day care
- Birthday parties
- Camp
- First Communion
- Bar/Bat Mitzvah
- Sweet Sixteen party
- Application fees for colleges
- Travel costs to visit prospective colleges
- SAT, achievement test fees, and tutoring costs
- Other tutors as needed
- Orthodontia
- Psychotherapy
- After-school activities
- Sports activities, uniforms, equipment, and fees
- Car, driving lessons
- Wedding

Wait a minute, you might be thinking. If all those items are extras, what am I paying child support for? Answer: food, shelter, clothing, telephone, utilities, and so on. Of course, depending on the amount of child support you are paying, your spouse may use some of the support for these extras.

Be careful, though. Anything you sign might come back to haunt you. Harvey, for instance, felt so guilty about leaving his wife, Jessie, that he agreed in writing to pay for each of their four daughters' weddings at the Waldorf-Astoria or someplace comparable. The daughters were only teenagers at the time. Unfortunately, Harvey's business took a turn for the worse. Although he could not afford the expensive weddings, he was obligated to pay for them. He went into debt to do so.

If you have a breakdown in negotiations, you can fall back on the child support guidelines, which really should be the floor for any child support award. Remember, that's the base level, and anything beyond is extra. Don't be afraid to seek help from your lawyers or a mediator.

When a Parent Is in Default

Being financially responsible for your children is so important that it is considered a crime to stop paying child support.

In 1992, the U.S. federal government passed the Child Support Recovery Act. This law punishes people who willfully fail to pay a past-due support obligation to a child who resides in another state. A judge can fine and imprison (for up to six months) first-time offenders. Repeat offenders can be fined and imprisoned for up to two years.

 **RED ALERT**

Even if your ex-spouse remarries into wealth, most courts will not require the step-parent to shoulder the expenses for someone else's child.

The U.S. Department of Justice Prosecutive Guidelines (1997) for this law state that the parent owing child support must be a person having the ability to pay but did willfully fail to pay a known past due (child) support obligation, which has remained unpaid for longer than one year *or* is an amount greater than $5,000, for a child who resides in another state.

This law has rapidly gained popularity as the crackdown against "deadbeat" parents has grown.

In 1994, the United States passed a law requiring all child support orders to provide for an automatic deduction from wages, unless the parents have otherwise agreed or the local court has waved this obligation. If a parent changes jobs, the new employer must be informed of the automatic deductions before they go into effect. The state can also seize some federal and state tax refunds to cover child support payments. It can also file a contempt of court charge, which can result in a fine or a jail term or both.

Of course, a private attorney can be hired by the custodial parent to help collect child support. The delinquent parent might also be required to pay the attorney's fee. Finally, there's always a collection agency, which usually charges a contingency fee.

In 1998, the Deadbeat Parent's Punishment Act came into play as well. In that law, anyone who owes $5,000 for more than one year or $10,000 for more than two years is subject to legal consequences. Punishment may include prison time of up to two years, and mandatory restitution is required.

When You Think You're Paying Too Much

If you and your ex-spouse are on friendly terms and you have been laid off from your job or have had a reduction in your pay, the first person to talk to is your former spouse. If you're lucky, she or he will be willing to reduce the amount of child support for a period of time until you get back on your feet. Or, your ex might agree to make a trade, such as less child support now but more later. Make sure that you and your spouse put your agreement in writing, and send it to the judge for signing.

If talking to your ex is not realistic, or if a judge decided your case, you can appeal his decision, provided you do so within your state's time deadlines. Consult with an attorney who is knowledgeable about how the appeals courts have ruled in such cases. In some jurisdictions, the higher court tends to defer to the lower court in child support matters, on the theory that the lower court judge had the opportunity to observe you and your spouse in court and may have reached a decision based on what he or she saw. Stated more directly, if the judge thought you were lying about your income, the appeals court might be inclined to go along with that judge's decision.

You can also return to court after a period of time—at least a year—if the situation has changed or if you were unable to prove something at trial that you can now substantiate. Peter testified that he could not afford the full percentage of child support because he suspected he was going to lose his job. The judge would not consider the possibility of Peter losing his job as sufficient to warrant his paying a lower percentage of child support. Six months later, Peter did, in fact, lose his job. He went back to court and was able to get a reduction in his child support obligation after a period of time had passed, and he was unable to find other employment after looking in good faith.

When You're Not Receiving Enough

What if the child support you are receiving no longer pays for your growing child's food, let alone clothing, shelter, and after-school activities?

If you're not having your payments made through the state payment agency (which should help you seek an increase), see an attorney. Your ability to have the payments increased depends in large part on the circumstances. In general, if you can show a judge that your children's economic needs are not being met, you probably have a good chance of getting an increase.

Insurance and Healthcare for Your Children

If a judge is trying your case, health insurance will be one of the items he or she will direct you or your spouse to maintain, unless you live in a country with universal health insurance. If you are negotiating a settlement, here are some things to consider:

If you have health insurance through your employer, keep your children covered. If neither you nor your spouse has health insurance through an employer, agree to allocate the cost of the premiums between you.

Be sure to include financial responsibility for uninsured healthcare costs in your settlement. Allocation can be in the same proportion that your individual incomes bear to your total income. If one of you is not working, then the other should pay all these costs.

Get a Qualified Medical Child Support Order. This requires employer-sponsored group health plans to extend health care coverage to the children of a parent/employee who is divorced, separated, or never married when ordered to do so by state authorities. Visit dol.gov/ebsa/publications/qmcso.html for more information.

If you and your spouse are negotiating, you should both agree to provide life insurance for the benefit of your children (assuming child support otherwise ceases upon the paying spouse's death). The parent who is paying child support should provide enough each year to cover his or her support obligation, which means that every year the amount of life insurance coverage needed lessens incrementally as the children get older. (Remember, child support usually ends when the child turns 18 or 21.) The amount of life insurance should include the paying parent's share of college as well, if you have agreed to include college expenses.

The parent who is not paying child support should also maintain life insurance coverage to help with college, if he or she can afford to do so, and if he or she is obligated to pay a share of college expenses.

Who should the beneficiary of the life insurance be? This is an emotionally charged issue, but it doesn't have to be.

Here are a few solutions. If your children are young, name your former spouse as beneficiary and hope he or she will use the money to care for your child. If the children are older, you can make them the beneficiaries, but you still have to hope that the children are taken care of. You can, of course, name a relative, but we don't recommend that. Your ex-spouse may justifiably express doubt as to whether the relative will ever use the money for the children at all. Alternatively, a custodial trust can be set up to continue paying child support.

The Least You Need to Know

- Try to include all important points in your agreement. In some states, it is easier to modify child support a judge ordered you to pay.
- Child support payments are not tax deductible for the paying spouse, but are tax-free for the receiving spouse.
- Each jurisdiction has its own guidelines for how much child support should be paid, and each has exceptions to those rules. Check your jurisdiction's child support guidelines. If you are still not sure, consult with an attorney before entering into a deal where you might be paying too much or receiving too little.
- Don't forget the items that add to the expense of raising children—parties, gifts, activities—when you negotiate child support.

Managing Your Money Solo

If you have been married for a short time, divorce might have only a minor impact on your finances. Before you married, you may have lived on your own, worked, and supported yourself just fine. If this is the case, you are one of the fortunate ones. It will be relatively easy for you to get back on your feet—financially, at least.

If you've been married for years, however, the lifestyle changes brought on by your new circumstances can be more profound. You'll find yourself far ahead of the game if you know what to expect. In this chapter, we present a guide to money management for the newly divorced.

In This Chapter

- Your financial profile, past and present
- Reestablishing yourself financially
- Selling your house, business, stocks, or other holdings
- Creating a budget you can live with

Expect Your Financial Situation to Change

There was a time—it might seem like centuries ago—when you casually went out to eat, vacationed at the Jersey shore, and thought nothing of buying your child the latest computer or toy. Now, you count every penny you spend. You hunt for sales and swallow your pride when accepting hand-me-downs for your kids. Dinner is, more often than not, pasta instead of a rib-eye steak. A night out on the town now means streaming a video from Netflix instead of a seat at the Super Bowl. In short, your former life seems so impossibly extravagant you can't imagine how you ever spent money so freely. You wonder if you will ever again be able to enjoy what you now consider the luxuries of a distant past.

Unless you are wealthy, it is likely you will need to live on a budget after your divorce. This is especially true if you have been married for a long time or if you have children.

For one thing, you and your ex-spouse each need a home. If there are children and custody is shared, both parents must sustain homes on less money than before. If one parent was accustomed to staying home with the children, that parent might now need to go out and get a job.

If one parent has custody, the other parent will have to help support the children while at the same time maintaining a separate household. The nonresidential parent might be required to provide support he or she feels he can little afford. If the residential parent does not work outside the home, the courts might instruct the working parent to provide spousal maintenance as well. Following divorce, some people start new families and must also help support them. (But be aware, the time-honored rule in these situations is: you must be financially responsible to your first family before you can be generous to your subsequent family.)

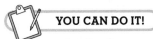 **YOU CAN DO IT!**

Juggling finances on a tighter budget requires looking for better prices on purchases, something you may find difficult as you have increasingly less time. But there are solutions. Many people we know have joined discount consumer clubs and buy purchases in bulk. Others shop for deals over the internet. You can save money, even if your time is limited.

Sharing the Responsibilities

In many instances, especially for those who have children, divorce will change your relationship with your former spouse but not sever it. As much as you might wish otherwise, you may still be bound by finances and parental responsibilities for years to come.

Even after you have left the marital home, your children will need your financial support and so might your nonworking ex-spouse. What's more, your earning power can always take a turn for the worse. If you don't get a cost-of-living increase, if you're laid off, or if your expenses are too high, you might have a difficult time making ends meet.

Here's a tale of woe: one evening, after the children had been tucked in and fallen soundly asleep, Helen informed her husband, Henry, that she had lost all feeling for him. No, she hadn't met anyone else, but she wanted to try. The long and the short of it: their marriage was at an end.

Helen told Henry that she wanted him to move out. Shocked and dazed, he began looking for an apartment nearby.

An independent web designer who went from gig to gig, Henry had a hard enough time paying the mortgage and bills when his family was intact. Adding a second household to his expenses forced him to moonlight, and his life became nothing but work.

Not that it's any consolation, but things were difficult for Helen, too. Indeed, any parent who maintains a home for young children assumes responsibility for their needs, including all the extra expenses that implies. You might receive a certain amount of help in meeting these responsibilities from your ex-spouse, but more and more, these days, a large part of the financial burden will fall on you. There's no getting around it. On the first of the month, you face a stack of bills that you must pay no matter what your income is.

 RED ALERT

> One friend of ours has refused job after job because she feels the entry-level positions are not commensurate with her experience. We have continually suggested she get in touch with reality. While many of her friends from college have been in the workplace for 20 years, she has spent 20 years at home. Her work at home was important, but when it comes to advancement in the workplace, she may have to step back a bit. Don't feel you have to take just any job, but be reasonable. It's better to enter the workforce and upgrade your skills in order to compete than to be overtaken by hubris while the world passes you by.

Helen, for instance, had to look for work after taking time off to be with her kids. Her new job, behind the counter at a coffee shop, was tiring and didn't pay much—but she did earn enough to contribute something to the mortgage, and the company provided her with personal health insurance, as well, a necessity in the United States.

If, like Helen, you have children living with you, you'll find yourself protective not just of your pennies, but also of your time as you juggle work, maybe some classes, and single parenting. You no longer have the luxury of sharing household responsibilities with a spouse.

 **SILVER LININGS**

For those exiting long-term marriages, finding a means of earning enough money to stand on your own can be the most important first step. Very few people are married to partners so well-off they can expect to receive support payments forever. For those whose husband or wife has "made it," you may be eligible for permanent financial support. Anyone in this situation should fight for all they are entitled to.

We are not telling you to stay married, and we are certainly not suggesting that Helen would have been better off in a loveless marriage, financial perks and all. For Helen, being married would have been an existence full of anger and angst. Helen gladly accepted her new challenges in place of the old, and though tired, she had no regrets. The new struggles were well worth undertaking in exchange for release from a life sentence with a spouse she didn't love. Nonetheless, it behooves you to understand the difficulties divorce might entail. Each person must decide, individually, which cross he or she can most easily bear.

Taking Stock of Your Finances

As soon as you're faced with the prospect of going it alone financially, call an accountant or divorce financial expert. An accountant—especially one familiar with your family's financial situation—is in a good position to help you develop a plan to get back on your feet.

If you don't want to go to a professional, you can work to get a handle on financial issues by listing your income, assets, and expenses. Then you will know if your current income is adequate. Notice that we haven't mentioned putting more debt on your credit card. Adding debt will ultimately lead you into a quagmire. It is better to cut back on unnecessary expenses or increase your income.

 YOU CAN DO IT!

Before you start looking for a job or maybe building a business, make sure you're heading in the right direction. Rank your interests and talents and see where that takes you. If all goes well, you'll be turning a bad situation, your divorce, into a good situation—beginning a new, fulfilling career. To get a foundation and ideas, there may be free or low-cost classes in your community or on the internet. They'll give you the skills and confidence to move forward with your search.

Carmen Carrozza, a former bank manager in Chappaqua, New York, has seen many people in the midst of divorce come through the door. The most uncertain are often women whose spouses have been the sole providers while they have been caring for the children. Even though these women worked for a few years before having children, they have been out of the workforce for too long to reenter at the same level, or the work they used to do has changed dramatically.

Looking for Work

If you haven't worked outside the home for a number of years, getting back into the workforce will take some time and getting used to. But it can ultimately reward you with far more than financial security. You will begin to feel self-reliant. You will meet new people. And you might even find you are distracted from the problems related to your divorce.

Discover the person you have not yet become. Recognize your innate talents. You're not just a great parent; get in touch with who you were before you had kids. To help you identify your natural aptitude, we suggest you list your special interests and abilities in detail. Use the list to help you focus your studies, your job search, and your goals.

Developing a Credit History

According to Carmen Carrozza, one of the most common concerns for those in the midst of divorce involves building personal credit. The task is far easier, of course, for people who can show they have assets or income, by way of steady support or employment.

Good credit is vital. If you have been working all along, your credit rating will not be affected by your divorce, unless you and your spouse had joint accounts and failed to pay those bills on time, or if you stopped paying them after the divorce was filed. If you have been relying on your spouse's income, on the other hand, you will have to establish your own credit history. Although the prospect seems intimidating, it's not as formidable as it sounds.

 **SILVER LININGS**

If you've been held responsible for a spouse's debt, you may seek recourse in the Innocent Spouse Rule, a provision in the U.S. Internal Revenue Code. Under this rule, if you can show that you are completely ignorant of your spouse's wrong-doing, you might not be held liable. (See irs.gov/Individuals/New-Rule-for-Innocent-Spouse-Relief.) If you're not sure if this rule applies to you, check with your accountant.

First, you must be able to identify your assets, like cash accounts, and your sources of income, including salary, interest, and, of course, maintenance (alimony). Because banks are seeking good credit risks, they will be looking not just at your income, but also at debts, credit history, collateral, and stability (how long you've been living in the same place). If you don't have enough qualified credit history, some banks may issue a *sub-prime* credit card. If you pay the entire bill every month on time, that will be a good start.

Another way to increase your credit score is to shop at stores that give instant credit; department stores, gas stations, and local stores are all good candidates. Begin by making small purchases on store credit, and pay your bills promptly. You can pay these bills with your sub-prime credit card. If you're diligent, you should have your own positive credit history in about a year.

Handling Your Debts

In addition to generating income and establishing credit, you will have to come to terms with your debt. You and your spouse may have joint debts. These would include a tax debt, a mortgage, a car loan, and credit cards. If you are not the spouse with deep pockets, you might have your name on the mortgage or car loan statement anyway; this means you are in debt—even though you have no income to offset the debt.

Third-party creditors, such as the IRS, banks, and stores, don't care whether you are getting maintenance or child support. They don't care if you are divorced. They just care about the money you owe them and how they will get it back. They are not bound by the divorce settlement. They will hold both you and your spouse liable for payment.

 RED ALERT

As far as the credit card companies are concerned, you remain responsible for all the joint credit card debt your spouse incurs whether or not you're divorced or have a separation agreement. The best way to protect yourself is to avoid shared credit cards. If you already have them, close the accounts and open a new one in your name.

Jim owned a construction company. One year, he hid income by simply not reporting it on his income tax statement. His wife, June, was shocked to learn that the IRS held her as well as her husband liable for his income tax evasion. She was not protected by their divorce settlement because the couple had filed their income tax statement jointly.

Living Within Your Means

You have already created a budget in preparation for your divorce settlement. But now that reality is settling in and your financial status has actually changed, it's a good idea to sit down and parse things out again, as mentioned in the beginning of this chapter.

As you did before, compare income and expenses, including such occasional items as tax payments, holiday and birthday gifts, and retirement savings.

Now put these two lists side by side. Add the totals for each column. How do they match up? Are you ahead or behind? If you're behind, put a star next to the expenses that are optional or that can be reduced. By how much can they be reduced? Is there any way you can eliminate or reduce expenses that are not starred? If you need help with this, consult your accountant or bank manager.

 Sample Income/Expense Statement

INCOME SOURCE	AMOUNT	EXPENSES	AMOUNT
Salary (net)	_____	Housing	_____
Child support	_____	Groceries	_____
Interest	_____	Clothing	_____
		Entertainment	_____
		House repairs	_____
		Car	_____
		Heat, elec., water	_____
		Children's extra-curricular	_____
		Childcare	_____
		Babysitting	_____
		Toys, gifts	_____
		Haircuts	_____
		Adult education	_____
		Vacation	_____
		Taxes or fees	_____
		Misc.	_____
		Savings	_____
TOTAL	_____	TOTAL	_____

If your living situation and financial status have changed for the worse because of your divorce, you might consider liquidating some assets or selling the house—if it was awarded to you—to help with your cash flow. Before you make this decision, be sure to speak with your accountant or a financial planner. Remember, your house is an asset as well as a home. If you have children, their emotional needs must be considered.

On the other hand, if you've received the house through a divorce settlement or judge's decree while your spouse has gotten the liquid assets, think carefully about whether you have enough cash to live comfortably in the house or whether you should move into less expensive living quarters. If the monthly payments on the house are small, you might as well stay where you are.

The sooner you assess your situation and come to terms with your financial situation, the sooner you will be able to take care of yourself.

The Least You Need to Know

- Divorce can mean more expenses on the same or less income. Depending on the facts of your situation, you might face the challenge of entering the job market. If so, be prepared to take that step.
- Establishing yourself financially means developing a good credit history.
- Creating a new budget will give you a sense of control over your finances.
- Give yourself some time to weigh all the pros and cons before deciding to sell your home after the divorce.

PART 4

Focus on the Children

Divorce is a time when you are necessarily focused on your own feelings. It is often difficult to think about anything but what is happening to you. Whether you are surprised to find your marriage coming to an end or you've been contemplating a separation for months, severing this relationship is all-encompassing.

If you have children, however, you have a dual responsibility: to yourself, and most importantly, to your kids. Your children know only the security and love they have had with the parents who have nurtured and guided them throughout their short lives. The thought of losing one or even both parents is frightening. The other life changes your children might experience—from changing residences to adjusting to a stepfamily—would disorient even the strongest, most experienced adult.

In the chapters that follow, we'll address your children's needs and your own as you cope with the aftermath of divorce. You'll learn how to help your children understand the changes their family is about to undergo, and how to move forward with your life.

Thinking About Custody

Once upon a time and long ago, you and your spouse lived together under the same roof as a family. You slept together, ate together, vacationed together, and, most importantly, raised your children together. One, or perhaps both of you, worked outside the home. Sure, you were overwhelmed by household chores; sure, you were tired from too many hours on the job. But there were the compensations: the pleasures of sharing time together as a family, as well as the opportunity to have some time alone while your spouse took care of the kids.

Now that you are divorcing, things have changed. For half the parents, this means a move to another residence. For these parents, the realization that they will likely be seeing the children less often can be painful.

The parent who remains in the home, on the other hand, is faced with the prospect of managing alone. Those who have not been in the labor force since the children were born will have the added burden of looking for work and then juggling work and single parenting.

In This Chapter

- Recognizing that custody is not ownership
- Is sole custody or joint custody right for your family?
- Choosing the children's primary residence

Before you make these changes, of course, you and your spouse need to put your differences aside to talk about how you will divide your responsibilities and arrange for the custody of your children.

Negotiating Custody

At first, the very concept of negotiating custody might seem alien. When you were a family unit, you both had custody—although you probably never thought of it that way. You were just your children's parents, nothing more, nothing less. Together, you decided where they went to school, what religion they practiced, and whether they would go through the ritual of getting braces or attending camp. It was natural in your family—as in most intact families—for you and your spouse to discuss these things and come to an agreement about what was best.

Once you and your spouse no longer live under the same roof, things will change. Now, the two of you will have to decide just how these decisions are made. Will one parent have the final say? What role will the other parent—the one no longer living with the children most of the time—assume? Will one parent feel overburdened with responsibility? Will the other parent feel cut off from his or her children, painfully disenfranchised from their lives? Or will the children alternate between the two of you, inhabiting different homes and bedrooms from one part of the week to the next? Do you think you can share the task of child-rearing, 50/50, even as you end your marital bond?

You must consider these questions as soon as possible. If you can put your personal animosity aside for the moment, you should be able to arrive at a practical, workable custody arrangement. If you can't (assuming you can afford it), court battles—perhaps lasting until your children are emancipated—might ensue.

Custody Is Not Ownership

Any negotiation, of course, is based on the assumption that you understand precisely what custody is—and what it is not. Let's begin with some definitions:

Legal custody. The parent(s) with legal custody has the legal right and responsibility to make decisions for the child.

Physical custody. The parent(s) with whom the child will live has physical custody.

Sole custody. One parent has the right to make all major decisions regarding the children, and the children reside primarily with that parent. The parent who does not have sole custody is called the "noncustodial parent," and—barring abuse, neglect, or abandonment—will have visitation rights, or "parenting time" with the child.

Joint custody. Joint physical custody means the children reside with each parent for an equal length of time. Joint legal custody means the children reside primarily with one parent, but both parents have an equal right to make major decisions about the children's lives.

 YOU CAN DO IT!

"Custody" is an unfortunate term that can make the noncustodial parent feel diminished as a parent. The terms "time-sharing" and "co-parenting" have become popular with psychologists working in the field of divorce and with many divorced people. The new phraseology emphasizes that both parents are still parents—a crucial concept for making life work after the cataclysm of divorce.

Custody does not mean ownership. Children cannot be owned like a car or a house. What custody does mean is that one (or both) parents have the final say in the decision making for major issues in child rearing (legal custody). Custody usually also determines with whom the children primarily reside (physical custody).

Understanding Custody in Your Jurisdiction

The advantage of negotiating a divorce settlement when you have children goes beyond saving time, money, and aggravation. It enables you to tailor your living and custody arrangements to your own children's needs without the cookie-cutter results most courts would impose. This fact alone is worth temporarily putting aside your angry or hurt feelings and trying to reach a settlement.

How to begin thinking about the emotional issue of who gets custody? Even if you plan to settle your divorce, it might help to be aware of the form of custody your jurisdiction prefers or presumes.

For example, in a jurisdiction that has a presumption of sole custody, if you are not able to come to an agreement with your spouse on custody, and your case goes to court, you will have to prove why joint legal—or maybe even joint physical—custody would be in the best interests of your child, given your family's circumstances. To repeat, this does not mean you can't agree to joint legal or physical custody in your own agreement, just that you'll have the burden of proof if you try your case in this situation. In a jurisdiction that has a presumption of some form of joint custody, on the other hand, if you go before a judge, he or she is likely to order a joint custody arrangement unless you prove it would not work for your family.

 SILVER LININGS

Child custody laws of many countries can be easily found online. In the United States, you can either search for your state's laws on child custody or go to the website of the American Bar Association, which lists all the states and their divorce laws: americanbar.org/groups/family_law/resources/family_law_in_the_50_states.html.

European Union member countries' custody laws are listed here: ec.europa.eu/civiljustice/divorce/divorce_gen_en.htm.

Canada: cba.org/CBA/sections_family/main/.

Australia: www.familylawcourts.gov.au/wps/wcm/connect/FLC/Home.

As you navigate your way through this important decision, your primary concern should be how you believe your own children—with their individual temperaments, personalities, fears, and needs—will thrive under a particular custodial arrangement. In particular, if you believe you cannot cooperate on a regular basis with your ex-spouse, you should not consider joint custody, no matter what the preference of your state.

Joint or Sole Custody?

For the sake of the children, the goals of divorcing parents should be the same: involvement of both parents in the lives of the children and mitigation of conflict between the parents. These two factors should dominate all others when thinking about custody.

While sole custody has historically been the most common arrangement after divorce, as women have entered the workforce in greater numbers and fathers have become aware of the benefits of more involvement with their children, time spent with the children has become more equitable. As time is shared more equally, joint custody has become an increasingly popular choice. Whether or not this makes sense for your family depends on a number of factors. Here are some considerations.

A joint custody solution gives a psychological boost to the parent who would otherwise be the noncustodial parent. But, even in a sole-custody situation, generous time-sharing (combined with open communication between parents) can create an environment where a noncustodial parent is significantly involved in the children's lives.

Sometimes it is difficult for mothers or fathers to handle the overwhelming burden of parenting children alone as they work to earn a living. For others, a new life means taking time and space for personal growth, something that primary physical custody would preclude. A man or woman frustrated about his or her own life will not be as effective a father or mother as one who is fulfilled. Rather than feeling guilty, a mother—most often seen as the primary caregiver—who decides to relinquish much of the daily childcare responsibilities may end up benefiting the children simply by being happier and self-assured. At the same time, the father can play a more active role with the children. Joint custody is a good solution for this family.

Is joint custody right for you? That depends a great deal on the ability of you and your spouse to get along. If you are to share decision-making, you must be able to sit down with your former spouse in a noncombative atmosphere and make decisions together. Shared values and parenting styles make this custody style more viable.

Long-term studies have shown that joint custody is a workable option only if the parents have an amicable relationship with each other, communicate well, and understand the nuances of their kid's day-to-day routines. Parents in this situation feel more involved in their children's lives than the noncustodial parent in the sole custody arrangement. On the other hand, in a family where one parent says "black" and the other parent says "white," the children are better off with a sole custody arrangement to reduce the possibility that their parents will fight over every decision that must be made on their behalf.

For parents not on friendly terms, joint legal custody, that is to say, joint decision-making, means more room for disagreement and continuation of conflict. These parents are more likely to return to court than parents who have one decision-maker (sole custody).

If you're able to communicate about the kids, are willing to live in close proximity to your ex, and have the time and resources to share physical custody, then it can be a great thing for everyone.

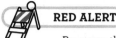 **RED ALERT**

Be aware that young children who do poorly with constant change, have difficulty adjusting to new situations, and seem to need a great deal of stability and security in their lives don't do well with joint physical custody. When evaluating your custody arrangement, the age and temperament of the children should be included in your calculations. This can also be addressed in your time-sharing schedule.

In short, if you can agree to most of the following statements, joint custody could work for your family:

1. I will communicate openly with my ex-spouse regarding the children's needs and activities.

2. I can be flexible in working with my ex-spouse and put my children's needs first.

3. I will never bad-mouth my ex-spouse in front of my children. On the contrary, I will show nothing but respect for my children's other parent.

4. I will respect my ex-spouse's right to have his or her own house rules and not undermine them.

Be honest with yourself. If your feelings don't allow you to accept these guidelines, then get some counseling. If that doesn't work, then joint custody is not a good choice for your family.

When Joint Custody Won't Work

Sometimes it simply isn't possible for divorcing spouses to interact amicably. Consider this situation: Candace and Bill had been snapping at each other for years by the time they decided to divorce. The manager of a medical clinic in the neighborhood, Bill couldn't keep his eyes off Marion, a lab technician 10 years his junior. Eventually, what had started out as an office flirtation turned into a passionate romance, and Bill asked Candace for a divorce. Of course, Candace was shocked. Despite the fact that she, too, was dissatisfied with the marriage, thinking about Bill moving out—to marry someone else—made Candace's heart race with anxiety.

When Bill decided it was time to work out the details of the divorce, he requested joint legal custody of the two children, Gwen, 14, and Martin, 12. The thought of giving up his role as decision-maker was too much to bear. Candace, humiliated by Bill's abrupt dismissal, wanted as little to do with him as possible and could not imagine sitting down to make mutual decisions for the kids.

In this situation, Candace and Bill would have to transcend their bitterness for joint legal custody to work. As long as the animosity continued, it would not be possible to share decisions about the children. If Candace and Bill's situation continued with ongoing conflict, as many of these situations do, joint legal custody would result in more fighting and perennial visits to court.

Determining the Primary Residence

Generally, the parent who has been most involved in the daily care of the children will wind up providing their primary home. Traditionally, this has been the mother, though fathers are increasingly assuming the role of primary caretaker. The court will ultimately look to the best interests of the children to make this decision.

The following is a checklist of routine care giving tasks that might help you decide which parent should maintain the primary residence for the children. Custody should go to the parent who has the most checks on the list. Many jurisdictions use similar criteria. Be honest with yourself when filling out the checklist. Your children will benefit, and you will be more comfortable with the outcome.

	TASK	MOTHER	FATHER
1.	Provides meals	❏	❏
2.	Holds and comforts children	❏	❏
3.	Changes diapers	❏	❏
4.	Dresses children	❏	❏
5.	Bathes children	❏	❏
6.	Plays with children	❏	❏
7.	Takes children to the doctor	❏	❏
8.	Stays home with sick children	❏	❏
9.	Reads stories to children	❏	❏
10.	Takes children to school or activities	❏	❏
11.	Puts children to sleep	❏	❏
12.	Communicates more closely with children	❏	❏
13.	Attends more school events	❏	❏
14.	Disciplines children	❏	❏
15.	Is called by children when they awaken during the night	❏	❏
16.	Who the children seek comfort from	❏	❏
17.	Arranges playtime with friends	❏	❏

Adapted from M. A., and C. B. Garrity. 1988. Children of Divorce: A Developmental Approach to Residence and Visitation. *Psytec: DeKalb, IL.*

The Noncustodial Parent

In a sole-custody arrangement, it's only natural for the parent without custody to feel cut out of the family at first. The parent with custody can help bring the other parent back into the picture by offering generous and flexible time with the children in the settlement agreement. If news about the children is freely shared, and the parent without custody goes to after-school activities and other public events, everyone will begin to settle in. The close relationship between both parents and the children can continue, albeit in separate homes.

Remember, even if the children don't live with you, your relationship with your children goes on, no matter what the official custody decision might be. You can and should continue to be involved with your children. If it's important to you, you can continue to share great times and impart the values you embrace. Whether or not you officially have legal custody or physical custody, you can still have a close and involved relationship with your kids.

A Parent Is Still a Parent

Custody is probably the most sensitive issue for parents going through a divorce (unless, of course, they are in agreement on that issue). In most cases, both parents have been putting their greatest effort into their children, so how can one parent be given sole custody, seemingly relegating the other parent to second place? That's why it is so important to emphasize that custody is simply a legal term, one that fails to fully define the profound meaning of parenthood. Difficult though it is to absorb, loss of legal or physical custody does not have to mean a break in the relationship between parent and child.

The Least You Need to Know

- Custody is not ownership. Both parents will always be parents, and the relationship the parents have with their children is usually within their own control.
- Joint legal custody can work if parents are cooperative.
- Joint physical custody can work if both parents want it and agree to live in close proximity.
- The children's primary residence should be with the parent who was the predominant caretaker of the children before the divorce.

Breaking the News

If you have children and you haven't yet told them about your intention to separate or divorce, this is the moment you're probably dreading. How can you break such news to your children when they look to you for love and security? What will go through their minds as you begin your discussion with them? How can you ease their fears while being realistic about the enormous changes about to occur?

This chapter will address these sensitive issues and provide guidance for addressing the needs of your children during this difficult time. The news of your separation will inevitably cause your children distress, but by taking the appropriate steps, you can help to mitigate their anger and fear.

In This Chapter

- When to tell your child about your separation and pending divorce
- What to say when you break the news
- Helping your child deal with grief, anger, and rejection
- Dealing with real abandonment by a parent

When to Tell Your Children

As soon as you and your spouse have made the decision to separate, it's time to tell your children, no matter how old they are. Even a toddler can understand, if addressed at his or her level. It is far more injurious to wake up one day with Mommy or Daddy gone than to be told in advance—preferably by both parents together—that one of you is moving out.

Telling your children sooner rather than later will ensure that they don't hear the news from another source or overhear you talking to someone else. Deception can promote fantasies about what is really going on, fears of abandonment, wondering about whether they will ever see their departing parent again, and a lack of understanding of the new realities they are about to face. If your children suspect information is being held back, a breach of trust might develop, becoming difficult, if not impossible, to repair.

How to Tell Your Children

Setting the stage for open, honest communication with your children is your most important job at this stage. Ideally, both parents should be involved in telling children about the divorce. Presenting a united front will help your kids by easing their fears of abandonment and will reduce a loyalty conflict—for example, it's all Mom's fault and Dad is the innocent victim.

If you have more than one child, gather them together for a family meeting to break the news. Having all the children together will give each child support from his or her siblings. Let the children know that both of you are available to talk to each of them individually or together again after the meeting. Be prepared for an avalanche of questions regarding the logistics of the divorce, custody, and visitation. Even money may be of concern to the children.

What to Tell Your Children

As always, your aim is to protect your children while being as open and honest as you can, given the circumstances and their ages and development. So don't go into all the gory details. However, children who are told nothing about the reasons for their parents' divorce are unnecessarily frustrated and have a more difficult time working things through.

Some children, especially older ones, might not be particularly surprised by the news. Alicia, a 13-year-old, recently had this to say: "My parents had been cold to each other for a long time. Sometimes, they would scream at each other, and all I wanted to do was run away. It came as no surprise when they sat me down and told me they were getting a divorce."

SILVER LININGS

Not all children will be surprised that their parents are divorcing. In some cases, when there have been nightly battles, children are actually happier knowing they'll never have to hear the shouting and name-calling again.

For children who have not been exposed to fighting, an explanation will go a long way toward helping them digest the news. Be as forthcoming as possible about why the marriage is ending, while staying appropriate. When speaking to your children in a group, use language that even the youngest can understand.

Telling the children that you are going to divorce and why is the toughest part of the family meeting. But it is only the beginning. Because children are centered in their own world, they need to have precise and concrete information about how their lives will change. By the end of the discussion with your kids, they should know:

- As much as appropriately possible—given their ages and maturity—about the reasons for the divorce.

- When the separation will take place.

- Where the parent who is moving out will live.

- With whom they will live during and after the divorce.

- When and under what circumstances they will see their other parent.

- Whether they will be moving into a new house or apartment.

- That they will have open communication with the parent who is moving out.

 RED ALERT

Don't bad-mouth your ex! Your children's relationship with their other parent is separate from yours. Respect their relationship. Trying to be objective about the reasons for your divorce is especially hard if you've been left or if you are battling it out with your spouse. For the children's sake, you must rise to the occasion. Even though it might seem to you that there is an obvious good guy and bad guy—as in the case of the infidelity of one parent—the reality is almost never that clear-cut.

Each parent should cover one or two points and then give the other a turn. To see how it works, here is one possible scenario. (Of course, you should modify the specifics, depending on the age of your children and your own situation.)

> **Dad:** As you may know, your Mom and I haven't been getting along for a while now. Although we were once happy together, we've grown apart. We tried to work things out and have been seeing a marriage counselor for quite a while, but, unfortunately, it hasn't worked.
>
> We're not getting along, and neither one of us is happy. This makes living together uncomfortable. So we've decided to live separately and then get a divorce. You have done nothing to cause us to divorce. It is not your fault. This is between your mother and me.
>
> **Mom:** I'm sure you know that we both love you very much. Just because your Dad and I have decided not to live with each other anymore doesn't mean that we don't want to be with you. Parents can divorce each other, but they do not ever divorce their kids. We will be your Mom and Dad forever. We will always be there for you just as before. You will always be taken care of. You will always have a home. Each of us will be with you, just usually not at the same time.
>
> **Dad:** I rented an apartment a few blocks away, and I'll be moving there next Saturday. You'll be living with your Mom and coming over to live with me every other weekend. We'll also get together once a week for dinner and homework help. We'll be sharing each holiday. I'll call you every night after school, and you can call me anytime. You'll have your own room at my apartment, and you can decorate it any way you want. (If the living arrangement is not yet settled, you can say, "The details haven't been worked out yet, but we'll let you know as soon as they are.")
>
> **Mom:** Your family will always be your family, even though Dad and I aren't going to be in the same house. Your grandparents, aunts, uncles, and cousins will still be your family—those relationships won't change.
>
> If you have any questions, you can ask them now, or you can talk to Dad or me later at any time. Remember, we'll always be there for you, and we love you very much.

If you and your spouse are in a heated battle, or if your spouse has left suddenly, a family meeting with both parents will probably be out of the question. Even though you might not know all the details of the living arrangements, you should tell your children whatever information you have, to give them a handle on the changes in their lives—but do not tackle this until you've calmed down.

When talking to your children, set aside your anger. Blaming one parent will only cause confusion. Because your children are emotionally attached to the other parent, they will feel conflicting loyalty. Not only will your child feel torn between his parents, but also, eventually, he might react against you to defend his relationship with the other parent.

When 12-year-old Michelle was told by her mother that her dad had moved out after a final blow-up the night before, Michelle was devastated. Her mother was so angry at her dad that she blamed him for all the ills of their marriage: she had to do all the housework, even though she worked; he would come home late at night; they never went out because he was too frugal; and other complaints.

At first, Michelle was sympathetic to her mother and understood her unhappiness. She felt angry at her dad for not being more considerate of her mother's feelings. But after a week had passed, Michelle started to feel guilty for having bad thoughts about her father. She missed him. She began to wonder whether her mother had told her the whole truth and even started developing feelings of resentment toward her mother; had her mother, she wondered, been instrumental in driving her father out of the house? The more her mother spoke against her father, the more difficult it was for Michelle to sustain a warm relationship with her.

Helping Children Cope With Divorce

No matter how "correctly" you explain things to your children, they will still experience a range of emotions, including disbelief, fear, anger, rejection, and grief. The only thing worse for parents than seeing their children suffer is being the cause of that suffering. Parents in the throes of divorce often find themselves in that situation, but they are too tied up in their own pain to take notice.

It is impossible to shield your children from all the hurt life brings. However, the breakup of a family and possibly the loss of one parent is surely one of the toughest hurdles for any child to overcome. This moment and the next year or two will test your emotional strength and your parenting skills to the limit. You think you're not up to the task? You are. You have no choice, and there is a lot of support for you in the community. Friends, family, psychologists, teachers, religious leaders, your lawyer, websites, and books are all there to help you manage this transition. Use whatever resources you need to acquire the knowledge and support necessary to help your children get through the initial shock, adjust to the changes about to begin, and adapt to their new way of living.

No matter how troubled your children might seem in the wake of your divorce, you can help them heal by viewing the world through their eyes. Karen Breunig, co-author (with psychologists Mitchell Baris, Carla Garrity, and Janet R. Johnston) of *Through the Eyes of Children: Healing Stories for Children of Divorce*, notes that parents must be aware of three overriding issues and deal with them up front:

Children fear that they will not be allowed to love both parents without interference. To address this concern, says Breunig, parents must remember that loving the other parent is a child's birthright. A child is partly like each parent, she notes, and "when you tear down your ex-spouse in front of your child, you're tearing down a part of your child."

Children harbor the fantasy that their parents will reunite. Parents must acknowledge that the child has these feelings, Breunig states, at the same time making it clear that reuniting is out of the question. "You must support your child in their grief," she notes, "so that he or she understands it's safe to talk about feelings without fear of rejection. You must listen to the feelings while, at the same time, telling the child that you and your ex will both be there to parent them, but that you cannot promise a reconciliation will ever take place."

Children may be emotionally damaged if exposed to too much anger and rage, even if those feelings are not directed at them. "Emotions run so high in a divorce," says Breunig, "that it takes tremendous adult responsibility to shield children from all the things it would be damaging for them to hear. People often can't control their feelings in the midst of an emotionally damaging divorce, but they can control how they act out those feelings in front of their children. If you've just found out that your spouse has been unfaithful and wants a divorce, it would be very difficult to hide the situation from a child, depending upon age. In such situations, it is not necessarily unhealthy for them to see your grief and sadness. But it can be quite damaging for them to see your rage or hear you lambaste the other parent. Children must be spared the pain of adult emotional business, as much as possible."

Dealing with Fears

Children of divorce are usually most fearful of abandonment and loss of parental love. It is crucial, therefore, that you take every opportunity to reassure your children that their parents love them and will always be there for them. According to psychologist Mitchell Baris, PhD, "What differentiates a parent-child relationship from any other kind of relationship is loyalty. Mom will always be Mom, and Dad will always be Dad, and nobody else will ever replace them. Even if the parents remarry, even if they'll be living in two houses, or even if one parent will be living far away, Dad will always be Dad, and Mom will always be Mom."

Let them know (assuming that one parent is not actually abandoning the family) that they will have a continuing relationship with both parents—even if, for the moment, you wish you would never see your spouse again! (If you have trouble saying things that you know are in the children's best interests but that stick in your throat, try viewing your spouse as their parent rather than your archenemy. Just for now, put yourself in his or her shoes.)

Dealing with Blame

Children are likely to blame one or both parents for the divorce. Sometimes—and of more concern—children blame themselves. Reassure your children repeatedly that the separation has nothing to do with them. Assure them that although parents can divorce each other, they cannot divorce their children—nor would they ever want to.

Dealing with Anger

Your children might not evidence or express anger until after the shock of the announcement has worn off. Anger, if not constructively channeled, can become outwardly destructive or self-destructive. Hidden feelings can fester and manifest in ways that seem unconnected to the separation.

Eric, for instance, had a close friend, Alex. They saw each other at school every day and often went over to each other's house after school. After Eric's parents announced their separation, he fought with Alex over everything. It seemed that Alex couldn't do anything right. Because Eric kept the news about his parents' divorce to himself, Alex didn't have a clue about what was going wrong. Alex stopped seeing Eric. Eric lost a best friend at a time he needed one the most.

To help your children work through this anger, make yourself available. Children need to know that their feelings count. Listen attentively when your children want to talk. Answer questions as honestly as you can. The more your children can express their feelings, the easier the adjustment will be.

When a Child Is Abandoned

What if, in the worst-case scenario, your spouse announces that he or she plans to abandon the family and have absolutely nothing to do with the children after the divorce?

If possible, it behooves you to convince your partner that the children need him or her in their lives, no matter what. Communicating this urgent message to a spouse who is threatening abandonment might be your best weapon against the devastation of parental loss. Ironically, some parents abandon their children because they, themselves, lack self-esteem. They think their children would do better without them. If your spouse harbors such feelings, you must do your best to explain how crucial he or she is to your child's well-being.

What if, despite your urgings, or completely to your surprise, your spouse actually just up and leaves? If this was a surprise to you, your own shock will make it monumentally more difficult to tell your children. You know intuitively that your children's self-esteem will be affected by your spouse's decision to cut them off. No matter how hard it is for you, it is far more damaging to your children because children don't have an adult's perspective on life or the inner resources to handle such extraordinary rejection and hurt. Your children might experience self-doubt, depression, and regression.

It is your job to pick up the pieces. If you are the parent who has remained, you must be there with all your love and support, making sure your children understand that there's nothing wrong with them. They are worthwhile and cherished by you. Instead, it is the parent who left who has the problems.

Remind your children that the flight of their other parent has nothing to do with them; they bear absolutely no blame. Also remind them that they still possess your constant, unconditional love, as well as the love and support of other family and friends. Be cautioned that it is unfair to give the children hope that someday their parent might return.

As the remaining parent, it is also your job to be on the lookout for the psychological side effects of rejection and abandonment. Your children might very well experience strong feelings of low self-esteem, a longing for the departed parent, and eventually anger. If there are any signs of depression after a three-month period, consult a psychologist.

The Least You Need to Know

- Telling your children that your marriage is ending is difficult but not insurmountable. If you and your spouse can manage to share this task, your children will benefit.

- Trust can be achieved by being as open and honest with your children as is appropriate for their age.

- Your children's sense of security will be enhanced if you and your spouse can assure them of a continued relationship with both parents.

- Try to work out the children's future living arrangements before you announce your plans to separate or divorce. Tell the children about these plans when you announce the divorce itself.

- Helping your children handle their grief, anger, and feelings of rejection will be your most important job in the coming months. If you are overwhelmed, seek professional help during this crisis period.

- Actual abandonment by one parent is a difficult scenario for children. Do what you can to prevent it, but if that's not possible, assure your children of your love for them.

Working Out Time-Sharing Schedules

Children of divorce not only suffer the trauma of a family split, they must also adapt to the stress of travelling from one parent's home to the other's and back again. Some adjust well to this involuntary lifestyle change; some have a harder time. In either case, children want to be involved with each parent but may have to put up with some inconvenience in the process.

This chapter addresses some of the issues that arise as your family adapts to the new routine.

When Parents Live Apart

To make shared parenting time work for the kids, it helps if each parent is tuned in to his or her children's individual and developmental needs.

Here are some tips for making co-parenting work:

- Cooperate with the other parent as much as possible.

- Keep each other informed of what's going on when it comes to a child's schooling, medical care, and social life.

In This Chapter

- Tips for successful time-sharing
- How to handle holidays
- Making time-sharing work when parents are at war
- When kids should have a say

- Establish a polite business relationship with the other parent.

- Be responsible in maintaining the time-sharing schedule. If a change must be made, work it out with the other parent in advance.

- Respect the rules of the other parent's household, just as you respect the rules of school and other public institutions.

- Don't send messages to the other parent through your children. Business should be conducted only between parents.

It's All About Attitude

To co-parent successfully, you must maintain a positive attitude. If you see your ex as your children's parent, rather than as your archenemy, you stand a better chance of making co-parenting work.

 **SILVER LININGS**

You have a great deal of control over the way your children handle life after divorce. By cooperating with the other parent, you are establishing a life pattern your children can carry into the future.

For example, don't criticize the parenting skills of the other parent. You may be tempted to comment on wrinkled clothing or messy hair when you pick up your children from your ex-spouse's home. However, unless there's a real cause for concern over safety, it is best to keep these comments in check. Your children will pick up on these negative statements, and it could damage their relationship not just with the other parent, but with you.

Likewise, don't focus on every negative comment your children make about the other parent when they're with you. Check your attitude: do you secretly relish these comments because you can't stand your ex and hope your kids support your view? Are you in competition with your ex for the kids' loyalty? Unless your children are saying something very disturbing about the other parent (physical or mental abuse, alcohol or drug abuse), any negative comments your children might make are often best taken with a grain of salt. Don't blow such comments out of proportion, and remember, your children might resent and distrust you if you cheer them on.

On the other hand, be realistic. Don't overcompensate for your negative feelings toward your ex by bending over backward to paint him or her as perfect. Nothing in life is all good or all bad, so how could it be that way for your children's experience at either home? Children should understand that there will be fun times and boring times, happy times and angry times, with each parent. In any case, portraying your ex as all good will have a false ring to your kids.

As you adjust to this new routine, keep any angry feelings you have toward your ex-spouse between you, your therapist if you have one, and your friends or family. Try to put a lid on your anger when you're with your kids. Sometimes anger comes out indirectly through a negative attitude towards things related to your ex-spouse. This might be confusing and potentially damaging to your kids. It's important to identify unconscious attitudes that you might not realize you express, because your kids' radar will pick them up.

What's your attitude toward your ex? Here's a quick quiz to find out. If you answer "Yes" to two or more of the following items, you need an attitude change!

- I hate my ex so much, I can't stand the thought of my kids being with him (her). _____Yes _____No

- When my kids come back from seeing their other parent, I tell them to take a shower or bath to wash my ex's presence away. _____Yes _____No

- When my kids tell me they had a good time with their other parent, it ties my stomach in knots. _____Yes _____No

- Whenever my kids say nice things about their other parent, my lips start to purse, and I'm silent, or I get the urge to say something really bad. _____Yes _____No

- If my kids report that their other parent is doing well and is happy, I get a sinking feeling in my stomach. _____Yes _____No

- I "accidentally" say things against my ex to friends or family within earshot of my kids. _____Yes _____No

- If asked, I can't come up with one good thing to say about my ex. _____Yes _____No

We hope this little quiz will tune you in to your feelings and bring them to the surface. Not only will this be beneficial to your children, but it might help you deal with some of the anger that is boiling inside you.

Age-Appropriate Time-Sharing

Although it's important for both parents to maintain a relationship with their children, schedules based simply on dividing up the number of days in a calendar year without regard for the children's age, psychological needs, or temperament can cause unnecessary stress; for very young children, ignoring these factors may cause permanent psychological harm.

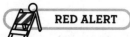 **RED ALERT**

If your very young child is grieving for the other parent, he will not be able to focus on his relationship with you. Give your child the time he needs to adjust to separation from his primary caregiver.

For most children, the ability to make transitions from place to place increases with age. For time-sharing to work, both parents must be attuned to their children's unique requirements and needs, as well as the general developmental pattern that most children follow from birth through the teen years.

Infancy to Two-and-a-Half Years

Infancy, psychologists agree, is a time for building an attachment to the primary caretaker. (Attachment to two primary caretakers, a mother and father, is increasingly common, too.) The infant's developmental task is to form trust in the environment. Long separations from the primary caretaker can result in symptoms of depression and regression and later may result in problems with separation and the ability to form relationships.

At this age, toddlers are beginning to develop a sense of independence. They are becoming aware of themselves and beginning to speak and walk. They can use symbols to comfort themselves, such as a picture of Mom or a toy she gave them.

Because the successful attainment of these developmental tasks lays the foundation for secure and healthy children, parents should design a schedule that fits a child's needs at this stage. The best schedule, say the experts, is short but frequent time with the noncustodial parent: short because infants and toddlers can't maintain the image of their primary caretaker for long, and frequent to enable them to bond with the noncustodial parent. Most psychologists agree there should be no overnights for very young children.

In cases where both parents share physical custody, frequent daily time with each parent is the ideal.

There are many innovative ways to share parenting responsibility at this stage. We know one couple who bought a second home in the wife's name following the divorce. Their child, a little girl, stayed on in the old house, now in the father's name. The parents shared custody by taking turns staying in the original family homestead. The "off-duty" parent lived in the new house. In short, the child had one stable home; instead, it was the parents who bore the brunt of constant change by moving back and forth. This model is known as "nesting" or "bird nesting" for the obvious reason that the young remain in the nest, as the parents come and go.

Two-and-a-Half to Five Years

This is a time of continued growth and individuality. These young children can now hold the absent parent in mind for longer periods of time. Their language is developed enough to enable these youngsters to express feelings and needs. They have more control over their feelings and bodily functions. This is also the age when children begin to identify more with the same-sex parent.

Although it ultimately depends on the temperament of the individual child, this is typically the age where time away from the primary caretaker can increase, and overnights can be introduced. If the child resists long periods away from her primary caretaker, short but frequent visits should continue until the child is better able to withstand longer separations.

Those who share physical custody must continue to be sensitive to their child's reaction to continual change.

Six to Eight Years

The hallmark of this period is development of peer and community relationships, a moral sense, empathy, and better self-regulation of impulses. Children develop a concept of themselves as they gain competence and master skills.

For children to develop normally, it's important during this age for the noncustodial parent to participate in the activities within the community in which the children live. At this stage, children thrive on consistent contact with friends, school, and extra-curricular activities. Although the length of time away from home can be increased for those ages six to eight, if a child is homesick, most child development experts recommend that the time away should be decreased to a tolerable level.

Nine to Twelve Years

During these years, children develop their academic, athletic, and artistic skills. They become more involved in community activity. There is an increased desire to maintain friendships and seek approval of peers, as well as growing self-awareness as they begin to evaluate their own strengths and weaknesses against the larger arena of the world.

As before, the noncustodial parent is advised to schedule visits, as much as possible, within the orbit of the child's home base. The closer children feel to the noncustodial parent, the more agreeable they will be to segments of time away from community activities and friends.

Thirteen to Eighteen Years

This period marks the beginning of psychological emancipation as children establish their personal identity more strongly than ever before. There is a mourning of the loss of child-hood as children relinquish dependency and the protection of the family circle to venture out on their own. Kids at this age are dealing with their sexual feelings. They are also beginning to see how to work within the rules and regulations of society.

At this age, children have generally come to count on a fairly established schedule and routine. Nonetheless, that may change as these teenage children seek to have input into the schedule so that it dovetails with their increasingly complex academic and social lives. It is difficult to force an adolescent into a schedule he or she did not help to create. In fact, if you are divorcing when your child is this age, don't be surprised if the judge meets with him or her to hear what he or she has to say. Many jurisdictions allow a judge to consider (but not necessarily defer to) the preferences of any child over the age of 12, giving due weight to the child's individual maturity and development.

Adopt an attitude of sensitivity and flexibility when it comes to the schedule you establish for your children. If your children are nearing adolescence, their social agenda will be paramount to them. Although spending time with their parents is very important (and sacred for the noncustodial parent), parents who respect their children's needs to develop a social life of their own will be helping them to grow normally.

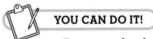 **YOU CAN DO IT!**

Teenagers often feel displaced in the wake of divorce, and the experts say that support groups of peers can often be particularly helpful. Do look to get your adolescent involved in a well-run support activity to help with the transition.

In situations where physical custody is shared, parents should consider living within a few blocks of each other in the same town. Expecting teens with school, sports, and social lives to "commute" is unfair.

Scheduled for Success

As the years pass, it is normal to revise a schedule so that children spend increasingly more time away from the primary home. As changes are made, however, parents must be sensitive to any signs that a child is being pushed beyond his or her capabilities. Remember that your relationship does not depend on the actual number of hours or days you spend with your children but on the degree of your involvement, concern, and openness to your children's emotional and developmental needs. Don't push your children beyond their temperament and capabilities.

One mother we know was allowed to see her daughter for two hours a week at a local mall, a temporary restrictive agreement that resulted because it was alleged that she used drugs. The mother was told she would have to participate in a 12-step program or some other kind of rehab before a more liberal schedule was allowed. The daughter missed her mother and treasured the time. The mother, meanwhile, felt two hours insufficient and, after two months in rehab, petitioned the court for extra hours at the mall. The judge granted the mother four hours at the mall, but so much time trudging around a mall after school was exhausting to the little girl. Though she loved her mother, she began to dread the exertion of the sessions and made excuses so she didn't have to go. The sessions resumed only when the mother promised the girl could go home when two hours were up. Remember, your children may love to see you and may miss you greatly, but they are still children, so any arrangement must be sensitive to their needs.

Most noncustodial parents, of course, are awarded far more time with their children than this unfortunate mom. Parents with liberal time-sharing or joint legal custody have been creative and flexible in myriad ways, designing schedules that range from alternate weeks at each parent's home, to rotating every other weekend, to living primarily at one parent's home. With shared custody the time-sharing can be as much as 50-50, depending on the child's age. You know your kids best, so think about what would work for them.

Finding a Routine that Fits

Different families have different needs, and it may take some trial and error to find a schedule that works for you, your kids, and your former spouse. In some cases, consulting with a child therapist may be helpful. This professional can recommend the best approach for your kids based on their ages and dispositions. A therapist may also be able to suggest ways to involve older children in the decision-making process.

Remember that you may need to try a few different arrangements before you find one that fits. For example, you may find that your young children are not adapting well to spending two nights in a row away from their primary residence. They're not sleeping through the night, and they have a hard time leaving their primary caregiver. In this case, it might be helpful to scale back so your kids are only spending one night with the noncustodial parent, while building in more weekday visits. If possible, introduce changes to the schedule gradually and incrementally.

At the other age extreme, your teenagers are likely more interested in being with their friends than with either parent. They are also burdened by more homework and usually many extra-curricular activities. On the weekends, they would feel left out if invited to a party but couldn't go because they were supposed to be with their other parent. In this situation, parents should be flexible to ensure their teenagers can thrive. If the situation cuts one parent off in deference to another, the family—including the teen—may need to rebalance priorities.

SILVER LININGS

According to Dr. Janet Johnston, an expert in high-conflict divorce at San Jose State University in California, if a 6-year-old expresses a clear preference about the schedule, parents should try to accommodate those wishes with these caveats: make sure the child is not just trying to please a parent, and don't let him know it was his idea! Children of this age can't handle the power of making the decision themselves. It's too frightening. Parents should listen to children from ages 9 through 12, and their views should be given consideration. By the time children are teenagers, they can be given more say in determining their schedule, but it is up to the parents to make the final decision.

Keeping the Joy in Holidays

Holidays are precious times of the year for many people, and you'll probably want to be with your children on these occasions most of all. Because they are so important, deciding how to divide the time can be difficult. It's essential that you agree on an arrangement that is fair to both parents and to the kids.

If Christmas is an important holiday in your house, you may find that alternating Christmas Day and Christmas Eve each year provides a good compromise. That way, each parent can share gift-giving and a Christmas tree with their children.

Jewish families may decide to split up the holidays or alternate them. For example, the parent who was not with children for Rosh Hashanah is with them on Yom Kippur. Hanukkah and Passover might be divided in half. Parents of other religions can use these examples for your holiday scheduling.

For some families, sharing school vacations may be more important than celebrating religious holidays. In this case, parents might decide to each take one break and alternate between winter and spring each year. The summer break allows more time for each parent to be with their children. Parents can divide the time when their kids are not in summer camp or other programs in which a child is not with either parent. If you have more than one child, you can swap kids with your former spouse so you can spend more time with each child.

Whatever you choose, keep in mind that your kids won't enjoy these special days if they're a source of bickering and resentment between you and your spouse. Embrace the holiday time you have with your kids, and do your best not to detract from the holidays they spend with the other parent.

Long-Distance Parenting

Although moving is sometimes necessary for employment circumstances, it's always better for both parents to stay within reasonable driving distance to the children. Once a parent moves far away, the children will be much less likely to see that parent on a regular basis, and they will probably have a stressful schedule—long summers away from the custodial parent with little contact during the school year. Added to that, they will usually have to travel long distances to see their parent.

The courts understand the negative impact when one parent lives too far from the child to have regular contact. Many states thus prohibit the custodial parent from moving out of state or beyond a certain distance from the noncustodial parent. In recent years such strictures have eased. This change was based on the premise that if the custodial parent is happy, the children will be happy, too. Restrictions against moving are not imposed on the noncustodial parent. Although a judge might refrain from getting involved in such decisions, negotiated divorce settlements can impose restrictions on moving for one or both parents.

Although it's not an ideal situation, if a noncustodial parent moves to another state or even another country, he or she can remain in close contact with the children. There are many modes of communication; find one that works for your kids and use it as frequently as possible. Maybe your toddler loves watching you play peek-a-boo on Skype, or perhaps your teenager is quiet on the phone, but eager to text.

When Steve moved from New York to Dallas for a terrific job opportunity, he still wanted to stay close to his children, Tim, 5, and Alex, 9. Steve called them every night before they went to bed. He also often sent emails, sometimes with photos of his new neighborhood or videos of himself taken by a friend. Steve also came up with some clever ideas for relating to his children while he was not with them. He told them to pick a television program they liked, and he would watch it, too. Later, they would talk about the show. He sent puzzles and riddles that the children could finish, and he would ask them how they did. Every six weeks, Steve spent a four-day weekend with Tim and Alex in their town. He also alternated school holidays with his ex-wife. In this way, Tim and Alex maintained a pretty close relationship with their dad, even though he lived a couple thousand miles away.

Time-Sharing in High-Conflict Situations

Divorce is often born of conflict. But when extreme conflict persists even after the couple has parted ways, the children of that marriage may find it difficult, if not impossible, to heal. Indeed, when parents cannot put their mutual anger aside, and when they sweep their young children into the conflict, they have ceased to protect their children.

Children of high-conflict divorce, torn between the two most important people in their lives, are often emotionally damaged by the struggle. According to psychologists, such children are often depressed and aggressive. Later, as adults, they may have difficulty maintaining intimate relationships. They are far more likely to divorce than adults who come from intact families or even divorced families at peace.

Time-Sharing Schedule Recommendations

Because open conflict is most likely to take place at the time the children go from one home to the other, many psychologists specializing in divorced families now recommend that the number of transition times be reduced in high-conflict situations. Here are some specific recommendations for time-sharing schedules when open warfare rages:

For moderate conflict. When parents function well on their own but fight when they are in contact with their ex-spouse, psychologists Mitchell Baris, PhD, and Carla Garrity, PhD, note that other creative solutions are necessary. Some of these may be minimizing transitions—packaging stays at each parent's home into one block per week. For very young children, the midweek visits might be eliminated. For older children, the visits might be consolidated each week. These may need to be handled by a neutral third party or take place in neutral places.

For moderately severe conflict. When there is constant litigation, and sometimes even physical threats or abuse between parents, children can suffer extreme emotional scars. In such cases, Baris and Garrity recommend caution. Mental health evaluation is mandatory, and supervised times with such a parent may be recommended if the safety of a child is a concern.

For severe conflict. In this situation, when children are at immediate risk of physical or sexual abuse, seeing this parent should be supervised and a full mental health evaluation conducted.

When Your Child Needs Help

Children of high-conflict divorce are often hit hardest, even when they seem upbeat on the outside. Parents who fail to notice the warning signs of a child in emotional trouble will pay a high price later. When does your child need help? New York psychologist Michelle Gersten, EdD, provides the following guidelines:

Maladaptive personality changes of extreme intensity or duration. If your child has changed in any major way since the separation, trouble may be afoot. Warning signs include inattentiveness, hyperactivity, aggression, shyness, or fearfulness. Maladaptive behaviors, of course, should set off alarms. Remember, all children involved in divorce may show minor difficulties, including eating and sleeping problems. But if these symptoms are short-lived, you probably don't have to be concerned. On the other hand, if a school-aged child who previously had healthy relations with her peers starts withdrawing from social activities, be on the lookout for trouble.

Regression. If your child has regressed to behaviors from earlier stages of development, seek psychotherapy. Examples might include a 4-year-old who now has frequent accidents, despite successful toilet training previously, or an 8-year-old who speaks in baby talk.

Extreme parental conflict. If the parents continue to fight in front of the child after the initial breakup, therapy may be required. If one parent is manipulative or continually undermines the other, psychotherapy for the child is indicated as well. (Psychotherapy for the parents would help, too.) In one case, a mother consistently failed to inform the father of plans and then told the child the father had simply failed to show. The father, in turn, told the child that the mother "just forgot." The stress of the situation was arduous for the

5-year-old boy, who became confused about his alliances and ultimately needed therapy to successfully relate to his mom and his dad.

The Role of the Parenting Coordinator

Researchers and practitioners, such as Mitchell Baris, Carla Garrity, and Janet Johnston, who work with families in high-conflict divorce situations, developed the concept of the *parenting coordinator.* The parenting coordinator, who must be familiar with family law, conflict resolution, mediation, family therapy, and child development, is not a mediator or a therapist. Instead, this third party works within the confines of the divorce decree to settle disagreements between parents as they pertain to the children.

A court orders the enlistment of a parenting coordinator in high-conflict situations in some states. The states that have passed legislation regarding parenting coordinators so far include Colorado, Idaho, Louisiana, New Hampshire, North Carolina, Oklahoma, Oregon, Texas, Massachusetts, and Florida. Depending on the state, the parenting coordinator may report regularly to the court and can speak to the children's therapist. The therapist is protected from litigation so that she can work with the children without being pressured or manipulated by either parent. In some states parents can decide in their settlement agreement to use a parenting coordinator to facilitate the parenting plan. The function and limitations of the parenting coordinator are usually determined by the courts.

 **DEFINITION**

> A **parenting coordinator** is an individual, perhaps a psychologist familiar with matrimonial law, who works with both parents to iron out any problems that may arise after the divorce decree is in effect. Sometimes parenting coordinators are assigned by judges, but parents can also voluntarily choose to enlist the aid of a parenting coordinator. For more information, check the website of the Association of Family and Conciliation Courts at afccnet.org.

The parenting coordinator can also be a facilitator between parents in high conflict. If one parent wants to send something to the children, he or she can send it to the parenting coordinator to make sure that the children receive it. The parenting coordinator may at times determine when the children are ready for increased time, which may have been shortened or curtailed because of the conflict. The court must approve any recommendation. The parenting coordinator maps out a detailed parenting plan, which is agreed to by all parties. In fact, your jurisdiction may require parents to file a "parenting plan" if custody is an issue in your divorce. (Some jurisdictions require a parenting plan for all families during the divorce process.) The more detailed the plan, the less room for conflict.

The plan below is tailored for parents in a high-conflict divorce. Points covered in the parenting plan might include the following:

Time-sharing schedule. Sets a drop-off and pick-up time and place, designates a means for transporting children between households, institutes a set plan for handling a refusal to visit, and decides who is responsible when children are sick.

Schedule change requests. A set protocol for trading days or making last-minute changes.

Phone call and Skype policy. Should they be regulated? Should children or the "other" parent be able to initiate phone calls or Skype in private at any time?

Toys and belongings. Provides guidelines for moving things between two households.

Boundaries or rules at other household. Neither parent can tell the other parent what rules to set; if abuse or possible abduction is suspected or concerns about parental judgment persist, the parenting coordinator, judge, or mediator must be contacted.

Pets. Establishes rules for moving them back and forth between homes with the children.

Advice from Those Who Know Best

Children of divorce have strong feelings and thoughts about how they should be treated by their parents. A word to the wise—heed the wisdom of the children.

Here are some recommendations to parents from veteran children of divorce:

- Recognize that we love and need both parents.

- Don't turn us into messengers. Mom and Dad should talk to each other directly.

- Don't say bad things about our other parent.

- Don't grill us about what is going on at our other parent's home.

- Don't ask us to take sides.

- Don't make us feel as if we're being disloyal to you if we enjoy being with our other parent.

- If you have something angry to say to our other parent, don't say it around us.

- Don't purposely forget important clothing or gear when we are going to our other parent's place.

How your children fare in the aftermath of divorce in large part depends on the degree of sensitivity you and your ex-spouse have towards your kids' needs. If you put your children's needs first and are able to take a step back from your own emotional turmoil, you will greatly relieve the stress on your children.

The Least You Need to Know

- One of the most difficult lifestyle changes children undergo as a result of their parents' divorce is moving back and forth between homes instead of living in one stable environment.
- Establish a polite business relationship with the other parent. Share important information about the children's academic, social, and health news.
- Time-sharing schedules should take the age and temperament of the children into account. The schedule should provide regular and predictable times for the children to be with each parent.
- The court can order a parenting coordinator to help with your parenting plan and make recommendations to the court for modifications. If your state does not yet recognize this professional function, a child psychologist can perform a similar role.
- Monitor your children's progress with the schedule. If they are not adjusting, modify the schedule.
- Never put your children in the middle of the fighting. Don't ask them to ally with you against their other parent.

Two Parents, Two Homes

Transitions are difficult for children, especially young children. Try to remember what it feels like when you stay at a friend's house; there's the strange bed and bathroom, the likes and dislikes of the person you're visiting, the different routines. The first night you might feel uncomfortable. You miss your own bed, your carpet, your morning coffee; you long to be free to look really grungy until you're done with your morning routine. Imagine this scenario, and you will begin to understand what your child's back-and-forth experience is like. To your advantage, you are an adult with an adult's perspective. Children, on the other hand, experience time differently. What might be just a weekend to you feels more like a month to a child. What might be a two-week summer vacation to you seems like a lifetime to a child.

In This Chapter

- Coping skills for children transitioning between households
- How your attitude can help your children
- When children refuse to go to the other parent's house
- What to do if you suspect abuse

Although your children love their other parent, the transition between households might still be hard because it is a major change in your children's reality. For them, every reunion is also a separation; every "hello" is also a "good-bye."

Each parent should give the children time to adjust to the transition and not get overly concerned with behaviors that seem unusual during the initial period after arriving at your home. Be sensitive. Read a book or do some other quiet activity with them. If they seem to need some space, finish what you were doing before they came over. In time, things will get back to normal.

Strategies to Cope with Change

Here are some ideas for helping your kids handle the transition from one parent to the other. You know your children best, so think about what makes sense for your family:

- Make a calendar with your kids. The calendar should include the highlights of their schedule, especially those times when they will be with the other parent.

- Remind them the day prior to the visit that they're going to see their other parent the next day.

- Depending on the age of your children, help them pack their bag the day before they leave. If they are school-aged, make sure that their homework is included.

- Have a young child choose his or her own traveling bag. His input into this symbol of his transition will help give him a feeling of involvement and control.

- To ease the packing and make them feel more comfortable when they are at the other parent's house, arrange to have them keep the basics (toothbrush, comb, pajamas, and so on) at both houses.

- Give very young children a traveling bear or other stuffed toy to help provide a sense of security.

- Let your child take a picture of the absent parent with him or her.

 SILVER LININGS

A child will probably get more one-on-one attention from his parents after the divorce than before the divorce. If one parent didn't spend much time with the children pre-separation, he or she might now spend much more time with them. The custodial parent may feel that this is just a ploy to reduce child support (more time spent might reduce support), but this may be the best news for the children.

Making the Exchange Smoothly

If you and your spouse or ex-spouse have a working relationship, the transition from one home to the other is easier on both the parents and the children. Children sense their parents' tacit approval and take with them the good wishes of the parent they are leaving. Even though the sudden change is stressful, knowing that the parent being left supports the departure and will be fine during their absence gives the children the foundation they need to cope.

Your Ex Is Your Child's Parent

We know we've said this before, but it's so important that it bears repeating. Keep your feelings about your ex-spouse to yourself. To lessen the uncomfortable feelings you might have when you face your ex-spouse during the exchange, see him or her through your child's eyes, as your child's parent. This technique will help keep your attitude positive during the exchange, which in turn will allow your children to feel okay about leaving you. And you really want your children to feel okay about leaving you. (Don't worry; they'll come back!)

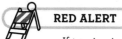 **RED ALERT**

> If tension is very high, as it might be at the beginning of the separation, it is better to have a third party make the exchange or have one parent drop off the children at school or an after-school activity and the other parent pick them up.

Shielding Your Children from Conflict

If you think you're delivering your children to the enemy, they will sense your tension.

Follow these guidelines for reducing parental conflict:

- Communicate only when necessary. If necessary, limit communication to email in order to reduce face-to-face exchanges.

- Keep a mental image of your spouse as your children's parent.

- Think of your parenting relationship as a business relationship.

- Don't get hooked into old patterns of fighting or being goaded into a nasty retort.

- Use clear and simple language without taking a judgmental or accusatory stance.

- Keep conversations as brief as possible.

- End any communication that looks as if it might escalate into a shouting match.

- When face-to-face with your ex-spouse during transitions, bury your feelings and exchange polite greetings. Keep it short.

- Don't discuss arrangements or other business with your ex-spouse during transitions.

- Turn the other cheek to any sarcastic or accusatory comments. Excuse yourself as quickly and politely as possible.

- Don't exchange checks and money in front of your children.

- Don't use children as messengers or delivery people.

- Have a positive attitude.

- Give a hug and a kiss goodbye to your children; wish them a good time.

- Smile. A happy parent makes for secure children.

Children Who Fight Visitation

In some cases, children will refuse to leave to be with the noncustodial parent. Here are some reasons why this might happen:

- A parent is not tuned in to the children's interests or is not actively involved with the children during their time together.

- Your children may be very young and anxious about separation from the parent who does the majority of caretaking.

- Open conflict is causing the children to appear to be aligned temporarily with one parent.

- In rare cases, there may be child abuse (which we discuss a little later in the chapter).

If your children don't want to leave their primary home to be with their other parent, having a good heart-to-heart with your ex-spouse should be the first step. The problem may be one that is easy to resolve, such as paying more attention to the children, a change in discipline style, or having more toys or other entertainment at the other home.

Either or both parents may unknowingly be causing the children's refusal to go. Following are two checklists, one for the custodial parent and the other for the noncustodial parent, unless custody is shared. Be honest. You're the only one looking at this.

PARENT Q&A	
I have done my best to encourage my children's visits with their other parent.	❏ Yes ❏ No
I do not give double messages to my children about seeing their other parent.	❏ Yes ❏ No
I make sure my children know that, although I miss them, I know they will be well taken care of.	❏ Yes ❏ No
I tell my children I am fine when they're away.	❏ Yes ❏ No
I make sure to pack everything my children need so their time with their other parent goes smoothly.	❏ Yes ❏ No
I understand it takes a while for my children to adjust to different surroundings, household rules, and customs. I don't pressure them to forget about their other parent when they're with me.	❏ Yes ❏ No
I make a mental note if, after a reasonable amount of time with me, my children are not adjusting.	❏ Yes ❏ No
I allow my children to speak to their other parent on the phone.	❏ Yes ❏ No
I don't do my work when my children are with me and are awake.	❏ Yes ❏ No
To stay involved with my children, I participate as much as possible in activities that center on their lives (Little League, dance class, play dates, and so on) instead of dragging them to things that are important to me but of no interest to them.	❏ Yes ❏ No

Go with the Flow

Sara, who was 12 years old, called her mother to tell her that she didn't want to go to her home one weekend. She said her girlfriends were having a slumber party, and she didn't want to miss it. Her mother insisted that she come instead of going to the party.

This wasn't the first time Sara had to miss a social event because that was her weekend to see her mother. She felt misunderstood and resented her mother for ruining her social life. Ultimately, Sara started to withdraw from her mother.

If her parents had been more flexible with the schedule, on the other hand, Sara could have had a more normal pre-teen social life and would have developed better relationships with her parents. She would have felt that they understood and cared about her emotional and social needs.

Six months after his parents divorced, nine-year-old Allen began refusing to go to his father's place for the weekend. When asked on several occasions, he wouldn't say why. Finally, he admitted that he was bored because his father would spend most of his time finishing reports for work, and Allen had no one to play with. When Allen opened up about his feelings, his father made sure to do his work after Allen went to sleep and devoted his time to him. That did the trick. From then on, Allen looked forward to his weekends with his dad.

What's your scenario? If your children are resisting going to your place, scrutinize the situation, and listen to what they tell you. Perhaps a simple change will turn things around for you, too.

The Anxiety of Transition for Young Children

Refusal to leave the primary residential parent is most common in very young children because they are too young to carry a mental image of the parent to whom they are most attached (usually their mother) and fear abandonment.

For these young children, the transition from one parent to the other can set off anxiety about safety and survival. According to Janet Johnston, a foremost researcher in children and high-conflict divorce, children up to six years old may continue to have difficulty if they have had "repeated distressing separations and maintain an anxious attachment to the parent. It is also possible that children under the ages of four or five do not have a sufficient understanding of the concept of time and, for this reason, are confused about the particular visitation schedule. Consequently, they are anxious about when they will be reunited with the primary or custodial parent."

If you and your ex-spouse get along, and your children are very young, the cause of your children's refusal to leave their residential home is likely normal, age-related separation anxiety. A parent's recognition of this and willingness to work with the other parent to ease his or her children's anxiety will go a long way toward building trust and bonding. Insensitivity, on the other hand, can result in continual resistance to leaving the primary residence and the eventual failure of the child-parent relationship.

When a Parent Is Maligned

If you think your ex has begun to wage a serious campaign against you with the kids (engaging in what's now called Parental Alienation Syndrome or PAS), you should suggest that your spouse and children see a mental health professional to aid their adjustment to visitation. If your ex refuses to seek help, you might be justified in seeing your attorney to request that the court mandate a mental health intervention, and perhaps a change in physical custody or visitation, depending on who's alienating whom. Complex situations such as this call for psychological—and perhaps, even legal—intervention for the entire family.

 YOU CAN DO IT!

Parental Alienation Syndrome shouldn't be a problem if you have a good relationship with your children. They're not going to buy the hard line that you're awful if you're really not. But, if you think your children are being brainwashed, discuss your suspicions calmly with them. You'll get a better feel for the true situation at their other home, and, hopefully, you'll be able to address any issues that arise. In case of true alienation, you must enlist the help of a therapist—and possibly address the damage by asking the court for help.

If you are the custodial parent in a heavily litigated case and your children refuse to visit their other parent, make sure that you are not bad-mouthing your ex-spouse in front of your children or sending them negative messages. If you want what's best for your children, you must put aside your feelings toward your ex-spouse and encourage your children to develop or maintain a relationship with their other parent. If your children lose the other parent because of your attitude, they'll risk low self-esteem and suffer feelings of abandonment—even if it seems as if they don't want to see that parent right now.

Rebecca's parents separated because her father was seeing another woman. Rebecca was eight years old when her father moved out. Her mother was in shock. When the shock wore off, the mother was filled with rage. She did not hide her feelings from Rebecca. Instead, she told Rebecca that her father couldn't be trusted and that he was insensitive and even cruel.

Rebecca couldn't bear to see her mother so distressed. She aligned herself with her mother against her father. Even though she had been close to her father before the divorce, her angry feelings prevented her from relating to him. She didn't even want to see him.

Rebecca's father accused her mother of brainwashing Rebecca against him. He went to court to try to gain custody. The litigation was heated and drawn out. Rebecca suffered terribly from the fighting and the insecurity of not knowing where she would be living. She continued to refuse to see her father.

Eventually, her father, who lost the custody battle, became less and less interested in fighting Rebecca's rejections of him. He and his girlfriend married and started a family of their own. As far as Rebecca was concerned, he found it easiest to just drift away.

What could Rebecca's father have done in this situation instead of giving up? For one thing, he might have let Rebecca know the door was always open for her. For instance, he might have continued to send regular emails and called, even if Rebecca didn't respond. She might have asked to see him again—in her own time. At the very least, she'd have concrete evidence to prove her dad still cared, despite her refusal to see him.

When your ex maligns you in front of your child, it puts your relationship at risk. Yet, psychologists note that a hurt, angry ex-spouse cannot always control the expression of powerful, negative emotions. They may be unaware of just how much they're damaging the child they love.

How do you handle this situation without drawing the child into yet more conflict? According to psychologist Karen Breunig, co-author of *Through the Eyes of a Child,* "The best thing that I would advise is to appeal to the better graces of the offending parent. Explain how damaging this is for the child, since the child identifies with both parents." It might also be useful for the offending parent to seek therapy.

If your ex remains closed to such suggestions, Breunig says you should discuss the situation with your child. Explain that you are going to try to work the situation out with the other parent and, if appropriate, assure the child that the statements made about you are not true. "Leave the lines of communication open so that your child can feel comfortable about checking these accusations with you, personally," says Breunig.

"Whatever you do," she concludes, "do not fight fire with fire. You will just be turning up the flames on your kid."

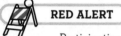 **RED ALERT**

Participating in open conflict—whether it is screaming at each other or making snide remarks—is the single most damaging thing you can do to your children. Although you have no control over your ex, you do have control over yourself. Don't get dragged into a fight. Stay cool.

If You Suspect Abuse

If your children seem fearful or refuse to see the other parent on a regular basis, you might have a genuine concern for their safety and even abuse. If this is the case, speak to your lawyer and a mental health professional before making any accusations to your ex-spouse.

The courts have seen a lot of child abuse charges in divorce cases. Many of these accusations turn out to be false statements made by an angry and vengeful spouse or by a parent who wants to limit parental access to the children. For this reason, your lawyer might call you in to discuss the facts behind your claim of child abuse. Your attorney will explain what constitutes child abuse in your state, according to case law.

On the other hand, if your children are victims of abuse, there must be immediate intervention, including the possible involvement of a psychiatrist, and a change in the visitation arrangement.

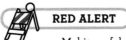 **RED ALERT**

Making a false allegation of child abuse is serious and can even result in a change of custody.

The Least You Need to Know

- Children who switch households regularly—different place, different people, different rules—carry a heavy burden. It takes time for them to adjust.
- Prepare your children well in advance of leaving your residence.
- Check your attitude! Your children need a positive relationship with both parents.
- Never engage in conflict with your ex-spouse in front of your children.
- If your children refuse to see their other parent, speak to your children if they're old enough. If necessary, consult with a mental health professional. If you are on good terms with your ex, discuss the problem with him or her. If you think you are a victim of Parental Alienation Syndrome (PAS), talk to your lawyer.
- If you suspect physical abuse of your children, contact your attorney immediately for advice.

Single Parenting

After your divorce settlement or trial is over and the shock has worn off, you will confront a different life. In your new role as single parent and single person, you will have to help your slightly smaller family navigate the rapids of life.

Because your children have a more limited perspective than you, you must help them deal with the fact that mom and dad are not living together in the same home. You will have to help them understand why they must split their time between two households, a situation that requires a period of adjustment as new patterns of living are set. This chapter will guide you through some of the obstacles you might encounter as a newly single parent in the alternate family structure created in the wake of a divorce.

In This Chapter

- The responsibilities of the custodial and noncustodial parents
- Juggling childcare, work, and your social life
- How to nurture your child
- Getting the most out of your time with your child

If You Are the Custodial Parent

If you are the parent who had been doing most of the caregiving for your children before the divorce, you are most likely the custodial parent in a sole custody arrangement, and you can expect some things to stay much the same. You will still be getting your children off to school, shopping for their clothes, and taking them to the doctor, after-school activities, and friends' houses if they're too young to go alone. It goes without saying that you will be shopping for their food and preparing their meals.

What's really different for you now? For one thing, you won't have backup for any of these responsibilities, and you'll be solo if you have to exercise discipline. If you were not the go-to parent for homework help, this task will be added to your list during the week. You might be the one pitching balls to your youngest or shooting baskets after school, even if you haven't done this before.

"But when will I get a break?" you might ask. Your break comes when your kids are with their other parent. That's a nice, solid break. Enjoy it!

Make the Most of Mealtimes

It might take some time to adjust to having meals with one parent missing. Not only will it remind you of your new marital state but, after a while, you might crave the company of other adults. What to do? Invite friends or neighbors over for dinner once or twice a week. Take your children out to restaurants so you can be surrounded by people, or just enjoy catching up with your kids' daily activities. Don't park them in front of the TV while they're eating or let them be on the computer or phone forever. Have your meals together. That will give all of you a chance to talk about the day's events and will provide a stronger sense of family—a good practice for every family but even more important for maintaining stability now that your children will be dividing their time between households.

 YOU CAN DO IT!

As a newly single parent, you might feel overwhelmed by the responsibilities—but when you think about it, there is support all around you. For young children, aside from day care centers, there are commercial play centers and recreational facilities. Your school-aged child will be able to participate in the school's enrichment activities, intramural sports, or clubs. Older children are already saddled with a lot of homework, and they'll want to get involved in after-school activities, as well as spend time hanging out with their friends.

Working Single Parents

Being a single parent is a juggling act. If you didn't work when you were married but do so after the divorce, you will most likely have to put major time and effort into developing your career. You will also need help with the kids when you aren't home. Before the divorce, maybe one parent stayed home to care for the children, or both you and your former spouse had work schedules that allowed one of you to be home when the kids got out of school. Now that you're single, those childcare solutions may not be an option.

Depending on the age of your children and your financial situation, you might need a full- or part-time babysitter and day care or nursery school. For older children, if you can afford it, having someone at home for their arrival from school will give them a feeling of security. Even young teenagers—although they won't admit it—feel more at ease if they know someone is looking after them.

Despite many safety concerns, some parents without funds still go the "latch-key" route, allowing older children to arrive home and let themselves in alone. Before you decide to follow this path, make sure you are familiar with the laws in your area. Many jurisdictions allow children ages 11 and older to stay home alone, but laws differ, depending on the location.

Even if leaving your child home alone is legal, you must still make sure the circumstances are secure and that your child is comfortable with the idea. Do you live in an apartment building with a doorman the children can call if there's a problem? Are there adult neighbors they can contact? As a general rule, children need the security and experience of an adult nearby through the early teen years, especially if the parent will be away for an extended period of time.

Finally, if you plan to leave your older children home alone, make sure they are armed with emergency phone numbers and strategies for dealing with an array of situations, from physical injury to prank phone calls.

An Issue of Discipline

Studies have shown that children do best with firm guidance combined with a lot of communication and affection. You may be tempted to overindulge your children to make up for the pain they are going through because of your divorce, but too much leniency has been shown to have a negative effect.

Frankly, a stricter attitude toward discipline seems to help children and teenagers more than an overly permissive style. This does not mean being irrational, controlling, or resorting to physical punishment. It does mean setting reasonable rules and expectations, discussing them with your children, and following through with previously established consequences if those rules are broken. At this unsettled time, children need definite boundaries and limits combined with a lot of patience, love, and understanding.

Caring for Yourself

One of the most important things you can do to support your kids is to take care of yourself. If you are an unhappy parent, it will have a major effect on your children. They look to you for strength and support. It's frightening to children of any age to see a parent lost to depression and removed from them emotionally; for many, the situation provokes anxious feelings of losing that parent as well, something especially painful at the time of divorce. To help them, help yourself by:

- Getting enough rest and exercise, and eating healthy foods.

- Putting yourself in places where you can meet new people.

- Getting busy with recreating your life. Start by renovating your house or apartment, even if it's just a fresh coat of paint and some new throw rugs!

- Taking an adult education class or volunteering.

- Seeing a therapist regularly, if necessary.

If you are the custodial parent, you have a lot on your plate. As long as your ex-spouse is in the picture, however, you are not entirely alone in raising your children.

 SILVER LININGS

If you and your spouse had been battling it out for custody and visitation, be grateful now that he or she wants to be active in your children's lives. Realize that the time your kids spend with their other parent gives you a much-needed break, allows your children to have both parents in their lives, and gives you help with the monumental tasks of parenting.

If You Are the Noncustodial Parent

The noncustodial parent will also be facing new challenges. Much of what is true for the parent with physical custody is also true for the noncustodial parent. The good news is that you have time for entertainment and your errands when the kids are with their other parent. Then, when they're with you, you can really devote that solid block of time to them. If you used to give little time to your children because you were too tired when you came home from work, you might not have developed the kind of fulfilling relationship you can now enjoy with the free time that comes from splitting the parenting duties post-divorce.

 YOU CAN DO IT!

Spending quality time with your children is the greatest gift you can give them. Communicating in a genuine way—really listening to them—will not only solidify your relationship, but it will also help them get through this tough time.

The noncustodial parent must make a special effort to maintain a close and loving relationship with the children. Here are some things you can do:

- Agree with your ex-spouse that each of you can have reasonable reciprocal communication with the kids by phone, text, or email when they're not with you.

- Send them photos of your time together.

- Attend the public sports, music, and arts activities both at their school and outside school.

- Don't shirk discipline in your home. Sometimes the parent who sees their children less often will avoid enforcing house rules for fear of alienating them. If possible, continue the same rules they've had all along, both for stability and consistency.

- Come to terms with your divorce so you don't communicate feelings of anger and hostility to your children. It's important to be emotionally available to your kids.

- We've said it before, but it bears repeating: treat your ex-spouse as a business partner. Be civil and courteous, and don't fight in front of the kids.

Don't Overdo It

You've probably heard the cliché about "weekend dads" (or moms) who spoil their kids by entertaining them at expensive places and buying more toys and gifts than they could ever hope to see at their other parent's home. This is a mistake. Your children need *you*, not lavish gifts that might assuage your guilt or show them what a great parent you are. Occasional trips to amusement parks, shows, and ball games are fine as part of hanging out with them. These special times together will cement your relationship and provide fond memories in the future.

 **RED ALERT**

> It's best if both parents can agree on a single disciplinary policy, so that children can't play one parent against the other. However, the reality is often different. If you've established certain rules at your place, don't expect the other parent to do the same at his or her home. Do continue with your disciplinary measures when your children return, if that's the deal.

Your Enormous Responsibilities

What are your practical responsibilities as a noncustodial parent? You don't have to buy the clothes for your children, since you're already paying child support, but it's always a good idea to have a spare outfit or two at your place just in case someone plays football on a muddy field, for example. Buying some toys for the younger kids is a must. If you cook, provide your kids with home-cooked meals, or even have them share in the cooking. If you're not into cooking, find great take-out.

Regarding discipline, the same is true at your home as for the primary residence. Firm discipline with a loving touch yields the best results.

What if your very young children are having a hard time being away from their custodial parent? If you can't comfort your small children after a reasonable amount of time, be flexible and hope your ex-spouse will be as well. Bring your children back and try again soon, maybe for a shorter time but more frequently. In the end, you will have earned your children's trust in you, and you won't have risked their emotional well-being.

A Life of Your Own

As a newly minted single parent, it may seem an impossible feat to care for your kids, work, and still have the energy and emotional strength to move forward with your social life. We know you might not believe it, but eventually, you will get your life together.

Building a New Career

One of our favorite examples of how an optimistic attitude can bear fruit is the story of Rebecca—a divorced friend of ours who has done an admirable job.

When Rebecca divorced, her two sons, Sean and Harry, were 7 and 10 years old. Her main occupation had been raising her boys, although she had begun a singing career before she had her first son. After the divorce, she decided to go back to school so she could become a music teacher. Meanwhile, she had some savings to live on but elected to work part-time as well.

Her children went to school on an early bus every morning. Rebecca had one class in the morning, did some shopping after the class, and then went to her job selling designer eyewear. A classmate of hers agreed to be at her home every afternoon when her children got home from school. When Rebecca got home, she made dinner, helped her kids with their homework when asked, and read to them before bed. After they were asleep, she did her own homework. Sometimes she fell asleep before she put on her pajamas.

When Sean and Harry were with their father, Rebecca did more school work, ran all her errands, and took in dinner and a movie with a friend. A year after the divorce, she forced herself to go on a date. She made it a point to fit one singles event into her schedule every month. She also joined a fitness club and worked out on her free weekends.

Rebecca is still single, but today, she's a success. Sean and Harry, now in high school, are top students as well as athletes. They both have an abundance of friends. And Rebecca is a music teacher proud of her children, her own professional accomplishments, personal independence, and new circle of friends.

Although it may not feel like it now, it's possible for you to find this kind of success, too. Staying involved and active while still caring for your children is a challenge, but it can be done.

Meeting New People

At some point during the healing process, you will be ready to meet new people (unless the reason for your divorce was that you had a new love in your life). How do you fit a social life into your busy schedule, and how will it affect your children?

The best time to become socially active is when your kids are with their other parent. That way, you'll be free to be you, not your kids' parent.

If you're fortunate and meet a person you click with, and your relationship becomes serious, be cautious about how you go about integrating your new love interest into your family life. Think carefully about the appropriate time to introduce him or her to your children after your divorce. Establish a stable relationship first. Make sure it's what you want before involving your kids. Children whose parents have divorced may be skittish about a new romantic involvement for mom or dad. Many children fantasize that their parents will reconcile, or they might see your new "friend" as taking time away from them.

Nurturing Your Kids

Whether your kids live with you 20 or 50 percent of the time, providing a welcoming, nurturing home for your children is the best prescription for a positive outcome. Organizing your schedule to adjust to the parenting plan, though it might be complicated, can be done; it's worth any inconvenience in order to develop a strong relationship with your child.

Take Byron as an example. Byron's daughter, six-year-old Michelle, lived with him three days each week, every other weekend, and one evening each week. When he picked her up on Friday evening from her mom's, he always took Michelle to her favorite Japanese restaurant. She could count on it. When they got to Byron's home, it was time for a bath and bedtime story. Before she went to sleep, Byron would help her call her mom to say good night. The rest of the weekend was spent on activities they could do together. On Mondays, Byron took Michelle to her kindergarten class. Because he was still at work when she was finished, he had a standing arrangement with a neighbor to pick her up and stay with her until he got home from work. Michelle was with her dad one more day and night. The last day, Byron took her to school, but her mother picked her up. Despite the patchwork of caretaking, it worked and became a routine for the family.

Whether you're the custodial or noncustodial parent, or if you share the time with your children equally, your kids need nurturing. As divorced parents, both you and your ex-spouse have to be mindful of your kids' needs at all times. Each of you is responsible for their physical, emotional, and spiritual health and well-being when they are with you—including giving hugs and kisses (number one on the list), goofing around, teaching them right from wrong, feeding them, making sure that they brush their teeth twice a day, and taking care of them when they're sick.

Once the wounds of the divorce process have healed and you have gotten used to the new family arrangement, everything will fall into place and become less overwhelming. Much of the anxiety you have felt during this trying time will lessen and then disappear after the legal issues are settled. It will definitely take time to get used to the changes that result from divorce. Eventually they'll become ordinary, the fog will lift, and you'll move on to better experiences.

The Least You Need to Know

- Parenting post-divorce is a challenge, but with good organization, support, and the right attitude, you will succeed.
- Single parents must be mindful of their children's needs during the delicate post-divorce transition time.
- The most successful disciplinary approach is firmness and consistency, with a lot of communication and affection. Ideally, the rules at each home should be about the same, assuming there are no philosophical differences.
- If you are dating, do so when you are not with your children. Don't introduce your new significant other to the children until you know you're serious.
- To get the most out of your time with your children, focus on them. Do activities you all enjoy, take care of their physical, emotional, and spiritual needs, keep the communication lines open, and give them a lot of affection.

Redefining the Family

Living in two homes is the norm for children whose parents are divorced. Sometimes, one or both parents will remarry. It's not uncommon for a parent to marry someone who already has children. In time, the couple might have their own child. When parents divorce, get remarried, and then start new families, it has a profound impact on the children. At a minimum, everyone involved will have to adjust to the new environment.

In the best of all worlds, the two families will be supportive and caring. The expanded family will bring variety and complexity but could also provide enriching experiences and close relationships.

In This Chapter

- Helping your children adjust to a stepparent
- Understanding the stepparent's perspective
- Creating a harmonious blended family

Helping Your Kids Accept Your New Spouse

If you and your significant other have gotten to the point where you both think it's time to live together and even marry, you must take steps to prepare your children for the change. Think about it: they will have to accept the fact that you and your ex-spouse will never be reunited, that you will have a new spouse or live-in partner, and that, potentially, they will have new stepbrothers or stepsisters. That is a lot to digest! Go slowly and proceed with caution.

Phasing in are the key words here. As we mentioned in Chapter 27, don't introduce your children to your new partner until you are sure about your own feelings about him or her. In many instances, your children will still be mourning the loss of your marriage—the family unit as they knew it. To see one of their parents with a new love interest can cause stress in the early period after divorce, so be sensitive and aware of their psychological needs.

Teenagers have been living in your well-established nuclear family for a longer time than the younger children and can be profoundly disturbed by a parent's new love interest. Take a reading on your kids from time to time by discussing similar situations—such as a TV show or perhaps another divorced family, where one or both parents remarried, so that you can judge their emotional readiness.

When you are ready to introduce your kids to your new partner, take it slowly. Going to a neutral place, such as the movies, a restaurant, or a walk around the block, might be the best way to ease into this difficult introduction. Let your kids gradually get to know your new partner over a period of time. When it feels right, open a discussion about your intention to marry or live together. Your kids might even initiate the conversation.

Don't expect them to welcome this new person (whom they may view as an intruder) with open arms. And don't be surprised if their reaction continues to be negative for quite a while. Accepting your new partner will take time. The more relaxed you are about it, the easier it will be for your kids to adjust. At some point after your children get to know the person you plan to marry, if he or she has any children, you and your partner should decide when the time is right for them to meet.

 YOU CAN DO IT!

Integrating your new partner into your children's lives should be handled sensitively and not rushed. Realize that, from their perspective, they are witnessing both the dissolution of the only family they have known and the remarriage of their father or mother. Put yourself in your children's place, and you will better understand how to handle this difficult adjustment.

The Dynamics of the Stepfamily

Although the stepfamily is an increasingly common institution, living in a stepfamily is not always easy. Each participant—the new parent(s), possibly the new stepsiblings, and perhaps eventually new half-siblings—adds to a changing dynamic within the stepfamily. Each will be coming to the family with their own emotional perspective and needs.

According to stepfamily counselor Jeannette Lofas, of the Stepfamily Foundation, Inc., as a new stepfamily adjusts, everyone is susceptible to feeling like an outsider as family members take on new relationships and roles. For instance, a 15-year-old girl might be used to sitting in the front seat of the car with dad, but when dad has a girlfriend, where should the girl sit? She will try to protect her territory.

If the stepparent also has children, there's the interaction of the children with the stepparent's children. Are they compatible—even superficially? Stepsibling relationships can be full of jealousies, turf-guarding, and other sundry emotions.

How about mixing and matching discipline styles? Is the stepfather a pushover compared to the biological dad? Or the opposite? Have the children who just moved into your house been raised to stay up to all hours while you expect your kids to go to bed at 10:30 p.m.? How will you set the rules so the new children and your children adjust to living under one roof?

 RED ALERT

Negativity toward an ex is extremely damaging to children under any circumstance. In instances where a stepparent is involved, any anger or criticism of the other biological parent can make the situation especially difficult and complex. When ex-spouses bad-mouth each other, children are caught in the middle, and feelings of guilt can emerge. This will make it more difficult than ever for the child to forge a relationship with the stepparent, even if that stepparent never says a negative word about the absent parent.

It's easy to see that achieving harmony with a blended family can be difficult. But Jeannette Lofas, who was born into a stepfamily and also married into a stepfamily, sees hope. She imparts some of her most valuable tips for the new, blended family:

Go slowly. Learn to partner with a new husband or wife through the creation of structure and discipline and the accumulation of couple strength. For instance, a single dad may have allowed the kids to stay up late or order dinner in. His new wife might not believe these things are appropriate, but if she tries to change things, the stepchildren will simply ignore her. She can easily slip into the role of "the bad guy," even if she states her point of view as gently as possible.

Find the right role. The stepfather or stepmother should not attempt to be parents to their stepchildren, even if the biological parent has died. Nor should they assume the role of friend. Instead, they should be seen as male or female head of household and a partner to the biological parent.

Leave discipline to the biological parent. The stepparent must not impose discipline on his or her own without the support of the biological parent. To do so always creates dissention, rendering the stepparent "the bad guy."

Look for ways to bond. Stepparents should attempt to bond with stepchildren by filling in where the biological parent cannot. For instance, a stepfather might play one-on-one basketball with a stepson or take stepchildren to see a movie; these are activities one can share without assuming the parental role.

Encourage a communicative atmosphere. One of the most important ways to facilitate the positive integration of all family members is to establish open, honest, and safe avenues for communicating feelings and differences of opinion. The adults should set the standard and allow structured and unstructured times for everyone to express their thoughts and grievances. This crucial step provides an outlet for everyone and can prevent a build-up of resentment and misunderstanding.

Easing the Transition

Adjusting to your new family structure will take time for everyone. Be sensitive to your children's feelings about your having a new partner. Listen to their concerns and take them seriously. If your child seems hostile, withdrawn, or is just not behaving as usual, insecurity about her or his relationship with you might be the cause. Reassure your child that your love for him or her has never been in doubt.

Remember that integrating everyone into a new stepfamily will require patience. The relationship between your children and their stepparent must grow naturally. Expecting too much too soon is bound to ruffle feathers. New roles within the blended family will be created as relationships take shape.

 YOU CAN DO IT!

You can't force a new stepparent or stepfamily down your kids' throats. Especially around this sensitive issue, pay attention to your children's cues. If your child regularly displays anger at his or her stepparent, talk to him or her privately and try to understand whether there are genuine issues that can be resolved or whether your child is having trouble accepting your new spouse. If, after listening to your child, you find the issue is not something specific that can be solved, consider consulting a psychologist.

The Stepparent's Point of View

As the stepparent, you will be facing many challenges. Since you've recently married, you're working on building a loving and supportive relationship with your new spouse. If you have your own children from a previous marriage, you want to be there for them as always. The most ambitious effort will be to develop a healthy relationship with your stepchildren.

To get your footing, take stock of your own emotions, priorities, and goals. Remind yourself why you decided to marry someone who has children, understanding the complexity this arrangement carries. Assuming you've given a lot of thought to this prior to marrying, how do you feel now that it is for real? Gaining insight into yourself at this time will bring to the surface any underlying misgivings you might have as you enter the new family situation. You will be able to work them through in your own mind before engaging with your stepchildren on an ongoing basis.

What are your priorities as you construct a mingled household? Will you put the well-being and happiness of your own children before your husband and stepchildren if there is an imbalance in family relationships, or is your marriage most important? How does the rapport with your stepchildren fit into your priorities?

Finally, what is your primary goal? Ideally, you consider the best outcome a harmonious blended family where everyone is respectful, caring, unselfish, and supportive. When walking cold into an unknown family situation where sensitivities are at their most vulnerable for everyone, you will have to rely on your strength, intuition, patience, and common sense to make it work.

 SILVER LININGS

> One way to strengthen family ties is to develop new traditions for holidays, birthdays, and other special occasions as well as routines, such as going out to dinner at a favorite restaurant on Fridays. Encourage the entire group to come up with the ideas and stick to them. You'd like to transform your hodgepodge family into a team, all on the same side.

One situation that can be particularly difficult for a stepparent is defusing the anger of a stepchild when the trigger for the anger is not obvious. You can't seem to extract any information from your stepchild because, well, maybe he doesn't know himself. He's not opening up to you; his biological parent can't get anything out of him either. More than likely your stepchild has not been able to accept the divorce and remarriage of his biological parent. If the anger persists, you and your spouse should consult with a psychologist for guidance or ongoing therapy.

At the same time, reflect on your own behavior toward this unhappy child. Are you favoring your own children without realizing it? Have you treated him with respect? Have you been supportive and caring? Have you shared activities together to promote bonding? Your own positive attitude and mature handling of your relationship will help avert intractable negative feelings and provide the basis for improvement in how he perceives you.

Half-Siblings, Stepsiblings, and the New Baby

It is no longer unusual for children of divorce to have many new relationships when their parents remarry. Although getting used to being part of a blended family is not easy, there are many positives. If parents have the right attitude, and sibling and stepsibling rivalries are worked out, having additional close relationships can be enriching to your children.

Half-siblings, who are biologically related through one parent only, often have closer ties than stepsiblings, who are not biologically related. That doesn't mean stepsiblings can't develop close relationships. Age, gender, life experience, and temperament have a lot to do with the way the new family interacts.

 SILVER LININGS

A blended family can be an asset to your children if everyone has the right attitude. Additional family relationships will enrich your children. If close in age with their step or half-siblings, they can become fast friends and provide mutual support throughout their lives. Stepparents can be positive role models who can offer love and a different perspective to your children's world view. Once adjusted to the new family structure, the children can begin to accept and feel comfortable with the new arrangement.

Some specific issues come up with half-siblings and stepsiblings in a blended family:

Jealousy over parents. Whose dad or mom is it? Children may feel possessive of their biological parent.

Sharing space. Children need their own space and privacy. Whose home is it? Whose room is it? Whose drawers are they? Whose bathroom is it?

Need for respect. Children's individuality should be respected. They should not be taken for granted, such as assuming older children will babysit for the younger ones. Children's wishes should be considered when making plans, and they should be told when plans are changed. Children should sense that you trust them and respect their place in the family.

Sexual relationships. Because stepsiblings are not related biologically, sometimes issues of intimacy can arise for adolescents and teenagers.

A new baby. Children in a stepfamily are often challenged by the arrival of a new baby—the product of one of their parents and their stepparent. This can be met with excitement or jealousy or both. The baby can be seen as eating up all their parent's time, a nuisance, and possibly an embarrassment if they think their parent is over the hill. Other children are able to enjoy the new baby and see themselves as the big brother or sister.

Each of these special issues should be handled carefully. Creating an atmosphere where communication is facilitated so feelings don't get bottled up is key. Making sure your children have the physical space, privacy, and respect they need to feel comfortable and secure will help prevent problems before they develop.

In short, being aware of the feelings of your children, your new spouse or significant other, and his or her children, if there are any, is the first step toward making it all work. If problems arise, listen carefully and try to think things through. Although it won't always be possible to please everyone in every case, sensitively negotiating with everyone involved will go a long way toward promoting harmony.

The Least You Need to Know

- When you have met the person you think will be your next spouse or live-in partner, introduce him or her to your children and let them get to know each other over a period of time. Allow their relationship to grow naturally.
- If your children feel that their importance to you has been overshadowed by your new family, reassure them that their relationship with you is special and that nothing and no one can replace them.
- Children should be raised by their biological parent, unless there is an emergency. The stepparent should not take on the role of the children's parent.
- Blended families thrive when everyone—including the children—has his or her own space and privacy and is treated with respect.
- Mutual respect, consideration, and understanding, as well as ample communication, will ease the way for your new blended family.

CHAPTER 29

Facing Your Feelings

Your spouse has moved out, you've negotiated a settlement and signed all the documents. The final divorce decree has arrived in the mail, and your attorney has gone off to fight other battles.

The distress of the divorce process is behind you, but it probably served to displace the more significant feelings caused by realizing your marriage has ended. These emotions might have emerged from time to time while haggling over the agreement, but now that things are settled, there is nothing holding these feelings back. Before you can move on to a new life, you will have to come to terms with how and why things went wrong. You will have to accept and understand your missteps and mistakes before you can feel psychologically whole enough to move on.

This chapter addresses these issues and offers strategies for navigating your emotional life post-divorce.

In This Chapter

- Dealing with grief, rejection, guilt, loneliness, and anger
- Regaining control of your emotions and your life
- How to cope when you miss your former life
- How to stop second-guessing your situation and move on without regret

Coping with the Emotional Fallout of Divorce

The end of a marriage can evoke intense feelings of grief, pain, and perhaps guilt and anger. You will grieve for the hopes and expectations you had for a lifelong partner and a family living together in a happy home. Along with grief is the pain of all your dreams evaporating, replaced by an existential emptiness. Infidelity will inevitably produce strong feelings of anger or guilt.

These emotions are quite natural following divorce. Even though you might not be able to imagine getting out from under the deluge of negative feelings, they will dissipate. This is only a moment in time, and time will be your greatest ally. The adage, "time heals all wounds," is especially pertinent to divorce survivors.

As the days and weeks pass, there are things you can do to put yourself on a healing trajectory. That journey may start with a sense of loss, but it will, over time, lead to a sense of renewal and a new feeling of empowerment over your fate and place in the world.

 SILVER LININGS

> It is common to pass through life without stopping to consider the consequences of our actions or being truly introspective. Given the stress of life today, exploring the inner self is often a luxury we feel we cannot afford. In the wake of divorce, it behooves you to go through an inner exploration. Consider this chance a gift—it may be painful at first, but it will enrich you in the long run.

If there was ever an opportune occasion for introspection and reflection, this is it. Depending on your level of functioning in the aftermath of your divorce, you may be able to work through this period on your own or, if not, seek professional help. Getting objective feedback from a pro can speed up the recovery process. He or she will be able to identify patterns in your behavior that might relate to your life before you got married.

"As you look into your feelings with the help of a professional," states psychologist Mitchell Baris, "you may even find that the problem is deeper than the divorce itself." Perhaps you are unable to recover because of a particularly difficult experience during childhood. Perhaps there is a long-standing reason, unrelated to your marriage, for your sense of failure and low self-esteem, if that's what you're feeling. If so, take this opportunity to learn about yourself and pursue meaningful change.

While you work to gain insight into yourself, consider joining a divorce support group. You can make friends and share your war stories with people who can really understand what you're saying. Lifelong friendships begin in these groups. As you heal, you can start the process of reinventing yourself by taking classes just for fun or to start a new career, if that's your goal. As you get involved in these activities and meet new people, you will be building a support system that will get you through this difficult period.

 RED ALERT

Some people have so much trouble coping with the pain of divorce that they resort to alcohol or drugs. Often, these people are immersing themselves in emotional numbness to escape their feelings. A word to the wise: it's better to feel the pain and get through it than to linger in emotional limbo. If you are having problems along these lines, seek support from your community or congregation, your friends, support groups both online and off, or, if necessary, get professional help.

Rediscovering Your Sense of Self

A healthy marriage will be supportive without being stifling. Each individual in the relationship will find it provides the confidence and freedom to develop an independent identity. In a marriage with a pattern of constant criticism and belittling, or one in which one partner controls the show, the berated spouse can develop an altered or diminished self-image—perhaps a toned-down version of the *Gaslight Syndrome*.

 **DEFINITION**

Gaslight Syndrome is a reference to a 1944 film directed by George Cukor, in which the husband surreptitiously creates evidence to convince his wife that she is insane. It has become clinical psychiatric terminology for one spouse trying to have the other labeled insane. A more common, less extreme form of this manifests as one spouse emotionally controlling the other. The partner being controlled suffers from self-doubt and loss of identity.

Our friend Shanna spent five years in a marriage trying to please an irascible, critical husband who found fault with everything—her eating habits, what she read, her clothes and weight, her philosophy of life, and her friends. Fortunately for Shanna, she had no children, and after a year of therapy, she felt ready to sever the bond. For six months after her divorce was finalized, Shanna lived in a studio apartment. For furniture, she used cardboard chests. Her bed was a cot, picked up on sale. For art, she had a single cartoon hanging on the wall: the picture of an Earth man, surrounded by aliens, in a bar in some godforsaken section of the cosmos. The caption: "When I've made it, I'll go back to Earth."

To Shanna, that said it all. She couldn't help feelings of anger, even rage, at her ex. At the same time, she felt a twinge of guilt: her husband had been truly devastated when she walked out.

Shanna eventually moved back to the town she grew up in to be close to her family, but not before she had bolstered her emotional resources. She had many issues to deal with in the aftermath of her divorce, and it took months before she was able, in the truest sense of the word, to return to the "singles" world to which she now belongs.

The issue for Shanna and most other survivors of divorce was a true loss of identity. After years, or sometimes decades, of living with another person, it is easy to accept, without question, their sense of who you are. In Shanna's case, that meant seeing herself as somehow stupid and lazy.

YOU CAN DO IT!

Sometimes, you can go home again. In the wake of divorce, it may be helpful to return to your roots. There, you might find the nurturing of old friends and family as well as inner strength you thought you had lost. You might also find some insight into your own role in the break-up of your marriage.

After 15 years together, Matt's overachieving wife, Jackie, informed him that she had met someone new and the marriage was over. "I never loved you anyway from the moment I married you," Jackie told him. "You're overweight, boring, nervous, and you have no taste." To Matt, it was like being cast out of the castle. Although he had found success in commodities trading, he had come from humble beginnings. He would now descend, he thought, to the wretched, untouchable world from which he had sprung.

It was difficult for Matt to see value in what were once his virtues—his honesty, grittiness, long-term friendships, and his ability to work hard. Instead, despite his high-powered career, he saw himself through Jackie's lens—a clumsy, inept pauper who had aspired too high and now must take the fall.

SILVER LININGS

Once you consider how your marriage might have perpetuated the worst in you, you may well view your divorce as the chance of a lifetime. When you finally get out of the environment in which negative images of you have been reinforced, you can start to view yourself in a new light, reflecting on your strengths and weaknesses, free of outside expectations.

Matt's image problem was typical. "After years of living with a spouse, you tend to internalize the labels and messages that you've heard repeated over time," says New York clinical psychologist Ellen Littman, a member of the faculty at Pace University and an expert on intimacy and self-image. "Messages like 'You're no good' and 'You're incompetent' tend to reverberate in your mind. If you've let your spouse define who you are, you are faced with the tremendous task of redefining yourself in a divorce."

Your new task: shedding the labels and creating new ones that fit the image of the person you have become.

Often, Littman notes, "people choose spouses who have qualities in common with people in the family of origin. Your role in your new family may echo your role in the old. Even if the labels are unpleasant, they can, therefore, feel safe." The trick, of course, is to replace a negative image with one that is more positive—and probably more realistic—instead of sliding back, once more, into old patterns. After all, if you are changing your life, this should be the place to start.

If you're still in the process of letting go, here are some tips for regaining your sense of self:

- See people and events based on their own contexts and avoid the tendency to project your past relationship onto these new experiences.

- If you feel exhausted or overwhelmed by your divorce, give yourself some time and space before jumping into another relationship.

- Reflect on what went wrong in your marriage. Perhaps if you can really understand what happened, you will be less likely to repeat the mistake.

It's Okay to Feel Angry

When do you get a chance to face your anger and express it, and who is it appropriate to express it to? "A tremendous amount of anger builds as a marriage dissolves," Littman says, "yet it's not wise to express that anger in front of your children or to your spouse. In fact, being in touch with all the anger might even be dangerous for you. Nonetheless, this high level of anger is inside you and often gets turned inward in the form of self-blame."

"Directing your anger at the perpetrator rather than yourself is the first step toward recovery," Littman states. "Many people are frightened by the intensity of their rage and feel that it is in some way unacceptable. They need to know that rage is an acceptable response when the very moorings of your life have been shaken, and you have had very little control over the destruction."

Says Littman: "The goal is creation of a new identity based on wisdom gained from the journey. This new identity should embrace your unique set of gifts."

Matt was lucky, at least in one sense. Already seeing a therapist, he explored his anger and his self-esteem issues before venturing out for romance again. He came to understand that he was shouldering more than his fair share of the blame and, without fear of repercussion in the therapist's office, expressed his inner rage. By purging his anger and examining the constraints Jackie had imposed on him, Matt was able to move on. A year after the day he'd been "kicked out," he was fathering his children as he never had when he lived at home.

 YOU CAN DO IT!

When you face your anger, you will be able to let go of it eventually. As you let go of your anger, you should be able to release all the negative definitions of yourself your spouse had convinced you were true.

Of course, violence is not an appropriate response. Some therapists specialize in helping clients get their anger out in a controlled situation. While you should recognize and accept your anger as valid under the circumstance, it's important to avoid letting it control you or get out of hand. Instead, assert your needs and complaints, but do so in a respectful way. Be alert to appropriate strategies for handling your anger. Are you holding it in? Is it morphing into feelings of depression? If so, let your therapist know, and if you haven't yet seen one, this would be a good time to start. The American Psychological Association has a booklet online that focuses on anger at apa.org/topics/anger/control.aspx?item=2.

Physical activity, like sports or dance, is another good way to let go of your tension and anger. If you're not already involved in a sport, gym, or dance class, maybe a friend or neighbor who works out can invite you to join his or her club. That will get you out of the house, where you can be with people, and help to get your juices flowing.

Dealing With Feelings of Guilt

All but the most narcissistic people feel terribly guilty about rejecting their spouses and hurting them deeply, not to mention destroying the nuclear family for their children.

You would be guilty—not just feeling guilty—if you brushed aside your spouse and recklessly caused your children harm by leaving the marriage without seriously trying to work things out. You made a commitment when you married, and if you had children, took on profound responsibility.

On the other hand, if you and your spouse—because the near-failure of a marriage is never entirely one-sided—made a strong effort to reconstruct your relationship, with professional help if necessary, then your guilt is unfounded. The option of staying in a marriage with children for the sake of the children has worked for some. This route requires strength, patience, and perhaps in your mind, sacrifice. But if you are the victim of relentless mental or physical abuse, or if, despite your best effort (including counseling), you cannot find satisfaction in your marriage, there is no reason to feel guilty. Such a marriage must be dissolved.

 RED ALERT

To sacrifice your needs for someone else is contrary to the concept of personal growth. Ultimately, a successful relationship must be built on a foundation where both people are coming from the position of positive personal growth and supporting each other's journey, together.

The Life You Left Behind

Even when you're well out of your marriage, it's natural to miss your life—afternoons in the yard, evenings with friends, and especially the kids. Brian, for instance, left his primary home to his wife and children. He found himself paying for their life in the house, even though he had no access to the premises and limited contact with his kids. "I just feel overwhelmed," he told us. "I'm 45 years old, and I'm experiencing a loss of alternatives. My money is committed, and I'm working to sustain a family I'm not even living with—and I don't get any of the positives."

Brian is frustrated, but he is not really seeing the reality of the situation, at least regarding his kids. He may not be living with his children, but he probably will be spending a good deal of time with them. He can have the same closeness as before, and perhaps the bond will even deepen now that he is taking care of them on his own.

As for his social problems, one solution for Brian is to get out into the world and meet new people. If he cannot make ends meet financially, he should be thinking about working toward a new career by going back to school—a good place to find new friends and interests while increasing his earning potential.

He might also want to develop additional parenting skills now that he will be taking care of his children without backup. He can take child development classes and read up on child safety issues. These classes are also a good place to make new friends.

YOU CAN DO IT!

Remember, if you are the noncustodial parent, feelings of loss can be repaired by throwing yourself into making a home for the children when they are with you. Think of things to do with your children that are ongoing and constant, something that they want to come to your home to do. Work on building traditions around their visits, whether it's Saturday morning pancakes or Sunday game nights.

When Doubt Lingers

It's not unusual, in the aftermath of divorce, to wonder whether you have done the right thing. In fact, unless your marriage has been complete hell—and that is not usually the case—you will still harbor residual feelings of affection for your spouse and the happy moments you spent together.

"Unless it's a situation of utter relief from the most adverse possible circumstances," says Dr. Mitchell Baris, "ambivalent feelings are likely to linger."

There is, quite simply, a period of wondering whether you could have worked it out or whether you simply gave up too soon.

One friend of ours began harboring such feelings, especially after his ex started calling him and asking him to be open, at least, to trying again. Her requests were especially tempting to him because she had been the one to end the relationship and push for the divorce in the first place. Just a year ago, he had pleaded with her to give the marriage a shot, and now, miraculously, she was doing just that.

But for our friend, things had changed. The experience had revealed to him his wife's fickle, callous side, and he had started dating someone new. Not only was he basically content again, but also he had no desire to plunge himself into the pain he had experienced as recently as a year before.

What should he do? A therapist wisely advised him to get together with his ex-spouse. "Don't be afraid," the psychiatrist told him. "You're thinking very clearly now, and you'll see things for what they really are."

RED ALERT

The temptation to be drawn back into the circle of your past relationship and all that it represents is real. Once the divorce is final, make it your business to establish your own life and center of activity. Make it your goal to move on.

Indeed he did. His ex-wife claimed she wanted a reunion, but within minutes of their meeting at a local coffee shop, she was commenting on his tie (too loud) and his hair (too short).

Our friend was cordial throughout the meeting but was able to walk away from it understanding he was well out of a relationship that meant nothing but pain. He had looked into the eye of the monster, after all, and he had prevailed.

The moral of the story: after your divorce, face your feelings head on. If your spouse has really been a louse or is just not right for you, you'll have the ability to see that, even if in your weaker moments you're still not sure.

Maintaining a Friendly Relationship

The divorce has been finalized and you're on your own. Your marriage, and all the pain it represents, is part of your past. Yet part of moving forward, for many, is learning to deal in a friendly, amicable way with their ex.

It seems like an oxymoron—two angry, divorced people ending up friends. Yet it is possible, according to Bill Ferguson, an attorney-turned-divorce consultant and author of *Heal the Hurt That Runs Your Life* and *Miracles Are Guaranteed*. The key is to end the cycle of conflict and restore the feeling of love. This does not necessarily mean "the husband and wife kind of love," he says, "but the kind of love that one human being extends to another."

 RED ALERT

The divorce courts are full of people who love each other. You may still love your ex, even after the divorce. This does not mean you should try to put your marriage together. Instead, remember that the goal is literally putting your divorce together, so that you can move on with your separate lives as friends.

This can seem like a daunting task if you are in the midst of conflict and angry feelings. How does one begin?

The first step, says Ferguson, is the realization that love is never enough to make a relationship work. In addition to love, a marriage also requires such elements as appreciation and acceptance—what Ferguson terms "the experience of love." That experience is destroyed by judgmental, critical behavior. Although it might be impossible to hold back such attitudes during the marriage, when the marriage is over, the cycle can end.

"To create and maintain this cycle of conflict," says Ferguson, "there must be two people participating, like a tennis match. When one person stops playing the game—when one person stops the nonacceptance—the cycle ends."

The key is clearly seeing the true character of your former spouse. "That person is the way he or she is, like it or not," says Ferguson. "When you can be at peace with the truth, you can see what you need to do. Maybe you need to move on."

Yet how do you break the cycle of conflict when you're hurt? "The first step," says Ferguson, "is realizing where the hurt is coming from." His notion is amazingly simple: "Your upset was caused not by what happened between you and your ex, but by your resistance to what happened. Now you must take your focus off what happened and, instead, work on healing the hurt that was triggered when the cycle of conflict began. Your anger and resentment are avoidance of the hurt. By facing the hurt, and coming to a place of forgiveness, it will be easier to be friends in the years to come."

"Trusting is one of the keys to letting go and being free inside," Ferguson adds. "However, this doesn't mean to trust that life will turn out like you want it to. Often life doesn't. The key is to understand that however life turns out, you will be fine."

The Least You Need to Know

- Allow yourself to experience the grief and pain. It's something you've got to get through, but don't hold onto it indefinitely.
- Reflect on what went wrong in your marriage. You can learn from the experience and avoid mistakes in the future.
- After your divorce, face your feelings about your spouse head on.
- In moments of loneliness, it is tempting to think you might find comfort and love again with your ex. While this is certainly possible, beware of this notion as a common, unrealistic wish among the newly divorced. Instead, call a friend and make plans to have dinner or see a movie.

Glossary

abandonment   The departure of one spouse from the marital home without the consent of the other spouse. In some states, this may constitute grounds for divorce.

action   A lawsuit. In matrimonial matters, it is usually a lawsuit for a divorce, an annulment, or a legal separation.

adultery   Engaging in sexual relations with someone other than one's spouse. In some states, this may constitute grounds for divorce.

affidavit   A sworn statement of facts. Affidavits usually accompany motions and are used to avoid having to personally appear in court to testify. However, sometimes you might have to appear in court even though you have prepared an affidavit.

alimony, maintenance, or spousal support   Payments made by one spouse to the other to assist with the support of the recipient spouse. Payments usually terminate upon the earlier of the death of either spouse, the remarriage of the recipient spouse, or a date decided by a judge or agreed upon by the husband and wife. Payments received are usually taxable to the recipient spouse and tax-deductible by the paying spouse.

appeal   A presentation, usually in writing, but sometimes supplemented by lawyers' oral arguments in court, to a court a level above the court that has decided an issue. The purpose of the appeal is to have the higher court reverse or in some way modify what the lower court did.

appellant   The person who brings the appeal.

billing rate   The rate at which an attorney bills a client for work performed. Many attorneys bill on an hourly basis, charging a certain amount of money per hour. Some attorneys bill per project, regardless of how much or little time it takes to do the work. This is also referred to as "unbundling" fees.

brief   A written presentation of a party's position. Lawyers most often submit briefs to argue appeals. Lawyers also submit briefs to support points of law made at the trial court level.

child support   A sum of money to be paid by one parent to the other to assist with the support of the couple's children. Child support is sometimes paid directly to a third party, such as a private school or a healthcare provider, rather than to a parent. In some jurisdictions, child support is paid to a state support collection unit, which in turn pays it to the recipient spouse. Child support usually terminates upon a child's emancipation. Unlike alimony, child support is not taxed as income to the recipient.

cohabitation   The act of living with someone. In some states, cohabitation may be grounds for the termination of support. In addition, some husbands and wives may agree when settling their case that cohabitation for a period of time (such as six months on a substantially continuous basis) will cause support to be terminated.

community property state   A state where all property (and typically income) acquired during the marriage is presumed to belong equally to both parties.

conflict of laws   Situation in which two or more national laws may be applicable to relationships (facts, contracts, family relationships, etc.) that are connected with more than one state. The conflict rules determine which country's domestic law is best placed to govern the legal relationship in question.

conflict resolution   A peaceful and mutually satisfactory way to end or significantly—and hopefully permanently—de-escalate a conflict.

constructive abandonment   The refusal of one spouse to engage in sexual relations with the other. In some states, this may constitute grounds for divorce.

contempt   The act of willfully violating a court order. Nonpayment of support when a spouse has the means to pay such support frequently gives rise to contempt adjudications in divorce cases.

cross-examination   The act of being questioned by the attorney representing the person on whose behalf the witness is not testifying.

cross-motion   A counter request made of a judge in reaction to a motion made by the opposing party.

cross-movant   The party filing a cross-motion.

decision   The judge's reasoning for why he or she directed something to be done or not done. Decisions usually accompany orders. Findings of fact and conclusions of law are the same as a decision. Decisions are sometimes referred to as "opinions."

defendant   The person who defends the lawsuit.

deposition   Answering questions under oath. In matrimonial matters, a deposition usually centers on a party's finances or child custody issues and is conducted in a lawyer's office or in the courthouse, but a judge will not be present. In some jurisdictions, the grounds for divorce may also be the subject of the deposition. A stenographer takes down everything that is said and later types it up for review by the parties and their attorneys.

direct examination   The act of being questioned under oath by the attorney representing the person on whose behalf the witness is testifying.

discovery   The act of revealing information so that both parties are fully informed of facts before trial. Discovery can pertain to finances or to one's physical or mental condition when those issues are relevant, such as when a spouse claims an inability to work due to an injury. Depending on the jurisdiction, other areas may be discoverable as well. Discovery methods include taking depositions, answering interrogatories, producing documents, and undergoing a physical.

dissolution   In many states, divorce is now called dissolution.

elective share   In some jurisdictions in the United States, an elective share entitles a spouse to receive a portion of the deceased spouse's estate, usually one-third, depending on the state law. This is intended to prevent disinheritance of a spouse. With this right, a spouse who was disinherited in a will, the elector, can challenge the will.

emancipation   The age at which a parent is no longer responsible for a child's support. The age varies by state. In some states, it may be 18; in others, 21. In addition, other events, such as a child getting married, joining the armed forces, or working full-time, if such events occur before the emancipation age, may also be deemed emancipation events.

ex parte   Latin phrase literally meaning "by, from, or for one party." An *ex parte* hearing is a proceeding brought by one person in the absence of another.

equitable distribution   A system of dividing property between spouses based upon what the judge considers to be fair. The law and precedent provide the judge with the factors to consider in making that determination.

exclusive use and occupancy of the marital residence   The right one spouse has to reside in the home in which the parties had previously lived together. Such right may be agreed upon or may be directed by a judge while an action is pending.

forensic   The term refers to applying scientific methods to legal matters and is sometimes used when an accountant performs a valuation of a business or a professional practice for distribution in a divorce. It can also refer to the process where a psychologist, psychiatrist, social worker, or other mental health professional is appointed to interview the parents and their children and make a recommendation to the court about who would be the better custodial parent. The mental health expert may also interview child caretakers, grandparents, teachers, and anyone else who has frequent contact with the children.

garnishment   A mechanism whereby support is sent by the paying spouse's employer directly to the recipient spouse and is deducted from the paying spouse's paycheck.

Gaslight Syndrome   A reference to a 1944 film directed by George Cukor, in which the husband surreptitiously creates evidence to convince his wife that she is insane. It has become clinical psychiatric terminology for one spouse trying to have the other labeled insane. A more common, less extreme form of this manifests as one spouse emotionally controlling the other. The partner being controlled suffers from self-doubt and loss of identity.

grounds   The legally sufficient reasons why a person is entitled to a divorce. Although many states are no-fault states—where no grounds need to be asserted other than incompatibility or irreconcilable differences—other states require the plaintiff to prove grounds, such as adultery, abandonment, or mental cruelty.

guardian *ad litem*   A person, often a lawyer, but in some states a psychologist or social worker, selected by the judge and assigned to represent "the best interests" of the children.

interrogatories   A series of questions that must be answered under oath, within a certain period of time, usually designed to ascertain a person's financial holdings and means of earning income or to address child custody issues.

joint custody   Sharing of the responsibilities for raising children despite a divorce. Joint legal custody can mean the children will live with one parent most of the time, but both parents will make major decisions. If the children divide their time equally between the two parents' homes, this is called "joint physical custody."

judgment of divorce   The written document that states that a husband and wife are divorced. In some states, this may be called a decree of dissolution. Typically, lawyers draft the judgment of divorce for the judge to review and sign. This document can contain a name change for one or both parties.

law guardian   A person, usually a lawyer, selected by the judge and assigned to represent the children of the divorcing parents or an incapacitated adult.

marital property   In general, property a husband and wife acquired during the marriage. Such property may also be called joint property. In some jurisdictions, inheritances, disability awards, and gifts received from a third party (that is, not the spouse) are not considered marital or joint property, even if a spouse received them during the marriage. Other exceptions may exist as well.

matrimonial property regimes   Matrimonial property regimes are the matrimonial property rights of the spouses. They are the sets of legal rules relating to the spouses' financial relationships resulting from their marriage, both with each other and with third parties, in particular their creditors.

mediation   A process whereby a neutral person—the mediator, who is usually a lawyer or social worker—works with the divorcing couple toward reaching a settlement agreement.

motion   A request made of a judge at a time an action is pending or at trial. Motions can be made in writing for the court to consider, or orally, such as at trial. In matrimonial cases, motions are typically made for temporary support, temporary custody, visitation rights, or to enjoin someone from taking money or property.

movant   The party making a motion.

noncustodial parent   The parent with whom the children do not live. Such a parent might not make day-to-day decisions but, depending on the definition of legal custody, can have a great deal to say about decisions regarding the children.

order   A ruling or "decree" by a judge, made orally or in writing, directing someone to do or refrain from doing something.

order of protection   An order directing one spouse to refrain from harassing or contacting the other. Violation of an order of protection can result in arrest and imprisonment.

perjury   The act of lying under oath.

petitioner   The person who first goes to court to file a request or petition for some kind of relief. Sometimes called the *plaintiff.*

plaintiff   The person who starts a lawsuit. Sometimes called the *petitioner.*

postnuptial agreement or separation agreement   A written contract entered into by a husband and wife, which sets forth all their present and future rights in the event of a divorce or a spouse's death. The parties may or may not be involved in divorce litigation at the time they sign such an agreement.

precedent   The use of previous decisions in cases factually similar to the case before a judge in order for the judge to decide how to adjudicate the present case.

prenuptial agreement   A written contract entered into by a couple who intend to marry but want to establish, before marriage, their rights in the event of a death or divorce after marriage. The validity of such agreements depends on state law.

pro se **divorce**   A divorce that is handled by the individual seeking the divorce rather than with the aid of an attorney.

record   All the evidence (testimony, documents, and exhibits) upon which a judge based his or her decision. When a party appeals a decision, it is necessary to compile all the papers and transcripts of testimony that the lower court used to decide the case and present that information to the higher court.

respondent   The person who has to defend or object to the appeal. The respondent also responds to the petition in the trial court and, in that case, may also be referred to as the "defendant."

retainer   A payment made to an attorney to secure his or her services. As the attorney works, charges are deducted from the retainer until the money is depleted. At that time, the attorney will bill on a weekly or monthly basis or ask for a new retainer.

retainer agreement   A contract signed by an attorney and client setting forth the billing arrangement to be instituted between the lawyer and the client. Some states require that a client's "bill of rights" be included in a retainer agreement.

separate property   Property a spouse acquires before the marriage and after an action for divorce has begun. In some jurisdictions, inheritance, disability awards, and gifts received during the marriage by one party are considered separate property. Other exceptions may exist as well.

sole custody   One parent has the right to make the major decisions concerning the children. Even where one parent has sole custody, the other parent often has the right to be informed and consulted, and to offer an opinion about the decision. Major decisions include religion, education, and health issues. Day-to-day decisions, such as the child's daily routine, are made by the parent who is caring for the child at the time. Under sole custody the child's residence is with the custodian, and the noncustodial parent has "visitation rights" (also called "parenting time" among other names).

transcript   The written presentation of testimony given at trial or in a deposition.

Index